RUMINATIONS on VIOLENCE

RUMINATIONS on VIOLENCE

Derek Pardue
Washington University in St. Louis

WAVELAND
PRESS, INC.
Long Grove, Illinois

For information about this book, contact:
 Waveland Press, Inc.
 4180 IL Route 83, Suite 101
 Long Grove, IL 60047-9580
 (847) 634-0081
 info@waveland.com
 www.waveland.com

Copyright © 2008 by Waveland Press, Inc.

10-digit ISBN 1-57766-508-2
13-digit ISBN 978-1-57766-508-3

All rights reserved. No part of this book may be reproduced, stored in a retrieval system, or transmitted in any form or by any means without permission in writing from the publisher.

Printed in the United States of America

7 6 5 4 3 2 1

*I dedicate this book
to my wife Selma Vital and our son André,
whose support and love provide me
with energy and a true sense of purpose.*

Contents

Acknowledgments xi
Introduction xiii

PART I
Theoretical Frames: Philosophy and Religion 1

1 **Two Meanings of Violence** 3
 Dustin Howes

2 **Exposing the Roots and Healing the Wounds of Religiously Sanctioned Violence** 23
 Peter Ellard

PART II
Violence as Part of the State and Colonialism 39

3 **Making Distance through a Violent Imagination** 41
 William Leggett

4 **Ethnic Riots in a Small Balkan Town: Understanding Hate and Violence in Macedonia** 54
 Robert Hislope

5 **The Afro Feast of Saint Francis of Assisi in Quibdó and Its Narratives of Amendment** 67
 Daniel Mosquera

PART III
Violence as a Family Affair: Gender and the Domestic Sphere 83

6   The Moral Imagination of Colombian Youth:
    Displacement, Survival, Paramilitarism and Peacemaking   85
    Victoria Sanford

7   Family Responsibility for Stopping Violence   100
    David Kaczynski and Linda E. Patrik

8   My Dad's Gun Collection   108
    Susan Graham

9   Is Violence against Women about Women or about Violence?   112
    Richard Felson

10 Impacting the Cycle of Violence One Child at a Time   122
    Carole Merill-Mazurek

PART IV
Narrating Violence 125

11 Journal Entries   127
    Leahanna Klement

12 Uberlinda   130
    Graciela Monteagudo

13 Negotiating Dangerous Spaces: Mundane Encounters
    with Prostitution and AIDS in Northern Thailand   134
    Ida Fadzillah

14 Convict Narratives from Postcolonial India:
    The Criminalized Woman in Phoolan Devi's Stories   144
    Basuli Deb

PART V
Violence as an Aesthetic 157

15 *Sou Marginal Mesmo* (I Am the Real Hoodlum):
   Using Violence as a Resource in Brazilian Hip Hop 159
   Derek Pardue

16 Omission, Silence, and Purity:
   A Statement on My Recent Work 173
   Conor McGrady

17 The Changing Qualities of Violence
   in American Popular Culture 181
   Jack Levin and Eric Madfis

18 Trigger-Happy 192
   Nadine Wasserman

About the Authors 203

Acknowledgments

The idea for this book could not have moved beyond the realm of possibility without the benefit of thoughtful dialogue. I want to thank my colleagues at Union College from 2005 through 2006, especially Sharon Gmelch in the Anthropology Department and Rachel Seligman, Mandeville art museum curator. Their support was fundamental in the early stages of the idea of *Ruminations*. At Washington University in St. Louis I would like to thank Amy Sapan for helping me edit and organize the texts and images in preparation of the first draft of the volume. Thanks also to my students in the courses "Ruminations on Violence" (Union College) and "Kill Assessment" (Washington University), whose feedback and comments helped shape the volume. I am grateful to Gayle Zawilla at Waveland Press for being so efficient and productive in editing. Her suggestions and comments have been wonderfully constructive.

Introduction

Violence pervades humanity as experience, public policy, narrative, and commodity. As an exercise of power, violence demands reflection. The goal of *Ruminations on Violence* is to discuss and analyze various contours of violence as it is made manifest around the world. Through such a discussion we can better understand and recognize the particularities of local forms of violence and the common threads of one of the most significant cross-cultural phenomena.

Ruminations began as an attempt to exercise global citizenship in the form of a public and collective document. The idea and title for this book project came to me as a result of my interaction with hip hop culture in the United States and Brazil. While working on my dissertation fieldwork with hip hoppers in São Paulo, Brazil in the late 1990s and early twenty-first century, I began to think more seriously about the diversity and complexity of violence in its physical and symbolic dimensions. In particular, I have been inspired by many Brazilian hip hoppers as they have transformed experiences of violence into cultural products, not only in the commercial music industry but also in the realm of popular education and negotiations with state departments of culture and health.

The choice of the word *Ruminations* in the title of this book is itself a reference to and a reflexive extension of the work of Chris Parker, alias KRS-One (Knowledge Reigns Supreme), world-renowned rapper and hip hop activist. His numerous recordings have always been popular as well as provocative. Early in his career, KRS-One understood the potentially special position hip hop could occupy in pop culture and society, a place of both entertainment and education or what he termed "edutainment"—the title of his 1990 recording. In addition, his participation in the foundational movement in the late 1980s to "Stop the Violence" is part of hip hop history. In 2003, KRS-One published *Ruminations*, a book detailing his various philosophies on life, history, blackness, and hip hop. As he reminds readers in his introduction, *to ruminate* has more than one meaning. One definition is "to chew cud or partially digested food," and the other is "to reflect on ideas repeatedly over a period of time." The spirit is the same in both literal and figurative connotations: a process of active reflection—breaking it down.[1]

---

[1] I recommend that readers of this book chew their food (i.e., the ideas presented in this text) well before swallowing—it will aid their "digestion" of the discourse on violence.

Ruminations on Violence is a collection of essays, stories, and poems, written by a range of people, including scholars, professionals, and performers from the areas of anthropology, sociology, criminology, philosophy, political science, literary studies, religious studies, community social work, and the plastic arts. Despite the variety of disciplines and perspectives represented here, the one unifying strand throughout is that violence is not a thing, but rather a dynamic, intersubjective force. Similarly, human beings—the agents of violence—can be defined not just as autonomous individuals but ultimately as producers and recipients of a wide range of social relations. Again, drawing from KRS-One, "we must first begin to see ourselves as events."[2] In other words, while this book contains thoughtful passages based on individual experiences of violence, the collective focus investigates violence as a social phenomenon rather than as solely an individual pathology.

Furthermore, the idea behind the book is not simply "violence around the world." Rather, the layout is thematic, moving from conventional anthropological and sociological issues of state-sponsored, ethnic, and domestic violence to media studies and popular-culture fields concerning the aesthetics and narration of violence. The eclectic nature of the collection is what makes this book stand apart from other texts on violence.

Ruminations on Violence fills a void in the literature. Most college courses and accompanying texts in the social sciences approach violence in one of two ways: as an expression of human behavior (a psychological perspective), or as culturally constructed and thus possessing multiple meanings and functions (an anthropological perspective). Within the latter category, a number of recent ethnographies and edited volumes have emerged within the subdisciplinary topics of anthropology of conflict and medical anthropology, taking their perspective from such prominent scholars as Philippe Bourgois and Nancy Scheper-Hughes.[3] In addition, there are several textbooks oriented towards the social work practitioner, written in a clinical manner with the purpose of training students to ease tense situations and assuage violent persons. While there is no doubt that such approaches are valid and productive, other dimensions of violence are represented by scholars in communication, media studies, and literature—all of which deserve the attention of social critics. Violence is not only a structural force of political and physical leverage but also a resource for creativity and storytelling. Violence, in essence, is a constitutive part of expressive culture and thus requires the careful scrutiny of social science.[4]

---

[2] KRS-One (2003), *Ruminations*. New York: Welcome Rain Publishers, p. 21.

[3] See Philippe Bourgois' *In search of respect: Crack in the barrio* (Cambridge, 1995); Scheper-Hughes and Bourgois' *Violence in war and peace: An anthology* (Blackwell, 2004); Bettina E. Schmidt and Ingo W. Schröder's *Anthology of violence and conflict* (Routledge, 2001).

[4] Cultural anthropologist Neil L. Whitehead made this point clear in his work on warfare and ritual violence in South America when he stated that "violence may be an expression of fundamental cultural practice and a sanctioned collective communication and exchange" (War and violence as cultural expression, *Anthropology News* [May 2005]:24).

CENTRAL THEMES

Ruminations on Violence is both applied and theoretical in its approach, containing cross-cultural case studies and personal testimonies as well as impressionistic essays and theoretical statements on violence as a powerful discourse.

Part I, *Theoretical Frames: Philosophy and Religion*, consists of two essays: political scientist Dustin Howes' "Two Meanings of Violence" and religious-studies scholar Peter Ellard's "Exposing the Roots and Healing the Wounds of Religiously Sanctioned Violence," offering readers a survey of two major epistemologies of violence. Human actors located in such wide-ranging fields as the military, tattoo art, sex industry, and corporate business explicitly or implicitly articulate violence drawing from mainstream interpretations of philosophy and/or religion. In the first essay, Howes provides a philosophical survey of how scholars have defined violence. In particular, he interprets a cadre of authors and organizes them into two themes: violence as a vector of physical force and violence as essentially "intersubjective" (significant through social relations). In the second essay, Ellard argues for a serious and critical reading of the Bible, discussing how it has been interpreted by a host of spiritual leaders and politicians as a justification for carrying out violent acts. While addressing extremism as obviously important in the current debate on religion and violence, Ellard focuses on "moderate" religious people to make the point that there exists a mainstream interpretation of the Bible, in particular, which has created a significant case for justifying violence. While certainly these two essays do not exhaust all the operative definitions of violence nor the religiously-inspired interpretations of conflict and violence, they do provide a necessary basis of theory, a toolkit of ideas that readers can use to more productively understand and interpret the essays that follow.

In short, readers are challenged to adapt the general arguments in Howes and Ellard to the case studies of violence described in the remainder of the book. How do the actors in each essay conceive of violence and power? Is it based on notions of success, upward mobility, memory, maturity, morality, family, ethnic hatred, colonialism, the "primitive," masculinity, or "might makes right"?

One of the most prevalent ways in which violence makes its presence known in the public sphere is through state mediation. In Part II, *Violence as Part of the State and Colonialism*, the authors treat such visible manifestations of violence in different but complementary ways. In his work on corporate office spaces in Jakarta, Indonesia, anthropologist William Leggett reveals how "Western" ex-pats use their understanding of the Indonesian state and European colonial history to create and maintain separation from Indonesian employees. His "Making Distance through a Violent Imagination" demonstrates how colonialism and discourses of "civilization" pervade even the most trivial of spaces such as corporate offices. In the fourth essay, "Ethnic Riots in a Small Balkan Town," political scientist Robert Hislope investigates ethnic-based violence in contemporary Macedonia. Rich in description and analysis, this essay challenges readers to think beyond ethnic divisions as either ungrounded, fabricated discourses or as simply "natural" facts. Hislope argues that such models of "constructivism" and "primordialism," respectively, do not explain the case of Macedonia as he makes a distinction between "expressive" and "actionable" hatred. In the fifth essay, "The Afro Feast of Saint Francis of Assisi in Quibdó and its Narratives of Amendment," literary scholar Daniel Mosquera describes and contextualizes a popular feast in the state of Chocó in the country of Colombia. Mosquera weaves the historical and ritual detail of the celebration to the social and political commentary embedded in the Feast. Ultimately, the Afro Feast is both a wonderfully expressive party and a sharp critique of the Colombian state due to the long-standing armed civil war, state abandonment of the Chocó state, and the persistent negative racialization of Chocó by state agencies.

In Part III, *Violence as a Family Affair: Gender and the Domestic Sphere*, violence is analyzed as a systematic expression of gender and family relations in contemporary societies. (The theme of family and gender is a significant factor in the two final sections as well.) In the first essay, "The Moral Imagination of Colombian Youth: Displacement, Survival, Paramilitarism and Peacemaking," anthropologist Victoria Sanford brings much-needed attention to the agency of child soldiers. Traditionally, scholars and pundits alike have explained children in times of war and armed conflict solely as victims, objects of adult actions and decisions. Sanford provides insight into the various motivations and intentions of children as they become armed soldiers for state militias, guerrilla forces, and independent peacemakers.

The remaining four essays in this section are located in the United States. David Kaczynski and Linda E. Patrik reflect on their roles during the 1990s as family members and negotiators involved in the infamous case of the Unabomber. In "Family Responsibility for Stopping Violence," Kaczynski and Patrik present a complex and compelling story of ethics and morality. Next, artist Susan Graham combines family memories, narrative, and aesthetics in her piece, "My Dad's Gun Collection." Graham draws in the reader as she remembers childhood scenes of her father's various guns around the house and then connects these memories to an emergent motivation to construct artistic replicas of her father's gun collection. Framed in the poetics of "an instant of stillness, suspension, where nothing has yet happened," Graham's short and sweet essay provokes a reflection on the gendered nature of family dynamics mediated through the presence of firearms.

In the ninth essay, sociologist Richard Felson presents his polemical view and analysis of domestic violence with the revealing title, "Is Violence against Women about Women or about Violence?" A response by sociologist Kristin Anderson and psychologist Jill Cermele follows. The final essay in this section is a report from Carole Merill-Mazurek, a multi-tasking program coordinator of the YWCA in Schenectady, New York. "Impacting the Cycle of Violence One Child at a Time" describes an innovative project of outreach between the YWCA and local public schools. Essentially, educators are able to elicit stories about domestic violence from children through the use of puppets. As so many scholars, community activists, and survivors have argued, to talk about violence is one of the greatest obstacles to overcome in the process of healing. For children, this can sometimes be even more difficult and traumatic. It is within this context that Merill-Mazurek's piece should be read.

Part IV, *Narrating Violence*, picks up the theme of elicitation and storytelling as part of an approach that configures violence as a creative human expression. The physical and symbolic dimensions of violence are not isolated but rather are overlapping layers of how we experience violence. One of the most powerful manners in which we negotiate violence is through narrative. We tell stories of violence on levels ranging from the personal to the global. We give testimonies of the present as well as imagine (and make links to) the prehistoric "noble savage" and/or futuristic utopias and dystopias. This aspect of violence is so powerful because it represents how we "feel" (empathize, sympathize with) the violence of others.

In the eleventh essay, student Leahanna Klement poignantly renders her experiences of college campus rape. In essay 12, political activist, anthropology graduate student, and veteran puppeteer Graciela Monteagudo writes a short vignette about "Uberlinda," a poor, marginalized woman from Monteagudo's home country of Argentina. Monteagudo implicitly links the devastating crisis of 2001 (i.e., political-economic violence) to the trials of Uberlinda. The final two essays in this section cast a wider net to demonstrate in more explicit ways the connections between narration, family violence, and national identities. In essay 13, "Negotiating Dangerous Spaces: Mundane Encounters with Prostitution and AIDS in Northern Thailand," anthropologist Ida Fadzillah discusses the stories young Thai women tell about themselves and about other young women who work in the sex industry. Fadzillah's analysis reveals young women's agency as they try to control the meaning of AIDS, client brutality, and the violent ramifications of being a sex worker. Finally, in essay 14 literary scholar Basuli Deb identifies the importance of the "criminalized woman" within Indian literature as both part of caste violence and a potentially radical feminism. Deb focuses her analysis on stories about the national icon of Phoolan Devi, born a lower-caste girl, who avenged caste violence and eventually was elected into the national parliament in 1996.

Part V, *Violence as an Aesthetic*, represents a departure from the conventional social science text on violence and moves the discussion to the intellectual spheres of communication, media, and popular culture studies. The first essay in this section comes from the editor, Derek Pardue. In *"Sou Marginal Mesmo:* I am the Real Hoodlum," I analyze why and how local hip hoppers in São Paulo, Brazil use and deploy violence as an aesthetic marker and comment on the variable but unbreakable link between violence and hip hop "reality." Next, artist Conor McGrady combines an analysis of his own drawings with social commentary on daily life in Northern Ireland. In particular, he draws attention to the role of state violence as a tool to maintain social order and enforce control of subversive or insurgent populations. In the seventeenth essay, sociologists Jack Levin and Eric Madfis qualify violence as a variable force within U.S. popular culture, investigating such issues as the contemporary marketing of murder and murderers in the United States as part of celebrity culture. The final essay, "Trigger Happy," written by art curator Nadine Wasserman, contextualizes the diverse treatment of violence by a group of artists.

With this mixed genre of voices and concerns, I have attempted to lay the foundation for the main message of the book: violence is a diverse, complex phenomenon. Understanding this message is the first step in the process of assessing the power of violence in the world and dismantling the negativity and destruction potentially associated with it.

INTERDISCIPLINARY/MULTIDISCIPLINARY APPLICATIONS

From the standpoint of pedagogy, these essays might serve as introductory passages to teach ethnographies, novels, and/or surveys. Especially at more advanced levels of social science or the humanities, these readings will complement foundational texts on violence, power, and identity. For example, Michel Foucault's discussion of the spatiality of power could work well in conjunction with William Leggett's essay; Gayatri Spivak's work could be used to accentuate the theory of subaltern voices in Basuli Deb's essay; or the perspective of Hannah Arendt might augment Victoria Sanford's observations in investigating the general relationship between violence and power.[5] In its scope and diversity, *Ruminations on Violence* offers the reader interdisciplinary and multidisciplinary perspectives that will help them to understand the difficult issues surrounding the complex phenomenon that is violence.

Derek Pardue

---

[5] Michel Foucault, *Discipline and punishment: The birth of a prison* (Random House, 1975) and a collection of Foucault's work by Colin Gordon (Ed.), *Power/knowledge: Selected interviews & other writings 1972–1977* (New York: Pantheon Books, 1980); Gayatri Spivak, Can the subaltern speak?, originally published in Cary Nelson and Lawrence Grossberg (Eds.), *Marxism and the interpretation of culture* (University of Illinois, 1988); Hannah Arendt, *On violence* (Harvest Books, 1970).

PART I

THEORETICAL FRAMES

Philosophy and Religion

Two Meanings of Violence

Dustin Howes

This essay explores the contested and slippery meaning of violence by identifying two contrasting trends in influential literature on the topic. First, in the work of thinkers such as Karl Marx, Sharon Marcus, Michel Foucault, Elaine Scarry, and others, violence is associated with our physical capacities and limitations. In each case, violence is understood as a means for changing the nature of our social relations, but its distinctive quality lies in its close association with the manipulation and destruction of the body. A second conception of violence can be clearly identified in the work of Jean-Paul Sartre, Pierre Bourdieu, Walter Benjamin, Jacques Derrida, Primo Levi, Emmanuel Levinas and others. Here violence is associated with profound fissures in our expectations as to how we ought to interact with one another. This "intersubjective violence" can consist of a word, a gesture or a look, either between individuals or as supported by institutions. Such violence can inspire fear, strike at the core of one's identity, or make a way of living and being impossible even without physical intimidation or destruction. The paper concludes by discussing some of the prospects for mitigating physical and intersubjective violence.

It should come as no surprise to those who have some background in contemporary philosophy that the meaning of the word *violence* is prone to instability, multiple usage, and contestation. In the work of J. L. Austin, Ludwig Wittgenstein and others, we are encouraged to notice that words are highly context sensitive (and are themselves creators of context). Yet it is perhaps strange, given the ubiquity of the term, that violence has rarely been the subject of sustained philosophical inquiry in the way that concepts such as religion, freedom, or the self have been. That is, we might expect that philosophers would not only invoke different meanings of violence, but that they would *openly* contest the term—a matter for explicit and serious discussion. Most surprising of all is the neglect of the term in political philosophy. If every political philosopher talks about violence, they do so typically as a back-

Written especially for *Ruminations on Violence*.

ground condition for politics and, in this way, violence becomes the meaning already assumed or a topic of secondary interest. Yet if words create context, and "violence" seems to frequently create the context for our meanings of politics, then it deserves a careful and sustained treatment in its own right.

In the following pages, I cull two meanings of violence from the Western philosophical tradition. This is a tricky task for a number of reasons. First, I navigate texts that span languages, cultures and time periods. Second, an author might develop a concept, for instance Foucault's "discipline" or Marx's "alienated labor," that we can usefully associate with violence and yet refrain from using the term violence, or even, as is the case with Foucault, specifically invoke violence as a contrast to that concept.

These difficulties raise the question: if we are not looking for the term violence itself, or at least not exclusively, then what exactly are we looking for? If there is a general sketch or hypothesis that precedes and guides the more precise inquiry into potential meanings of violence, it is the following: I am interested in drawing together and thematizing the ways in which human activities can cause a high degree of suffering among others.

THE FRAGILITY AND ABILITY OF BODIES

The most obvious place to begin a discussion of violence is the body. Whatever ambiguities and difficulties in the term *violence*, ordinary usage suggests that certain actions by one body upon another, such as rape, murder, and torture, normally fall within the purview of the term. As we will see shortly, these quintessential instances of "physical" violence are not really reducible to physical interactions. However, their frequent association with violence indicates that we would do well to start with our physical capacities and limitations in developing conceptions of violence.

Modern philosophy provides us with many explicit—and more often, implicit—understandings of the nature of our physical being. Among the most compelling, and one that provides a useful framework for this discussion, is Thomas Hobbes' assertion that human beings share a particular kind of natural physical equality. He writes:

> Nature hath made men so equal in the faculties of body and mind as that, though there be found one man sometimes manifestly stronger in body or of quicker mind than another, yet when all is reckoned together the difference between man and man is not so considerable as that one man can thereupon claim to himself any benefit to which another may not pretend as well as he. For as to the strength of body, the weakest has strength enough to kill the strongest, either by secret machination, or by confederacy with others that are in the same danger with himself.[1]

Here, Hobbes states that the human body is characterized by fragility and ability. By some measures, human beings are quite robust—for instance, we

---
[1] Hobbes, 13:1, 74.

are stronger than many species of animals and our immune systems can ward off many forms of disease. However, our physical durability and stature are overwhelmed by our abilities with respect to that stature. A turtle or a deer cannot kill one of his/her own. Yet each "man," notes Hobbes, has the ability to kill every other person and each of us is in turn capable of being killed.[2]

This unique way of framing our natural condition has often been de-emphasized by Hobbes scholars in favor of treatments of the role of pride or mistrust in the state of nature. However, the notion that we are fragile and capable can help us identify, in a wide range of literature, a whole host of physical possibilities and vulnerabilities that attend the human body.

For Marx, for instance, labor is related to the special capacities of human beings with respect to the material world. Whereas other animals work to meet their physical needs, we humans continue to create and shape the world around us even after we have satisfied our own basic physical needs. This can imbue human labor with a special quality, whereby we become what Marx calls "conscious beings" or "species beings." Yet this remarkable potential to express ourselves through the objective world (Marx mentions science and art) can be transformed into our greatest liability. Indeed, our ability to manipulate the material world beyond what is physically necessary can be turned on other human bodies and used to alienate them from their own activities. When this happens, Marx says, the proper relationship between our conscious self and the material world is reversed in that: "a conscious being makes his life activity, *his essence*, only a means for his existence."[3] Whereas Hobbes is concerned with our ability to kill one another, Marx suggests that alienating another from her or his labor relates to *our capacity to deprive and our vulnerability to being deprived* of basic necessities such as adequate food and shelter. The upshot is that our physical ability to create institutions that play on our physical vulnerabilities allows us to alienate other human beings from the very activities that make them unique.

Elaine Scarry's analysis of torture provides us with another example of our physical capabilities and vulnerabilities. Scarry describes all manner of ways for us to use our sensory capacities to cause one another pain including: confinements that contort the body; implements that poke, prod or burn the flesh; and assaults on our most sensitive nerve endings to name but a few. Indeed, she notes that, in torture:

> Each source of strength and delight, each means of moving out into the world or moving the world in to oneself, becomes a means of turning the body back in on itself, forcing the body to feed on the body: the eyes are only access points for scorching light, the ears for brutal noises; eating, the act at once so incredible and so simple in which the world is literally

---

[2] Though Hobbes's argument potentially sets the stage for radical equality, it is also inflected with masculine and racialized notions of the body. See Mills 1997, Pateman 1988. More recently, see Hall 2005.
[3] Marx, 63.

> taken into the body, is replaced by rituals of starvation involving either no food or food that nauseates. . . . The prisoner's body—in its physical strengths, in its sensory powers, in its needs and wants, in its ways of self-delight . . . is made a weapon against him on behalf of the enemy, made to be the enemy.[4]

In this way, Scarry describes sufferings that complicate and add nuance to the notion of fragility. Our bodies are robust in the sense that they can endure the most profound pain, and yet this strength is precisely the fragility that allows us to experience torture. If our bodies could not survive such things, the pain would not be possible; once the body perishes, torture has ceased. With respect to our abilities, Scarry suggests that it is the transforming of the pain of another into our object that is the crucial "utility" of torture. Indeed, we can mobilize our bodies to handle other bodies in a particularly horrifying way: We can operate in the space between life and death by perceiving *the possibility of eliciting and sustaining the pain* of another living, sometimes barely alive, body.

Thus, if Hobbes points out that we are capable and vulnerable in that we can kill and be killed, thinkers such as Marx and Scarry show us that our capabilities and vulnerabilities can extend to physical interactions that fall short of killing or even trifle with life at the boundary of death. Other thinkers help fill in other aspects of our vulnerability and capability. Hegel's analysis of slavery is perhaps most closely related to Hobbes' work, at least in the sense of giving pride of place to our potential for killing one another. Yet Hegel argues that we can enslave one another by calling attention to another's mortality and thereby *hold her or him in fear of death*, even without killing them. Foucault looks to Marx in developing a political economy of the body, but hones in on the ways in which the state cultivates a micro-physics of power. In doing so, he keeps the body front and center and demonstrates that discipline and punishment function because our bodies can be dismembered and destroyed—and also *incarcerated, trained,* and *routinized.*

Theorists who grapple with rape highlight a patriarchal social reality where men are much more likely to rape and women are much more likely to be victims of rape. However, in attempting to denaturalize this reality, feminists have persuasively argued that rape cannot inhere in the sex of bodies. Sharon Marcus remarks:

> [L]anguage structures . . . the would-be rapist's feelings of powerfulness and our commonplace sense of paralysis when threatened with rape.
> As intractably real as these physical sensations may appear to us, however, they appear so because the language of rape speaks through us, freezing our own sense of force and affecting the would-be rapist's perceptions of our lack of strength.[5]

---

[4] Scarry, 48.
[5] Marcus, 390.

Implicitly, the argument here is that women and men are *not* decisively more or less strong with respect to one another. Instead, in line with Hobbes's notion of natural equality, the potential to rape and vulnerability to be raped revolves around *sexual capacities and vulnerabilities* which extend across the human form. In fact, gender norms, rape scripts, and linguistic structures have created men who seem to believe that they are capable of rape but not vulnerable to being raped (by a woman). It seems that Marcus wants us to understand that women are just as physically capable of raping as men, and men are just as physically vulnerable to rape as women. Analyses of rape, then, detail yet another aspect of our physical capability and vulnerability—the sexual aspects of our bodies.

Hobbes's rather simple and straightforward observation that we are each equally fragile and able helps us notice the insights and assumptions of other thinkers as they relate to the character of the human body. Taken together, these thinkers provide us with a rather stark view of what is physically possible among us.

However, this discussion also helps us notice that cataloguing the fragility and ability of our bodies is inadequate. Rape, torture, alienated labor, slavery, discipline, and punishment are clearly not reducible to the physical possibilities that attend them. First, if our capacity for deprivation, pain and confinement mean that there are many opportunities for us to inflict suffering on one another, such capacities also mean that there are opportunities for us to regard one another as worthy of care and concern. Our capacity to hold others in fear of their lives may mean we take action to ensure that they do not feel threatened by us. For example, our capacity to inflict pain and kill others may mean we take special care in following safety precautions at a work site or driving a vehicle. If an employee is unable to pay his or her power bill, an employer may take that opportunity to forego greater profits and begin to provide a living wage. In other words, the simple existence of certain physical possibilities and vulnerabilities does not determine our actions. Second, the physical vulnerabilities and capabilities that make phenomena such as murder, torture, alienated labor, and rape possible can take place independently of torture, alienated labor, and rape. When performing medical procedures we sometimes deprive others of food and drink and/or cause great pain, but we do not usually speak of such procedures in terms of alienation and torture. Instances arise when one person kills another as an act of mercy, and those who take a life under such circumstance usually do not think of such actions as murder. The indeterminacy of particular physical acts is perhaps most obvious with respect to our sexual capacities and vulnerabilities. Rape turns the pleasure centers of victims against them and the pleasure centers of perpetrators into weapons, yet a particularly rough act of consensual sado-masochistic sex may be more physically injurious than a given instance of rape.

These examples suggest that not all instances of physical harm constitute violence. Yet surely these physical possibilities are deeply intertwined with, and indeed make a certain kind of violence possible. What, then, is the relationship between these physical possibilities and violence?

Physical Violence

Hobbes begins with this idea, that we are vulnerable to being killed and capable of killing, in order to help us understand why our natural condition is a state of war. In doing so, he introduces our physical possibilities alongside a bundle of assumptions about human motivations and purposes.[6] While Hobbes's assumptions are sensible and powerful, they cannot and are not intended to explain the wide variety of situations mentioned above. What is required then is a generalized understanding of the relationship between human purpose and our fragility and ability. That is, it seems that what distinguishes sado-masochistic sex from rape, or mercy killing from murder, has something to do with the *purposes* that animate physical actions.

Another theorist of war, Prussian general Carl von Clausewitz, offers a more helpful analysis in this regard.[7] In Clausewitz's theory of war, we find ideas that help us gain purchase on the sort of phenomena we have discussed thus far. He writes:

> *War is an act of violence intended to compel our opponent to fulfill our will.*
> Violence arms itself with the inventions of Art and Science in order to contend against violence. . . . Violence, that is to say, physical force (for there is no moral force without the conception of States and Law), is therefore the *means*; the compulsory submission of the enemy to our will is the ultimate *object*.[8]

Three things stand out here. First, Clausewitz squarely places war in the realm of the physical. War is an act of violence, and violence is understood to be synonymous with physical force. Second, the action of war is instrumental: Violence is not an end in itself, but a means to another end. Third, the ultimate object of war relates to a *subjective* aspect of one's "opponent." If the means of war are physical, the ultimate end has to do with a change in the nature of another's will.

The notion that we can use one another's bodies as means to ends can be found in each of the texts we have examined thus far. For instance, according to Marx, our labor is alienated from us for "the *pleasure* and the life-enjoyment for another."[9] Hegel describes almost precisely the same relation between lord and bondsman,[10] and Foucault's concern with "the political

---

[6] For instance, he urges us to recognize that every human being is likely to consider his or her own judgment superior to the judgment of others (at least in matters that concern the person under consideration), and that human beings want to survive and have a natural right to do what is necessary to secure that end.

[7] In relying on Clausewitz we need to be cautious. Much of what he says applies specifically to warfare and not the conception of violence I will develop here. Further complicating matters, Clausewitz regularly uses the term violence (or terms that are translated as such) in ways that are mostly, but not uniformly, consistent with my understanding.

[8] Clausewitz, 101.

[9] Marx, 65.

[10] Where "thing" refers to the body of the slave, Hegel (1977, para. 190, 96) writes: "For the lord . . . the immediate relation becomes through this mediation the sheer negation of the thing, or the enjoyment of it."

economy of the body" builds on just this sort of thinking. For Marcus, rape is a way of creating gendered understandings of bodies that suggests to men that they can use women's bodies for their own purposes; indeed, the "horror of rape is not that it steals something from us but that it makes us [women] into things to be taken."[11] Likewise, while denying that torture can be a means to any useful information, Scarry suggests that torture is in fact an instrument to other ends when she states that "the fiction of power [is] the final product and outcome of torture."[12]

In fact, the notion of instrumentality is associated with our fragility and ability in both ancient and contemporary texts. Machiavelli makes the case for "[w]ell-used cruelty (if one can speak well of evil)" that can be used to "ensure one's subjects benefit in the long run."[13] Aristotle writes that "[w]ar must therefore be regarded as only a means to peace ... as means to acts which are good in themselves."[14] And Malcolm X invokes the right of African Americans to pursue justice "by any means necessary" while leaving no doubt that "any means" includes the use and destruction of bodies.[15]

In this way, we see that what seems to be at stake in our physical fragility and ability is the potential for using that fact to achieve some sort of change in the world. Yet Clausewitz is even more specific: he points out that the end which attends these means and the purpose that motivates our actions are *not* physical. First, the "political object" we have in mind when we target the will of another can be just about anything. Thus, his insights are easily imported into all the various contexts we have dealt with thus far: peace, the good, pleasure, power, the construction of femininity, self-preservation, or justice for African Americans can all comfortably qualify as "political objects" in this broad sense. Second, if our "object" is subjective, then our real target when we take up another's body is subjective as well. The means is another's body, but the "object" is their will.

Taking these aspects of Clausewitz's analysis together—the manipulation and destruction of the physical body, the use of that body as a means, the subjective nature of our purposes, and the fact that we are targeting subjectivity—helps us to determine our first meaning of violence: *Physical violence is the use of another's body in order to guide, submit or destroy their will for some purpose.*

There are many implications of conceptualizing violence in this way; here we should mention two, if only as a way of organizing the many diverse contexts covered by such a definition. First, if our particular purposes (Clausewitz's "political object") guide the use of the physical means, we should note that our purposes could relate to individuals or groups. The above discussion of fragility and ability relates to one individual raping or

---

[11] Marcus, 399.
[12] Scarry, 57.
[13] Machiavelli, 8, 30.
[14] Aristotle, 7:14:12, 317.
[15] See Breitman 1970.

killing another individual for individual pleasure or retaliation for a perceived wrong, as well as to institutions that kill and rape, or elicit work and discipline from thousands, in the name of a grand ideological vision. In both cases, the nature of the political object determines what sort of physical actions are taken in order to achieve that subjective end.

Second, in Clausewitz's work there is an instructive vacillation between the idea that the ultimate purpose of war is the "submission of the will" and the possibility that our purposes might be so important that war will involve "extermination."[16] This is important because it reveals that this conception of violence entails both the possibility of manipulating another's body in order to change the character of subjectivity and simply destroying another's body in order to eliminate the possibility of subjectivity being expressed at all. In both cases, we find that physical violence may or may not achieve its goals. Physically harming someone may not change their will at all (or only temporarily), and killing someone may turn them into a martyr— producing unintended effects among others who are still alive. But the point is that physical violence dreams of using or destroying the body in order to ensure a particular subjective end.

In order to develop an adequate definition of "physical" violence, we found it necessary to incorporate subjectivity. Indeed, violence is not only between bodies, but also between *living* bodies—even if it results in the destruction of life. Yet if physical violence relates to human purposes, goals, and ends, it raises the possibility that violence has less to do with the character of our bodies and more to do with our character per se.

PRIMO LEVI AND THE PROBLEMS OF RECOGNITION AND FREEDOM

Developing an alternative, nonphysical conception of violence requires that we delve into the nuances of our subjective relationships, just as we delved into the subtleties of our physical fragilities and abilities. However, the difficulties entailed in describing the nuances of subjectivity suggest that, instead of invoking numerous examples as we did in exploring our physical fragility and ability, we might be better served by a more extensive analysis of one particular example. Ideally, we need an instance and description of the problems of subjectivity that is not inattentive to or entirely removed from the

---

[16] He writes: "If the aim of the military action is an equivalent for the political object, that action will in general diminish as the political object diminishes, and in a greater degree the more the political object dominates. Thus it is explained how, without any contradiction in itself, there may be Wars of all degrees of importance and energy, from a War of extermination down to the mere use of an army of observation" (Clausewitz, 110). In effect, the "ultimate object" referenced above—the submission of the enemy's will—is conditioned by a more practical, subjective and circumscribed "political object" of the particular actor in a particular time and place. The political object—our purpose—can involve just about anything, but what it is matters because it guides and characterizes the means we use to achieve it.

more usual meanings and understandings of violence and yet provides us with a way of thinking about our ability to cause suffering that is not dependent upon the physical factors we have already discussed. In Primo Levi's *Survival in Auschwitz,* we find just that. In fact, alongside a careful description of one of the most physically destructive institutions in the history of the world, Levi provides us with a perspicacious analysis of the subjective factors at play in Auschwitz.

Primo Levi was an Italian chemist captured by the Nazis in 1943. When the chapter "Chemical Examination" begins, Levi has spent three months in the Lager. He is weak and starving as a consequence of forced labor, pitiful rations, and the generally appalling conditions in the camp. In the Lager, persons able to demonstrate a talent of value to the industrial complex that is part of Auschwitz are more likely to survive. When a Chemical Kommando is formed, Levi volunteers; it is a potentially life-saving opportunity to be "a specialist." However, in order to qualify for the commando, Levi has to take an oral exam given by one of the three German chemists who work in the Polymerization Department at Auschwitz.

When Levi and the Kapo Alex enter the office, Alex introduces him to a Doctor Pannwitz as "'. . . an Italian, has been here only three months, already half kaput . . . *Er sagt er ist Chemiker.* . . .'"[17] Alex is dismissed and Levi and Pannwitz are alone. Pannwitz sits "formidably behind a complicated writing table" and Levi, Häftling 174517, notes that it is ". . . a real office, shining, clean and ordered, and I feel I would leave a dirty stain whatever I touched."[18] The next moment is perhaps the most painful and puzzling of Levi's life:

> When he finished writing, he raised his eyes and looked at me.
> From that day I have thought about Doktor Pannwitz many times and in many ways. I have asked myself how he really functioned as a man; how he filled his time, outside of the Polymerization and the Indo-Germanic conscience; above all when I was once more a free man, I wanted to meet him again, not from a spirit of revenge, but merely from a personal curiosity about the human soul.
> Because that look was not one between two men; and if I had known how completely to explain the nature of that look, which came as if across the glass window of an aquarium between two beings in different worlds, I would also have explained the essence of the great insanity of the third Germany.[19]

That Levi is not prone to hyperbole, that his tone is so often muted in the face of suffering, makes the passage that describes these first moments of his interaction with Pannwitz stand out. He also suggests that the circumstances he is attempting to describe test the limits of his formidable explicatory capa-

---

[17] Levi, *Survival in Auschwitz,* 105.
[18] Ibid., 105–106.
[19] Ibid.

bilities. In this way, he conveys both the immense power and subtle opacity of "that look."[20]

In Levi's description of his experience with Doctor Pannwitz, we find a distinctive way of thinking about what can go wrong in our interactions with others. Of course, much of what goes wrong here is due to the sort of factors we have already discussed—that is, it is clear that any interaction between a prisoner and a higher-up in Auschwitz is inflected by the surrounding physical violence. Part of what is so painful about this interaction for Levi is that the profession he loves, his capacity to think about and practice chemistry, is turned into a means for survival. During the exam, Levi says that Pannwitz searches for "some utilizable element"[21] in him. Coupled with the ever-present possibility of being "selected," Levi's experience can be understood as lying somewhere between Marx's alienated labor and Hegel's slavery. Yet Levi's description of his interaction with Pannwitz, while not entirely excluding such interpretations, seems to specifically resist the idea that his encounter with Pannwitz is explicable in terms of the physical suffering of Auschwitz. Instead he posits the reverse: something about their *social* interaction—something about "the nature of that look"—is at the heart of the physical demolition and institutional structures that constitute the "great insanity."

There is, of course, no dearth of philosophical works concerned with problems that arise out of interactions between subjects. With Levi's description of his interaction with Pannwitz in mind, we can identify two crucial themes in such works. The first relates to the difficulties that surround our attempts to know one another, or, the problem of recognition. The second concerns problems that arise from our simply being together, or, what we might loosely refer to as the problem of freedom.[22] With respect to both recognition and freedom, we find the most useful articulations of the problems in Jean-Paul Sartre, Maurice Merleau-Ponty, and Emmanuel Levinas.[23]

---

[20] As readers, we cannot be sure of exactly what is happening during the exam. That I find myself devoting more words to the experience than the individuals who had the experience seems dangerous. Indeed, perhaps the most important aspect of Levi's response to the situation is his curiosity as to—and acknowledgement of his inability to know—exactly what Pannwitz is thinking. As I discuss below, this helps us understand certain aspects of intersubjectivity. That fact, does not, however, give me license to trample upon the defining moments of Levi's life. Put another way, while what I say here will undoubtedly be an incomplete and distorted representation of his experience, I hope that the reader will at least have a better understanding of why that is the case.

[21] Levi, *Survival in Auschwitz*, 106.

[22] I say "loosely" because the meaning of freedom is highly contested even among the related works I deal with below.

[23] The problem of recognition has become something of a preoccupation for contemporary philosophy. Most authors rightly turn to Hegel as a founding thinker on the issue; however, because his exploration of recognition is so indelibly characterized by the physical aspects of the master-slave relation, other phenomenologists are more helpful in explaining the sort of thing that Levi describes.

The problem of recognition is distinct in the work of each of these thinkers, but taken together they provide us with a robust rendition of the difficulties we face in trying to know one another. First, for all three thinkers the human subject is fundamentally irreducible, yet finite and separated. This implies, paradoxically, that there is a kind of necessary primordial recognition of others, but also that the obstacles to fully knowing others are ultimately insurmountable. Pannwitz cannot help but recognize that Levi is in front of him—he looks at him—but clearly he does not know him. This is perhaps best expressed in Levinas' question: "Who is it?"[24] Levinas argues that this is a necessary question of social interaction and intersubjectivity. On the one hand, we would never pose this question if we did not already recognize another of some sort. And yet, of course, the question itself demonstrates that we do not know who it is that presents her- or himself to us.

Sartre suggests that this relationship is reciprocal: not only can we not know another, but we also realize that the other does not know us. He memorably describes our interactions with others and our self-apprehension through others as being like looking into a clouded mirror.[25] In part, what is so disturbing for Levi is that when he looks at Pannwitz's look, he finds that his reflection is utterly unrecognizable.[26]

Yet if all of this is apropos to Levi's experience with Pannwitz, Levi also adds something important to the mix. As the examination proceeds, Levi recalls his knowledge of chemistry and feels he is able to convey his professional identity to Pannwitz. Yet there is no sign that Pannwitz's general demeanor toward Levi is affected by that realization. Levi is *not* reduced to a simple recognition of his physical presence and gains much more than the simple acknowledgement of his social presence. He secures recognition of the fact that he is a chemist. Yet the result for Levi is not an interaction "between two men," but a profound sense of the human capacity to parse what we know from what we do not know of one another. In this way, Levi shows us that the problem of knowing one another is almost unimaginably elastic. Indeed, if being in the presence of one another elicits a minimal knowing of one another, Levi shows us that something much more than minimal can be utterly insufficient. Pannwitz is somehow capable of comprehending and yet not comprehending, seeing and yet not seeing. As Levinas might say, Levi encounters our capacity to render someone else both visible and invisible at the same time.[27]

---

[24] Levinas, 177.
[25] Sartre, *Being and Nothingness*, 327.
[26] Drawing on Hegel, Sartre is prone to connect the problem of recognition with objectification. He suggests that the primordial recognition that inspires the question as to who someone is, is analogous to our relationship to objects of the material world. Thus, we find ourselves looking at one another as objects, and relating to the strange unknown "nothing" of the other in ways that are terrifying and tend to reduce subjectivity to objectivity.
[27] Levinas, 61.

14   Part I: Theoretical Frames

Merleau-Ponty and Levinas suggest that one of the reasons we encounter problems of recognition is the "surplus of the social relation":[28] the active and affirmative plurality of human subjectivity. Against Sartre's focus on objectification, Merleau-Ponty and Levinas argue that we have difficulty recognizing and knowing one another because we are unpredictable beings that overflow and exceed the capacity of others to apprehend us and vice versa.

However, these features of subjectivity not make it difficult for us to know one another, they also potentially create problems in our simple being together. Sartre argues that even if we could completely know one another we would still be plagued by "the scandal of the plurality of consciousnesses".[29] Merleau-Ponty argues that:

> The criminal fails to see his crime, and the traitor his betrayal for what they are, not because they exist deeply embedded within him as unconscious representations or tendencies, but because they are so many relatively closed worlds, so many situations.[30]

While Merleau-Ponty generally has a more sanguine view of intersubjectivity, here he suggests that we are existentially bound to potential harm of and from one another as a consequence of the fact that we are embedded in particular intersubjective situations. Levinas describes the potential for danger in our simply being together in even more stark terms, when he argues that "freedom discovers itself murderous in its very exercise."[31] Here Levinas suggests that the simple fact that we *are*—the "facticity of power and freedom"—and that we exist in the context of community, means that we can be "murderous."

His choice of words here is both instructive and potentially misleading. Levinas does not mean to say that by simply existing and exercising freedom we commit murder in the physical sense. In fact, he strangely partitions off "freedom" from other aspects of who we are. Alongside his idea of murderous freedom, Levinas suggests that "the face" has a welcoming and open disposition, so that the "face to face" is peaceful and yet "nonetheless maintains the plurality of the same and the other."[32] Levinas invokes the phrase "murderous freedom," then, to emphasize the gravity of his claim that our existing together as separated and finite subjects means that we will necessarily come up short—well short—of our conceptions of moral perfection. According to Levinas, in coming to grips with my very existence as a subject I realize that by being and doing I am necessarily going to harm and destroy others and have indeed actively been doing so.

Again we find that Levi's description of his interaction with Pannwitz is consistent with much of what these philosophers say about subjectivity and that his lived experience adds nuance and depth to their claims. First, in read-

---

[28] Levinas discusses this in terms of the Myth of Gyges (Ibid., 221).
[29] Sartre, *Being and Nothingness*, 329.
[30] Merleau-Ponty, *Phenomenology of Perception*, 444.
[31] Levinas, 84.
[32] Ibid., 203.

ing "Chemical Examination" we might come to the conclusion that irrespective of problems of recognition, Levi might still encounter "that look." That is, it could be that the simple ineluctable difference between their perspectives and dispositions might allow for the moment that so troubles Levi.[33] Moments after describing Pannwitz's look, Levi writes:

> One felt in that moment, in an immediate manner, what we all thought and said of the Germans. The brain which governed those blue eyes and those manicured hands said: "This something in front of me belongs to a species which it is obviously opportune to suppress. In this particular case, one has to first make sure that it does not contain some utilizable element." And in my head, like seeds in an empty pumpkin: "Blue eyes and fair hair are essentially wicked. No communication possible. I am a specialist in mine chemistry. I am a specialist in organic syntheses. I am a specialist...."[34]

Here Levi clearly means to indicate that he is uncomfortable with the thoughts that Pannwitz's look inspires in him, they are like "seeds in an empty pumpkin." But when Pannwitz looks up from his writing table, it is as though "the scandal of plurality" confronts Levi directly. He is stuck there, confronted by Pannwitz's disposition and perspective, one that is utterly at odds with his most basic understanding of how one ought to relate to another. Pannwitz and Levi are confined to "so many relatively closed worlds, so many situations." In the fact that another person and a would-be colleague can be this way, Levi finds a demonstration of the murderous potential of "freedom."

INTERSUBJECTIVE VIOLENCE

Levi's encounter with Pannwitz, then, helps to illuminate and assist in the navigation of two of the more pernicious aspects of subjectivity described in contemporary political thought. However, there is more to be done. At times, existentialist and phenomenological thinkers seem to suggest that relations between subjects are always necessarily characterized by a degree of pain and suffering. To the contrary, just as our physical fragility and capability mean that physical violence is always a possibility but do not necessitate or adequately explain physical violence, the character of subjectivity suggests that intersubjective violence is always possible but not an indelible feature of every interaction between people. Likewise, while not every aspect of our physical fragility and ability is related to physical violence (our susceptibility to illness for instance), not every difficulty that arises between subjects is usefully understood to be intersubjective violence. Therefore, we should try to sketch out with a bit more clarity whether any, or what sort of, interaction might deserve the name.

---

[33] We might even interpret Levi's desire to see Pannwitz outside of the Lager, his curiosity about "the human soul," as indicative of his desire to sort out whether their encounter is due to a problem of recognition or a matter of fundamentally divergent ways of being.

[34] Levi, *Survival in Auschwitz*, 106.

Part I: Theoretical Frames

We should begin by noting that many thinkers implicitly or explicitly conceptualize violence as inherent in the nature of our relationships. A prominent theme is the idea that violence is the law or the breaking of the law. In *Crito,* Socrates argues that he cannot disobey the death sentence of the Athenian jury, because to disobey the law of Athens would be akin to doing violence to one's parents.[35] Likewise, in Sophocles' *Antigone,* Creon invokes his status as a father and the ruler of Thebes when justifying his death sentence for Antigone by saying, "he that breaches the law or does it violence/or thinks to dictate to those who govern him/shall never have my good word."[36] In both instances, violence is something done *to* the law by simply acting and being in a way that does not accord with it, as contrasted with the conspicuous physical punishment and killing practiced by the state itself.[37]

Contemporary philosophers who take up the issue offer a more nuanced perspective. In his "Critique of Violence," for instance, Benjamin suggests that certain kinds of strikes can be considered violent or nonviolent, and the difference seems to be in part a matter of whether they break the law.[38] In "The Force of Law" Derrida, drawing on Socrates and Benjamin, seems to suggest that the law itself, and the police as an embodiment of the law, are indicative of violence.[39] In both cases, physical violence is at issue, but at the same time Benjamin and Derrida clearly mean to suggest that the simple existence of a certain kind of strike or a particular set of government strictures can be violent. That is, law can be violent simply by embodying a way of being as opposed to physically punishing or harming citizens.

Serious attempts to describe violence as something indicative of intersubjectivity are, perhaps not surprisingly, also found in the work of the three phenomenologists we discussed above. Merleau-Ponty is the least interested in violence, though he does say at one point that perception itself can be violent.[40] Sartre's *Notebooks for an Ethics* and Levinas's *Totality and Infinity* provide perhaps the most thoroughgoing discussions of violence in the Western philosophical tradition and each deserve discussion beyond what is prudent here. In the *Notebooks* Sartre explicitly argues that violence should be understood as "a type of relation to the other";[41] and in *Totality* Levinas implies that violence is at the core of our most intimate interactions, associating it

---

[35] Plato, Crito 50b–51c, 91.
[36] Sophocles, ln 715–719, 187. A subsequent reference to violence, however, suggests that Creon himself commits violence in his refusal to bury Polyneices and his "burial" of the living Antigone because in doing so he acts against the natural order of things. Sophocles, ln 1144, 202.
[37] Wolin (24) cites Thucydides' use of the term to denote "the violation of the constitution"; fn. See Thucydides, 8:53, 568.
[38] Benjamin 1978.
[39] Derrida, 1992.
[40] Merleau-Ponty 1985, 421. See also Merleau-Ponty 2002, 2.
[41] Sartre, *Notebooks for an Ethics*, 215.

with murder[42] and death,[43] but also with injustice,[44] "seduction," "flattery,"[45] "the naïveté of being,"[46] feminine equivocation,[47] and "enjoyment being broken up."[48] In Sartre's case, however, the discussion always seems to circle back to objectification, making it difficult to discover exactly what distinguishes "the type of relation" we are seeking from physical violence. Levinas's desire to preserve the peaceful and ethical character of "the face to face" produces a puzzling attempt to cordon off "murderous" freedom from the rest of subjectivity.

Yet if the term violence is frequently associated with aspects of intersubjectivity, none of these thinkers really offer us a unifying conception that can help guide our thinking on the subject. Some themes have come to the forefront in the foregoing pages. Misrepresentations of ourselves in others, mischaracterizations of others in ourselves, ways of being that are at odds with one another, understandings that are incompatible—these are all attributable to the fact that we are separate, habitual, and creative beings in community with other separate, habitual, and creative beings. If we are bound by the strictures of the possibilities of subjectivity, then social interaction unavoidably involves experiencing profound difficulties. Sometimes those interactions are painful enough to warrant the name violence. We can conceptualize this sort of violence in a more general way: *Violence occurs when we encounter a disposition that is at odds with, prevents, or destroys our own.* Violence is the experience of discordant dispositions.

If some measure of this intersubjective violence is common enough, the experience of dispositions that severely compromise our capacity to be, or that stop our disposition in its tracks, are not so common. The interaction between Levi and Pannwitz is instructive. Certainly the other members of the Kommando might have found Pannwitz's look offensive, but Levi's is a special and particular feeling of disjuncture. Levi could have never guessed that he would encounter a chemist in Auschwitz who would look at him in that way, a being who could separate Levi's capacity to do science from nearly every other feature of his being. That particular disposition and way of being shatters Levi's ability to comport himself as he otherwise would. In Levi's literary work, it is clear that his professional identity is entirely integrated with his understanding of himself and the world. To encounter someone who acts as though such things can be disintegrated is the penultimate offense. We might even say that the driving force and overarching theme of Levi's writings after Auschwitz is an attempt to repair this breach, to make his identity coherent again by describing how science is deeply intertwined with love, literature, and everything human.[49]

---

[42] Levinas, 233.
[43] Ibid., 224.
[44] Ibid., 70.
[45] Ibid., 180.
[46] Ibid., 171.
[47] Ibid., 264.
[48] Ibid., 164.
[49] *The Periodic Table* is probably the exemplar in this regard, mixing autobiography and fiction while interweaving scientific insights and concepts. See Levi, *The Periodic Table*, 1984.

18   Part I: Theoretical Frames

In this way, we see that violence can involve a word, a gesture, or a look. But as those who understand the law and the breaking of the law as violence suggest, and as the very fact of the context of Auschwitz makes clear, intersubjective violence often involves ways of being and dispositions as enacted by institutions or cultures. Pierre Bourdieu describes what he calls symbolic violence in Kabyles communities in Algeria. He argues that the common practice of showing extraordinary generosity involves "'socially recognized' domination, in other words, *legitimate authority*":[50]

> ... The gentle, invisible form of violence, which is never recognized as such, and is not so much undergone as chosen [is] the violence of credit, confidence, obligation, personal loyalty, hospitality, gifts, gratitude, piety—in short, all the virtues honoured by the code of honour. . . .[51]

According to Bourdieu, these sets of expectations and values create a habitus that allows for certain people to rule over others, most dramatically in the relationship between a "master" and a *khammes*, who receives only a very small share of a crop that (in some cases) he alone works.[52] In this way, Bourdieu describes a kind of violence that is grounded in social relations and yet orders and adjudicates among bodies. The code of honour "involves no abstract discipline, no rigorous contracts, and no specific sanctions,"[53] yet Bourdieu identifies it as the source of domination among Kabyles and is bold enough to call it "violence."

Surely for many Kabyles, Bourdieu's use of the word "violence" would sound strange, just as describing legitimate institutions of American government such as airport security or freedom of speech as violent would sound strange to many Americans. However, when people enact ways of being that prevent or destroy the possibility of others being and doing in ways consistent with their identity and dispositions, it is usefully described as such. For some, being searched or screened at the airport is a fundamental violation of their understanding of who they are and what the role of government is.[54] For some, freedom of speech means that the American media are free to represent African American communities in ways that strike at the core of their self-understanding. Likewise, when people overturn extant repressive institutions and cultural norms, they are enacting ways of being that prevent those who enact the status quo from being as they may. Intersubjective violence plagues the human condition wherever the difficulties of living with one another are so pronounced that the experience of discordant dispositions strikes at the heart of who we are and/or fashion ourselves to be.

---
[50] Bourdieu, 192.
[51] Ibid.
[52] Ibid., 190.
[53] Ibid.
[54] For instance, Giorgio Agamben's Jan. 2004 piece in *Le Monde* describes why he resigned his position at New York University rather than being subjected to new American security procedures (http://www.artistsnetwork.org/news11/news570.html).

THE PROSPECTS FOR MITIGATING VIOLENCE

Both conceptions of violence developed here defy easy moral assessments and calculations. Very few people would argue that physical violence and intersubjective violence, when understood in these ways, are never justified. In fact, most people would probably argue that, in certain scenarios, we will be compelled by political necessity or moral duty to harm or destroy others' bodies for subjective purposes or to act in ways that exclude or destroy others from being as they may. However, with these conceptions of violence in hand we might ask: what are the prospects for mitigating our capacity to cause one another suffering? That is, what are the prospects for a credible pacifism, if these are indeed viable meanings of violence?

Of course, I can offer only a cursory assessment of the prospects here, but a few important points can at least initiate the conversation. First, I argued above that intersubjective violence is in some sense unavoidable because of the nature of subjectivity. Sartre, Merleau-Ponty, and Levinas argue persuasively that we cannot fully know one another and that, even if we could, we would create ways of being that are unpredictable and, at times at least, at odds with the habits and practices of others. In fact, we find that "nonviolent" social movements sometimes exacerbate intersubjective violence in the sense of highlighting and magnifying the discordant dispositions that characterize a society. When Mahatma Gandhi led Indians in a march to the sea to make salt, he confronted the expectations and destroyed the legitimacy of the British colonial state that prohibited such actions. When Rosa Parks and Martin Luther King led the bus boycott in Montgomery, Alabama, they incited a crisis and fundamentally challenged the habits of the white power structure. Of course, such actions were in response to systems and institutions that made it impossible for Indians and African Americans to live in ways consistent with their own self-understanding. In effect, by way of civil disobedience and mass direct action, nonviolent movements respond to intersubjective and physical violence by enacting ways of being that make it impossible for repressive structures to function. In doing so, they threaten the habits and identities of oppressors and in that way practice and exacerbate intersubjective violence.

Yet in doing so such movements attempt to attend to, confront and resolve long-festering problems that generate intersubjective violence over the long run. H. J. N. Horsburgh describes Gandhi's method of *satyagraha* in this way:

> A Gandhian appeal operates on two levels, not only challenging opponents to recognize the justice of a certain cause but also to develop an attachment to satya [truth] itself, thereby entering into a co-operative inquiry into human needs. It also attaches more importance to a co-operative pursuit of truth than to the recognition of the truth, which the specific cause is thought to represent. Thus, it holds particular disagreements in perspective, insisting that a fundamentally co-operative relationship is

possible between those who disagree about even the most important specific issues.[55]

In effect, nonviolent movements accept the basic premise that we are stuck in relationships with others. By refusing to take up the body of another in order to achieve subjective ends, pacifism understands that the human needs of both oppressors and the oppressed are at stake. In order to unearth and grapple with long-standing and seemingly intractable difficulties, the person who practices satyagraha (a satyagrahi) may exacerbate difficulties in the short run but hopes to initiate a conversation that can make for a more settled future. What's more, if nonviolent activists destroy and undermine extant habits and institutions, they exhibit a willingness to embrace suffering as a demonstration of good will, the seriousness of the issue at hand, and the ongoing pain and unacceptability of the status quo.

We might also note that by implicitly accepting the ineluctable nature of subjectivity pacifists are on to something else. In fact, the issues that surround intersubjective violence indicate that physical violence cannot overcome or reliably determine the character of subjectivity. That is, in light of the problems of recognition and freedom, attempts to manipulate the character of subjectivity by way of one another's bodies are, at best, temporary solutions to more difficult problems. Indeed, pacifists argue that they produce no more consistent results than demonstrating a willingness to take on and endure physical suffering.

This point becomes particularly salient given the definition of physical violence developed above. If what is at stake in physical violence is subjectivity, then the use of physical violence provides us with very little certainty as to its outcome. Pacifism suggests that the hopes and dreams of would-be practitioners of physical violence will come to naught—we might amend that and say they will *often* come to naught. Killing people can ensure that others never act, talk, or do again. However, killing cannot determine how other people will react to such death. Physically harming and threatening people can reliably produce screams and suffering, but the conclusions that people draw from such suffering (i.e., whether or not to change their will) are not so foreseeable. Sometimes threatening and killing people can cause people to conform to certain notions of how we ought to be. However, on other occasions attempts to physically manipulate and destroy others will produce precisely the opposite effect. Causing physical suffering in order to change people's ways of being, or simply destroying ways of being altogether, does not ultimately produce predictable subjective results.

Currently, the most powerful military in the world has found that attempting to use physical violence to create a certain kind of society in Iraq is entirely ineffective. Tensions and fissures in society, many of which consti-

---

[55] H. J. N. Horsburgh, *Non-Violence and Aggression: A Study of Gandhi's Moral Equivalent of War* (London, New York [etc.]: Oxford U.P., 1968), 162.

tute instances and examples of intersubjective violence, have not been reduced by physical violence; if anything physical violence has only heightened the sense of frustration and disagreement among Iraqis. Pacifists might point out that if Iraqis and Americans are eventually able to create a more stable Iraq, it will be a consequence of efforts to take up the underlying question of how Iraqis (and Americans) ought to live with one another—that is, the questions and problems that drive the physical violence in the first place.

While pacifist methods will never produce a world where people do not cause one another to suffer, they do highlight the fact that our attempts to improve our condition by physically destroying and manipulating one another are unlikely to produce satisfactory results over the long term. Instead, nonviolent social activists embrace the responsibility of confronting our various ways of imagining how we ought to live together, our diverse habits and dispositions, and our capacity to create new ways of relating to one another. While such processes can be tremendously painful and tumultuous, they acknowledge the realities—and violence—of subjectivity. In that way, at least, they hold out the hope of a more humane approach to the contradictions and difficulties of human togetherness.

References

Aristotle. *Politics.* Translated by Ernest Barker. Oxford; New York: Oxford University Press, 1998.

Benjamin, Walter. *Reflections: Essays, Aphorisms, Autobiographical Writings.* Translated by Edmund Jephcott. New York: Harcourt Brace Jovanovich, 1978.

Bourdieu, Pierre. *Outline of a Theory of Practice.* Cambridge; New York: Cambridge University Press, 1977.

Breitman, George (ed.). "The Founding Rally of the OAAU." In *By Any Means Necessary: Speeches, Interviews and a Letter by Malcolm X.* New York: Pathfinder Press, 1970.

Clausewitz, Carl von. *On War.* Translated by J. J. Graham. New & revised ed. Harmondsworth: Penguin, 1968.

Derrida, Jacques. "The Force of Law." In *Deconstruction and the Possibility of Justice,* edited by Drucilla Cornell, Michel Rosenfeld and David Carlson. New York: Routledge, 1992.

Hall, Barbara. "Race in Hobbes." In *Race and Racism in Modern Philosophy,* edited by Andrew Valls, pp. vi, 293. Ithaca, NY: Cornell University Press, 2005.

Hegel, Georg Wilhelm Friedrich. *Phenomenology of Spirit.* Translated by Arnold V. Miller. Oxford: Oxford University Press, 1977.

Hobbes, Thomas. *Leviathan: With Selected Variants from the Latin Edition of 1668.* Indianapolis: Hackett Pub. Co., 1994.

Horsburgh, H. J. N. *Non-Violence and Aggression: A Study of Gandhi's Moral Equivalent of War.* London, New York [etc.]: Oxford U.P., 1968.

Levi, Primo. *Survival in Auschwitz: The Nazi Assault on Humanity.* Translated by Stuart Woolf. 1st Touchstone ed. New York: Simon & Schuster, 1996.

———. *The Periodic Table.* Translated by Raymond Rosenthal. 1st American ed. New York: Schocken Books, 1984.

Levinas, Emmanuel. *Totality and Infinity: An Essay on Exteriority.* Pittsburgh, PA: Duquesne University Press, 2001.

Machiavelli, Niccoláo. The Prince. In *Selected Political Writings*. Translated by David Wootton. Indianapolis: Hackett Pub. Co., 1994.

Marcus, Sharon. "Fighting Bodies, Fighting Words: A Theory and Politics of Rape Prevention." In *Feminists Theorize the Political*, edited by Judith Butler and Joan Wallach Scott, 385–403. New York: Routledge, 1992.

Marx, Karl. *Karl Marx: Selected Writings*. Translated by Lawrence H. Simon: Hackett, 1994.

Merleau-Ponty, Maurice. *Humanism and Terror: An Essay on the Communist Problem*. Boston: Beacon Press, 1985.

———. *Phenomenology of Perception, Routledge Classics*. London; New York: Routledge, 2002.

Mills, Charles W. *The Racial Contract*. Ithaca: Cornell University Press, 1997.

Pateman, Carole. *The Sexual Contract*. Stanford, CA.: Stanford University Press, 1988.

Plato. *The Last Days of Socrates*. Translated by Hugh Tredennick and Harold Tarrant, Penguin Classics. New York: Penguin Books, 1993.

Sartre, Jean-Paul. *Notebooks for an Ethics*. Translated by David Pellauer. Chicago: University of Chicago Press, 1992.

Sartre, Jean-Paul. *Being and Nothingness*. New York: Washington Square Press, 1993.

Scarry, Elaine. *The Body in Pain: The Making and Unmaking of the World*. New York: Oxford University Press, 1985.

Sophocles. *Sophocles*. Translated by David Grene. 2nd ed. Chicago: University of Chicago Press, 1991.

Thucydides. *History of the Peloponnesian War*. Translated by Rex Warner. Rev. ed. Harmondsworth, UK: Baltimore: Penguin Books, 1972.

Wolin, Sheldon S. "Violence and the Western Political Tradition." *American Journal of Orthopsychiatry* 33 (1963): 15–28.

2

Exposing the Roots and Healing the Wounds of Religiously Sanctioned Violence

Peter Ellard

Since September 11, 2001, many writers of all leanings have written articles and books about the violence perpetrated by Muslims. Much of what has been written has critiqued sections of the Quran, traditions of the Prophet Muhammad, and later expressions of Islam.[1] Some have called upon Muslims to follow the lead of Western enlightenment Christianity. Others have offered apologetic responses highlighting the noble nature of Islam co-opted by a few extremists. Some writers have turned the focus on Christianity's rich tradition of religiously sanctioned violence. This has included exposés on scripture and traditions across denominations.[2] While this essay will add to the latter conversation, it also will seek to focus not on the extreme elements of the religious fundamentalists, but on how moderate religious people—and most believers fall within this category—continue to sanction the violence in their sacred texts and thus leave the ground fertile for extremist cooptation of those texts. In the end, we will offer our own "modest proposal," which seeks to radically alter the conversation and to begin to pave the way toward healing a fractured world.

Written especially for *Ruminations in Violence*.

---

[1] For two such readings, see B. Lewis, *The Crisis of Islam: Holy War and Unholy Terror* (New York: Modern Library, 2003); P. Berman, *Terror and Liberalism* (New York: W.W. Norton, 2003); John Esposito, *Unholy War: Terror in the Name of Islam* (New York: Oxford University Press, 2002). See also chapter 4 in Sam Harris, *The End of Faith: Religion, Terror, and the Future of Reason* (New York: W.W. Norton, 2004).

[2] Jack Nelson-Pallmeyer, *Is Religion Killing Us? Violence in the Bible and the Quran* (New York: Trinity Press, 2003); Regina M. Schwartz, *The Curse of Cain: The Violent Legacy of Monotheism* (Chicago: University of Chicago Press, 1997).

The violent acts carried out by the 9/11 hijackers, the Branch Davidians at Waco, Aum Shinrikyo in Tokyo, and Paul Hill in Florida were the work of radical extremists within the respective religious traditions. Men carried them out—almost all of the active participants were male—who listened to their leaders or their leaders' interpretation of sacred texts, which sanctioned the violence they undertook. In no case do we have people carrying out religiously sanctioned violence after acknowledging that those acts contradict their sacred texts. That is, there is no case where they recognize that the Bible or Quran forbids this action and then say, "I will undertake it anyway because I have been inspired to do so by my leaders, my conscience, or my own well reasoned logic." These extremists still had to perform extreme feats of mental gymnastics to obtain their interpretation of the texts in order to justify their actions. Indeed, the interpretative process of those who kill children as combatants and take down buildings with thousands of people in them makes for fascinating case studies. It is my contention that moderate Christians—those who position themselves between the extremes within a given tradition and who seek to maintain the current status quo—must serve as an example to others and decommission from the ranks of the sacred what Phyllis Trible has called "texts of terror."[3]

As has been noted by many scholars, the very term "violence" is contested. While it is easy to center on a definition akin to "harm to persons or property," it is more difficult to come to consensus on the definition of "person" and "harm." While shooting and killing someone is clearly violence, adjusting the tax system so the burden falls disproportionately on the most vulnerable and thus indirectly causing "harm" has been cause for less condemnation.[4] While acknowledging the limited scope of the focus on the physical violation of another's person or property, this will remain our central focus. Still, it will become clear that our conclusions could easily be applied to any functional definition of violence.

WE LIVE IN A VIOLENT WORLD

It has become a truism to state that since the dawn of recorded history people have lived in conflict. Contrary to those who look toward an Edenic past of peace and brotherly love, there never was a time when conflict was not a part of the human condition. Rousseau's ruminations in his "Discourse on the Origin of Inequality"—where he pictures an idyllic time before humans first laid eyes on and then hands on a piece of private property, and a time when the noble savage (always male) lived on his own, stopping only to mate without emotion—was both a flight of literary fancy and poor anthropology.

---

[3] Phyllis Trible, *Texts of Terror: Literary Feminist Readings of Biblical Narratives* (Philadelphia: Fortress Press, 1984).

[4] See Robert B. Miller, "Violence, Force, and Coercion," in Jerome A. Schaffer (ed.), *Violence* (New York: David McKay, 1971), 25.

Indeed, contemporary evolutionary biology reveals that humans developed out of and within the same conflictual and competitive world that we see today in the world's prairies, jungles, and forests.[5]

Violence is a natural part of the universe and of the human condition. Our central focus here is on what Jack Nelson-Pallmeyer calls the "violence of God traditions."[6] This refers to those texts and traditions which place punishments or threats of violence as divinely authoritative—as part of God's thoughts, actions, or plan. It also refers to those texts that present violent images of God. That violence exists and perhaps has to exist among nation states is not in question. What is in question is the use and abuse of religion to support, instigate, and further violence.

We are not blind to the fact that there are other, sometimes more compelling reasons why people participate in violent acts of terror. However, our focus is precisely on the religious element. Andrew Sullivan offers some suggestions on this theme. After acknowledging that the history of Christianity, as well as Islam, is filled with religiously sanctioned violence, he writes; "It seems almost as if there is something inherent in religious monotheism that lends itself to this kind of terrorist temptation. And our bland attempts to ignore this—to speak for this violence as if it did not have religious roots—is some kind of denial. We don't want to denigrate religion as such, and so we deny that religion is at the heart of this. But we would understand the conflict better, perhaps, if we first acknowledged that religion is responsible in some way, and then figure out how and why."[7]

RELIGIOUSLY SANCTIONED VIOLENCE IN OUR TIME

We acknowledge that violence carried out by religious extremists is rooted in various layers of cultural, political and economic realities.[8] With Sullivan, however, we feel it is necessary to focus on the religious roots of the problems and the religious pieces of the puzzle, which will form the path away from such tainted traditions. We begin with three vignettes on religiously sanctioned violence.

The Army of God

In 1993, Paul Hill, a Presbyterian minister, shot and killed Dr. John Bayard Britton. In an online posting entitled "Why Shoot An Abortionist?", written before he was executed, Hill explained the religious sanction for his actions. He wrote:

---

[5] Richard Wrangham and Dale Peterson, *Demonic Males Apes and the Origins of Human Violence* (New York: Houghton Mifflin, 1996).
[6] Jack Nelson-Pallmeyer, *Is Religion Killing Us? Violence in the Bible and the Quran.*
[7] Andrew Sullivan, "This *is* a Religious War," *The New York Times Magazine* (Oct. 7, 2001): 45N46.
[8] Jessica Stern, *Terror in the Name of God: Why Religious Militants Kill* (New York: Harper Collins, 2003).

> I realized that using force to stop abortion is the same means that God has used to stop similar atrocities throughout history. In the book of Esther, for instance, Ahasuerus, king of Persia, passed a law in 473 B.C. allowing the Persians to kill their Jewish neighbors. But the Jews did not passively submit; their uses of defensive force prevented a calamity of immense proportions. In much the same way, when abortion was first legalized in our nation, if the people had resisted this atrocity with the means necessary it would have saved millions of children from a bloody death. It is not unwise or unspiritual, thus, to use the means that God has appointed for keeping His commandments; rather it is presumptuous to neglect these means and expect Him to work apart from them.[9]

Indeed, since Michael Griffin murdered Dr. David Gunn outside a clinic that performed abortions in Pensacola, Florida, in 1993, seven clinicians or doctors have been killed and there have been 17 attempted murders. Since *Roe* was enacted, there have been 173 arson attacks, 41 bombings, and 89 attempted attacks.[10] Many of the people involved in these acts are "God-fearing" Christians who frequently cite biblical passages to support their actions.

The last five years have shown a marked downward trend in violence at abortion clinics and against abortion providers. However, the Army of God, a loose affiliation of radical anti-abortion Christian terrorists, remains active and committed, in the name of God, to disrupt access. The Army of God is a fringe group. However, the sacred texts they use to support their actions can be found in millions of homes across the land. The sanctified violence sits silently, waiting for the next individual or groups of individuals to read, ponder, and validate as God's commands. Those who call themselves "pro-life" in the United States do in general not support these acts of extreme violence. Moreover, American clergy across denominations have spoken out against such violence. To date, however, there has been no condemnation of the image of God presented in the Book of Esther, which shows divine sanction for the slaughter of the Jews' enemies, "including the wives and children" (Esther 8:11).

Apocalypse Now: Waco, Texas

Our second example is David Koresh, the leader of the Branch Davidians, an off-shoot of the Seventh Day Adventists. He was a longtime student of the apocalyptic tradition of the Adventists and saw himself as a prophet who would fight alongside Christ against the Babylonians: the U.S. government. At Mt. Carmel, the Davidian compound later renamed Ranch Apocalypse, Koresh and his followers lived in isolation—except for trafficking in firearms—of the local people. There in Waco, Texas, they sought to prepare for earthly destruction to accompany the coming of Christ. The conflict in

---

[9] Paul Hill, "Why Shoot an Abortionist?" (http://www.armyofgod.com/PHillonepage.html)
[10] The National Abortion Federation maintains extensive clinic violence statistics on their Web site (http://www.prochoice.org/).

1993 with the FBI and ATF was an accident of timing exacerbated by ignorance on the part of the government forces. Without any real knowledge of the workings and "rationale" of a millennialist apocalyptic religion like the Davidians, their actions fed into the paranoia and prophecy of the Davidians and may have contributed to a violent confrontation that was avoidable. Still, David Koresh and his followers were prepared for the violence and indeed saw it as a necessary outcome of any true reading of the scriptures and the signs of the end times in the world around them. In short, they believed that the violence in which they saw themselves taking part, with or without the actions of the federal employees, was foretold and sanctioned by God.[11]

Koresh and many of Davidians were burned to death in the fire that accompanied the assault on the compound. Many of his followers are still active. Their interpretation of the apocalyptic literature is clearly at odds with that of the majority of American Christians. Still, the passages of Bible that speak about the end times are there for anyone who wants to read them. Moreover, if we look at the success of the "Left Behind" series of books and film, we can see that there are many people who are waiting for the right signs. They believe that God and God's plan are ultimately behind the violence that plagues our world.

"With God on Our Side": U.S. Domestic and Foreign Policy

If it were just the radical fringe of human society who see in the pages of scripture the recipe for how God has acted, currently acts, and will act in the world, and how violence is sanctioned by that same God, there might not be as much cause for concern. However, arguably there are millions of Americans who recognize in the recent events of history the signs of the end of the world that they read about in the Bible. These texts, moreover, are some of the most violent in the whole canon of scripture.

Two recent books, Ester Kaplan's *With God on Their Side*[12] and Kevin Phillips' *American Theocracy*,[13] describe in great detail the influence that the "religious right" has on the current administration. They list many appointments, beginning with then Attorney General John Ashcroft, of Christian fundamentalists to significant positions—which, in and of itself, is perhaps not a problem. What may be a problem is that these individuals openly seek to use their version of biblical morality as they carry out their jobs. The results may include seemingly innocuous things like covering up half-nude statues in the Justice department or insisting that the bookstore at the Grand

---

[11] Dick Anthony and Thomas Robbins, "Religious Totalism, Exemplary Dualism and the Waco Tragedy," in *Millennium, Messiahs & Mayhem*, edited by Thomas Robbins and Susan Palmer (New York: Routledge 1997), 261–284.

[12] Ester Kaplan, *With God on Their Side: How Christian Fundamentalists Trampled Science, Policy, and Democracy in George W. Bush's White House* (New York: New Press, 2004).

[13] Kevin Phillips' *American Theocracy: The Peril and Politics of Radical Religion, Oil, and Borrowed Money in the 21st Century* (New York: Penguin, 2006).

Canyon carry a book that describes how the canyon's creation can be understood from a Creationist perspective.[14] However, it may also have far more serious implications.

More pertinent to this essay is that many within this powerful constituency believe that God is following a script encrypted in the pages of scripture and is using the United States as a tool toward the ultimate conclusion of the rapture and the end times.[15] Indeed, Phillips argues that this constituency, deeply rooted in a biblically based view of the God of war and the apocalypse, wields influence on U.S. policy especially as it relates to Israel and to the war in Iraq. Among the strongest base of the Republican Party—those who vote in the primaries—most believe that we are living in the end days and that the war in Iraq (Babylon) is a part of God's divine plan as outlined in the scriptures. Furthermore, some of these people are in positions of real power.

Lieutenant General William Boykin, Deputy Undersecretary of Defense for Intelligence and a senior policy maker in the "War on Terror," recounted in 2002 an experience he had while viewing aerial photography of the scene of the defeat of U.S. forces in Somalia in 1993. He said, while addressing a church audience in full military uniform, that he could see or sense the presence of Satan in the photographs. He said he saw in the photographs "the principalities of darkness. It is a demonic presence in that city that God revealed to me as the enemy." At another presentation at a church, when referring to the U.S. military enemies, he said that our "spiritual enemy will only be defeated if we come against them in the name of Jesus."[16] Whether or not the invasion of Iraq was a good idea is a topic for another conversation, but this is a man responsible for decisions concerning U.S. foreign policy. The idea that there are those in the government who believe that Jesus/God is marching into war on the side of the United States is extremely disconcerting. Still, even a casual read through many Biblical texts can leave the reader believing that these leaders have ample support for the violence they perpetrate.

Another example reflective of a similar mind-set is found in the thought of Supreme Court Justice Anton Scalia. In a talk to the Divinity School at the University of Chicago explaining why the death penalty is perfectly legal and ethical, Scalia, who considers himself a devout Catholic, cites St. Paul as support for his position: "The core of his message is that government—however you want to limit that concept—derives its moral authority from God." Seeking to differentiate Americans from Europeans, Scalia states that people in the United States "are more inclined to understand, as St. Paul did, that government carries the sword as 'the minister of God' to execute wrath on the evildoer." In affect, Scalia is stating, as he does elsewhere, that his under-

---

[14] Chris Mooney, "W's Christian Nation," *American Prospect*, 14(6), June 1, 2003.

[15] For an overview of the history of American Fundamentalist Christians and their view of the role of Israel in U.S. foreign policy see Donald Wagner, "The Evangelical-Jewish Alliance," in *The Christian Century,* June 28, 2003, 20–24.

[16] William Arkin, "The Pentagon Unleashes a Holy Warrior," *Los Angeles Times*, Oct. 16, 2003.

standing of the Bible and Christian tradition is a central component of his judicial philosophy.[17]

BIBLICAL PORTRAITS AND A HISTORY OF RELIGIOUSLY SANCTIONED VIOLENCE

There are several excellent studies of the violence and portraits of a violent God in the Old Testament/Hebrew Scriptures.[18] We highlight here just a few passages to demonstrate the nature of the issue.

The thirteenth chapter of the book of Isaiah offers us a glimpse of God whose day comes "cruel, with wrath and fierce anger to make the earth a desolation, and to destroy its sinners from it." These sinners included anyone who—along with other heinous crimes—said the word God, ate the wrong food, worked on the wrong day of the week, or dishonored his or her parents. This would also include those who worshiped other Gods. These sinners will have "their infants dashed to pieces before their eyes . . . and their wives ravished."[19] However one wishes to contextualize this passage, in order to understand it within its historical milieu, one reads here the sanctification of the killing of innocent babies and the rape of women. In times of war, God is often portrayed as fighting on the side of the Israelites as they destroy their enemies. God also fights against the "chosen people" when they go astray. In the book of Jeremiah God says to the Israelites; "I will fight against you with outstretched hand and mighty arm, in anger, in fury, and in great wrath."[20]

One additional reference will suffice our present purposes. If we turn to Numbers 31: 1-20, we see a stunning example of religiously sanctioned violence. Here Moses is commanded by God to slay all the males of neighboring tribes and burn what remained behind. The striking part comes when the commanders return from their victorious battle and Moses is very angry. The text reads:

> And Moses was angry with the officers of the arm, the commanders of the thousands, and the commanders of the hundreds, who had come from service in the war. Moses said to them, "Have you let all the women live?" Behold, these caused the people of Israel, by the counsel of Balaam, to act treacherously against the Lord in the matter of Pe'or, and so the plague came upon the congregation of the Lord. Now therefore, kill every male among the little ones, and kill every woman who has known man by lying with him. But all the young girls who have not known man by lying with him, keep for yourselves.

---

[17] Anton Scalia, "God's Justice and Ours," *First Things*, May 2002, 17–21.
[18] Jack Nelson-Pallmeyer, *Is Religion Killing Us? Violence in the Bible and the Quran;* Regina Schwartz, *The Curse of Cain: The Violent Legacy of Monotheism* (Chicago: University of Chicago Press, 1997).
[19] Isaiah 13: 9, 16.
[20] Jeremiah 21:4.

30   Part I: Theoretical Frames

The vindictive, merciless violence of this scene is bad enough. More disturbing is the fact that there is no hint here of any moral uneasiness with Moses' actions. There are scores of similarly morally suspect texts of violence that rise to the level of sadism and terrorism. Jack Nelson-Pallmeyer offers a thorough list of such disturbing texts within the Old and New Testaments. More specifically, Phyllis Trible points to texts which highlight violence against women—Hagar, Tamar and the daughters of Jephthah, along with those who remain unnamed.[21] While scholars can debate the historical and literary critical elements of the texts, mothers and fathers—perhaps the parents of David Koresh, Paul Hill and General Boykin—read these texts to their children.

Dealing with these "Texts of Terror"

What do we do with texts like these? How do we retain their status as divinely inspired? How do we measure the impact that such texts have, on ordinary people as well as those in positions of political power, who see the Bible as the unerring word of God?

We are reminded here that since the words were first collected—and long before that in oral traditions—these texts have been interpreted and reinterpreted to fit the prevailing view of God of the day. We are also cautioned that the words should be understood within their context. This, however, fails to cover their horrific content and the horrific actions ascribed to God. In his work on violence and religion, Leo Lefebure tells us:

> In pondering the biblical trajectory of holy war, Origen recognized that an uncritical acceptance of the scriptures can lead to erroneous ideas about God, specifically regarding violence; and he used the criterion of what is fitting and proper for God to determine what was to be taken as literal and what as allegory in the scriptures. Augustine used the criterion of *caritas*, self-giving love, to make this determination. Passages that condemn *cupidity* and teach *caritas* are to be taken as literal; those that appear to violate this rule must have another, allegorical meaning. Thus each author has an interpretative strategy that could reverse the direct literal sense of the biblical texts that command violence in the name of God.[22]

The problem of course is that even through all the varied interpretations, the vitriolic texts remain. The images of a mean and angry God are still there for millions to read and to imitate, just waiting for people like Koresh, Hill, and Boykin to come along and adopt them as their own.

It is just too easy to rely on the adage of "a few bad apples" or that the people were not acting like good Christians, or that they were misguided and operating from a poor interpretation of scripture. The "violence of God" traditions—from the gruesome murder of Hypatia in the fifth century, to the tor-

---

[21] Phyllis Trible, *Texts of Terror: Literary Feminist Readings of Biblical Narratives.*
[22] Leo Lefebure, *Revelation, the Religions and Violence* (New York: Orbis, 2000), 128.

turing, dismembering, and burning of heretics under the guidance of Church officials; to the Crusades, the slave trade, and the wild and rampant anti-Semitism that flows throughout Christian history—remained strong. Moreover, at every turn, these violent acts were done with what was thought to be the explicit support of the sacred texts. In truth, it is difficult to read the history of Christianity any differently from that of the rest of human culture. Ours is a history of violence, the roots of which lay in our scriptural traditions and in ourselves.

AUTHORITATIVE OPPOSING VOICES

Scripture has many faces. For every text in support of violence there are also texts of love, compassion, forgiveness, and redemption. Countertraditions in the Old Testament present images of God as loving Wisdom. In the Rabbinic traditions and throughout Christian history there are many voices opposed to these wide and varied traditions of religiously sanctioned violence. Still, the "texts of terror" remained. Over the last century the American Catholic Bishops have written extensively on many topics, including the violence of nuclear weapons, the violence of Appalachian poverty, and the violence of economic injustice. They have spoken out against abortion, capital punishment and, more recently, the war in Iraq. Still the texts remain. Indeed, the pontificate of John Paul II was filled with many official apologies on behalf of the *actions* of individual Catholics—though not of the Church itself. Still, short of indicating that the way they had been interpreted was no longer authorized, the texts of sanctified violence remain.

Today, the interpretative process continues. Many moderate Christians find solace in the fact that as Western liberal Christianity grew, it adopted and adapted the texts to meet its newly enlightened senses. Many of the texts of biblically sanctioned violence have been reinterpreted by appeal to authority, by an appeal to the individual conscience, and by an appeal to reason. However, even when religious leaders condemn violence and selectively edit by skipping difficult parts in Sunday services, the seeds of violence remain. These seeds, once sown, are nourished and periodically reaped.

There is an oft-quoted, unattributed line to the effect of: "Show me an issue, and I'll find a scriptural citation to support it." Unless a community has one authoritative voice on interpretation, individuals will reinterpret the words many times over. There is no getting around this, and it is not normally a cause for alarm. Still, the blatant image of God as a violent, jealous, unbalanced psychopath appears time after time as a reason for the actions of extremists and religious terrorists. Along with love thy neighbor and justice for the poor comes vengeance upon the wicked and condemnation of the enemy. Along with heaven, there is hell. We are also told that for those who wish to remain Christian, we can't just erase or pick and choose the pages of scripture to our liking as if we were at a buffet. Perhaps it is time to reconsider this prohibition.

32   Part I: Theoretical Frames

Lynn White, Walter Rauschenbusch, and Larry Rasmussen

As we begin to seek a pathway out of the malaise of the "violence of God" traditions, we look to the past for insight. We can take our first clue from Lynn White, a mid-twentieth-century scientist whose 1967 essay, "The Historical Roots of Our Ecological Crisis," caused a great deal of reflection and reaction on the part of Christians.[23] Essentially, White argued that the religious consciousness of the modern Western Christian world, beginning in the fourteenth century, forms the root cause of the modern ecological crisis. His essay produced a whole genre of critiques and follow-up studies. Often forgotten, however, is White's final plea. He argues that if a religious worldview got us into the problem of environmental degradation, then it is religious voices that must get us out of it. Exactly how religion can be employed in this endeavor is a topic of much debate. One contemporary theologian offers us a suggestion.

I once hosted a lecture given by Larry Rasmussen, then the Reinhold Niebuhr Professor of Social Ethics at Union College. In his talk on Christian ecological theology, Rasmussen spoke of the late nineteenth-century proponent of the Social Gospel movement, Walter Rauschenbusch, who challenged Christian pastors and theologians to continually "do their first works over." He called on people to closely examine their traditions, practices, and interpretations of scripture. While Rauschenbusch had spoken of the need to reread the Gospel and refocus its implications on justice for the poor, Rasmussen spoke about how theologians need to rethink all basic ideas as the current state of the environment necessitates our doing so. Both of these theologians have a point. One could argue that given the current state of religiously sanctioned violence in the world, Christians need to go back and do our "first works" over. It would seem fitting to start with the canonicity of sacred texts themselves.

If religion is part of the problem, then religion needs to be part of the solution. It is possible that leaders of religious institutions, parishes and other groups, both ordained and lay, need to step up and refuse to validate those passages of scripture in which God or heroic people celebrate violence. While we may need to acknowledge that a distinction between vindictive, preemptive violence, and violence which comes as a result of self-defense, images and stories such as those we have related hardly fall within the latter category. It is indeed possible that these texts need to be excised from the ranks of the holy, the ranks of the inspired. As we look for guidance on such delicate matters, we would do well to look in unfamiliar places. We turn here to explore an additional perspective from an area to which we might not think to look for insight: that of rationalistic atheism.

God, Heaven and Hell: One Atheist's Educated Opinion

In his book, *The End of Faith: Religion, Terror, and Future of Reason*, Sam Harris picks up the mantle of Bernard Russell. Harris does not seek to simply

---

[23] Lynn White, Jr., "The Historical Roots of Our Ecologic Crisis," *Science,* 155, 1203 (1967).

present the basic tenets of Christian and Islamic faith as untenable. Rather, he presents the very psychic structure of religious faith in general as being thoroughly irrational, destructive, and beyond redemption. Although the text has its flaws, in a series of bold and highly critical expository chapters Harris condemns faith-based religious understanding as a deterrent to the flowering of a rational society. Moderate religious adherents are, in Harris's mind, as much a part of the problem as are religious extremists.[24] This is because moderates often seek to soften the uncomfortable parts of the tradition only to give support to the faith based—albeit abhorrent—extremist views.

In one section of the text Harris asks the reader to look at the basic precept of heaven and hell in the Christian and Islamic view of the afterlife. The basic premise—and the majority of American Christians hold this position—is that some people (or their souls) will go to heaven to enjoy some kind of life of peace and happiness with God, while some (most) will be carted off to hell to suffer for eternity. According to this fundamental story of creation, sin and redemption, God has created a world whose outcome, based on human choices or on predestination, is eternal violence sanctioned by God. Now perhaps, as many are told by their parents and preachers, this hurts God more than it hurts the "sinner." Still, it has to hurt the sinner an awful lot.

Liberal theologians and college chaplains across America have gone to painstaking ends to soften this picture of what is to many a fundamental part of their faith. The end result is one that mirrors a poor magician's slight of hand and art of distraction. Harris makes the reader ponder the reality beyond the many passages of the Jewish, Christian, and Islamic Scriptures—some of which we highlighted above—which present a brutal God of unquenchable wrath and destruction. In short, Harris calls on us to ask: What can we expect of a religion where the central eschatological premise is eternal, divinely sanctioned violence? Is this still acceptable? Harris leads us to consider that if judgment will produce violence, if the end product is violence beyond Dante's most vivid imagination, then it is a short step for religious fanatics (who were once in the mainstream, listening to these stories at the feet of their grandparents) to bring that violence onto this side of the created order. In short, the Branch Davidians were simply trying to "work with God," to partner with God, to help the end-time destruction and punishment begin. This is precisely how people like General Boykin and Pat Robertson, with his television audience in the millions, view current U.S. foreign policy.

The Alien Question

If we think Harris is on the wrong track with regard to atheism serving as the only option, we are in good company. Research indicates that the vast majority of Americans believe in God, and many believe that the Bible is the literal word of God. Even though some of what Harris has to say is tenuous

---

[24] Sam Harris, *The End of Faith: Religion, Terror, and the Future of Reason* (New York: W.W. Norton, 2004).

and even dismissible, still, he does cause us to stop and reconsider the texts and teachings we hold to be sacred. For example, try the following variation of a commonplace hypothetical thought experiment. Imagine that years from now beings from another planet finally make their way to earth, long after humans have exterminated each other through war or have made the planet a toxic waste dump incapable of supporting human life. These aliens are very interested in finding out what this lost species was all about and, being of religious inclination, they peruse our most sacred texts—specifically, some of the basic precepts of the Hebrew and Christian scriptures as well as Christian eschatological theology. These alien visitors might reasonably conclude that the violence that brought about our end was the natural outcome of the violence practiced and sanctioned by God and as outlined in the pages of scripture and in Christian doctrine.

But wait, you protest, what about all those passages about love your neighbor and your enemy, and what of the redemptive compassion of the cross and the moral outline of the Sermon on the Mount? These texts would survive as well, but a valid reading—from an alien point of view—might be that these texts lost out to others that espoused violence, wrath, vengeance, and destruction. These aliens might ask, "Why did these people not follow the precepts of love and compassion instead of the texts of terror and violent images of God? Was there not a way to pragmatically insure a peaceful existence where excess power is held in check, while the norm was not a state of perpetual war and violence?" We might ask ourselves the same questions.

THOUGHTS OF A PRIEST, A HERETIC, AND THE THIRD PRESIDENT OF THE UNITED STATES

I had the good fortune one afternoon in the early 1990s to act as chauffeur for the theologian Thomas Berry, who had been a guest speaker in a graduate class. I had the chance to ask him about one of his suggestions about putting the Bible on the shelf because we no longer know how to read it. I asked him if he was serious. After all, these texts have guided Christians and Jews for thousands of years. In his reply he said, "There is good and there is bad in its pages. However, we as a consumerist, petroleum-based culture have become so hypnotized by ourselves and our corrupt images of God that we now read the text with blinders on. We read as if blind." Instead, Berry argued that people need to return to the book of nature and the story of the universe and listen, learn, and grow. Berry concluded by saying that at some point in the future we will be able to take the sacred texts down off the shelves, and then with a fuller sense of the human, terrestrial, and cosmic journey that we are on, read them anew.

Others have taken a stronger stance than Berry. One of them, a person known to us as Marcion, remains a shadowy figure of the early church. The wealthy son of a bishop, what we know of him comes down to us through the voices of his detractors. In his lost work, *Antithesis*—cited by the "church fathers"—he outlined what he had seen as the problem reconciling the gospel of love and forgiveness of Jesus with the wrathful and vengeful God of the Old Testament. Marcion—who was one of the earliest anti-Semites of the Christian tradition—taught that the Church should reject both the Hebrew Scriptures and the Hebrew God. Moreover, Marcion could not reconcile what he saw as discrepancies in the four gospel accounts and what he claimed to be the "Judaizing" of the Jesus message. Marcion sought to "cut and paste" a version of the New Testament, using only the Gospel of Luke—minus the birth narrative, genealogy, the story of the temptation of Jesus, and any mention of John the Baptist—and the ten Pauline epistles. All texts, however, were neutered of any perceived connection to the images of the God revealed in the Old Testament. He sought to reveal a canon of scripture that was more in keeping with his view of reality and his image of God. While we are not stating our support for the specifics of Marcion's editorial ideas, nor with his ignorance concerning the Jewishness of Jesus and Jesus' inherently Jewish understanding of God, he does call on us to ponder the nature of the canon of scripture.

History reveals that Marcion was excommunicated from his church in Rome in 144 of the common era. Still, he spread his views throughout the remainder of his lifetime, and Marcionite churches existed for several centuries in many parts of the ancient world. Moreover, his actions may have played a key part in forcing the orthodox Christians—in this case the side that won the debate— to establish the first clear canon of accepted sacred texts. His unique approach to biblical adaptation proved to have more of an impact than that of the third president of the United States.

Thomas Jefferson took a similar approach in his own cut-and-paste version of the New Testament, often called "The Jefferson Bible." Unlike Marcion, what the father of the Declaration of Independence did was to exclude all passages about miracles and prophesy. He sought to highlight a humanistic, Socratic, enlightenment Jesus. Jefferson wrote:

> Among the sayings and discourses imputed to Him by His biographers, I find many passages of fine imagination, correct morality, and of the most lovely benevolence; and others again, of so much ignorance, so much absurdity, so much untruth, charlatanism and imposture as to pronounce it impossible that such contradictions should have proceeded from the same Being. I separate, therefore, the gold from the dross.[25]

---

[25] Thomas Jefferson, from a letter written to the Unitarian minister and Dutch scholar Francis Adrian can der Kemp, and cited by Forest Church in the Introduction to *The Jefferson Bible* (Boston: The Beacon Press, 1989), 28. Similarly, in a letter to William Short he wrote, "We find in the writings of [Jesus'] biographers matter of two distinct descriptions. First, a groundwork of vulgar ignorance, of things impossible, of superstitions, fanaticisms and fabrications. Intermixed with these, again are sublime idea of Supreme Being, aphorism, and precepts of the purist morality and benevolence, sanctioned by a life of humility, innocence, and simplicity of manners, neglect of riches, absence of worldly ambition and honors, with an eloquence and persuasiveness which have not been surpassed" (*The Jefferson Bible*, 29).

Jefferson lived in fear of his ideas being made public, as he was very much aware that his creative editing would have been received as many times more radical than the revolutionary writings of his youth. Jefferson also made the connection to the violence traditions, writing: "I learned that what made religion good and necessary also made it prone to intolerance and violence." In addition, he makes reference to the art of the interpretative process as he writes, "In the midst of problems rooted in land, oppression, discrimination, or any number of other historical grievances, religion is often called on to justify human violence with subtle or not so subtle reference to 'sacred' texts, divine mission, or moral purpose."[26]

Jefferson's musings come in private letters and from a single mind, clandestinely hidden away from a public not yet ready for such intrigue. I do believe, however, that we are obliged to acknowledge that, as with Marcion, he had a point. Though their particular choices for what to keep and what to leave intact may not necessarily be deemed valid, Christians today may need to take a similarly bold initiative with regard to the Bible's "violence of God" traditions and its "texts of terror." Otherwise we are left to celebrate and teach our children about a God of remorseless violence, vengeance, and wrath. This will be an extremely difficult process. There is a lot at stake.

A Modest Proposal

I was once at a meeting in a college Pax Christi group—an international Catholic Peace organization—discussing whether or not to join in religious service with ROTC members on the campus. The idea behind the gathering was that even though the two groups disagreed (we were trying to get ROTC removed from Fordham's campus), we worshipped the same God and were called to be brothers and sisters at the altar of sacrifice. During our discussion, one of our members stood up and said, "I am not sure that we worship the same God." It was a powerful moment. It continues to disturb my psyche, and twenty-odd years later I think he was right. It might be that Christians who think of God as love, and who seek peace and justice, may need to take a stand and say, for example:

> My God—or his angel—did not fly over the Egyptian people and kill the firstborn of all the land. It didn't happen. Even as a made-up story filled with layers of metaphor and open to many possible interpretations, this narrative no longer functions and must be jettisoned from the ranks of the holy. Further, even if such events—like Moses ordering the death of the children and women of the slain enemies—reflect an historical event, God had nothing to do with it, and if someone else worships a God, or an idolatrous idea of God, who acts in this way, then we do in fact not worship the same God.

---

[26] Ibid., xi.

At the conclusion of one of his chapters in *Is Religion Killing Us*, Jack Nelson-Pallmeyer argues that in the face of violence we need to stand up and actively resist interpretations of scripture which extol violence, and in fact that "doubting the authority of 'sacred texts' that legitimate violence is an essential act of faithfulness."[27] Perhaps this "doubting" needs to be systematically formulated by communities of believers so that they can declare that certain texts are no longer to be understood as inspired.

The truth is that a clandestine editing and skipping over of these "difficult" texts happens all the time in churches and homes. While the idea of a "salad bar" use of the Bible may seem untenable, it is in fact what people have been doing this since the first words were written. Any student of modern biblical criticism can demonstrate how the Bible itself underwent constant change, including additions and subtractions, throughout its developmental history. It comes to us in its current form because at some point in their history a community of people determined that "this part is in the canon of scripture and those writings are not."

The heart of our modest proposal is that this debate needs to continue. Perhaps sections of the Bible can be transferred to a new section designated as "formally determined to be inspired by violence-loving forbearers." Religious leaders and communities need to be empowered to say, "This one has to go," or "the God that we believe in did not say that, did not do that, and does not call on us to imitate." People may reasonably conclude that certain passages and images of God need to be censored—not from view or further study, but from the ranks of the holy.

As we present this proposal, we need to recognize that these are not just fringe texts. Let us return to the Passover story alluded to above. This story, recounted each year for thousands of years, marks for the Jewish people a central point of historical intervention by God on behalf of His chosen people. It also serves as a central text for Christians, who see in it a foreshadowing of Jesus' passion, death and resurrection. Here, as outlined in the Book of Exodus, God—or God's agent, with God's sanction—carried out the murder of thousands of firstborn children and animals. Passing over the houses of the faithful who have smeared blood on their doorways, death envelops the land of Egypt, and none are spared. This text might be close to the top of the list of texts which are declared to be unreflective of a God to be worshipped in a world bent on defeating intolerance, injustice and religiously sanctioned violence. While the Egyptians of Moses' time may have been unjust slave owners, the murder of all their children in their sleep can no longer receive the stamp of sanctification and be seen as "Godlike."

Acts of religious-sanctioned violence will continue. As long as the seeds of the condoning of violence remain as inspired texts, the possibility of the next "God-sanctioned" bomb blast in a subway or invasion of a foreign country remains inevitable. Much to Harris's chagrin, religious faith is not going

---

[27] Nelson, 97.

away any time soon. Religion serves, among other things, to bolster love, forgiveness, compassion, and acceptance. There is much magnificent content in the Bible, as there is in other religious texts. However, there is chaff among the wheat.

One immediate question that rises is: "Who gets to the make the call on what to keep as authoritative and what to put on the shelf?" It is a fair question. I can only say—and this is perhaps what distinguishes my proposal from previous ones—that the community should be allowed to make the call. But again, communities already do so; they just have not formalized it. If people find themselves within a community which refuses to cancel the divine authorship of certain texts, they can foment change from within, or they can find alternative communities. This does raise the prospect that different communities will honestly disagree on what goes, what gets an asterisk, and what stays. It bears repeating that, in truth, this "editing" has been happening for hundreds of years; and the reality is that many communities do not read the same passages. When was the last time you heard a sermon on Numbers 31 and Moses' call to "keep the virgins for yourselves"? This covert editing needs to come to the surface and be formalized. Years of biblical exegesis reveal clearly that the texts are products of believing communities. Religious communities validate the scripture; the scriptures do not appear first and then validate the community. Much confusion will arise, and much disagreement might follow. Still, in the face of the religiously sanctioned violence in our world today, other choices seem to be few. Religious leaders, preachers, theologians, and liturgists may need to adopt a variation of what feminist theologians have called the "hermeneutics of suspicion" and approach the texts armed with the knowledge that they arise out of a violence-legitimating context. Then they must excise those parts of scripture and tradition which promote, legitimize, and sanction violence. In the end, this modest proposal may be just what is needed to come to terms with the blood on our hands and in our texts. It may be just the spark to ignite the move forward—away from the images of a tormenting God and away from religiously sanctioned violence.

Part II

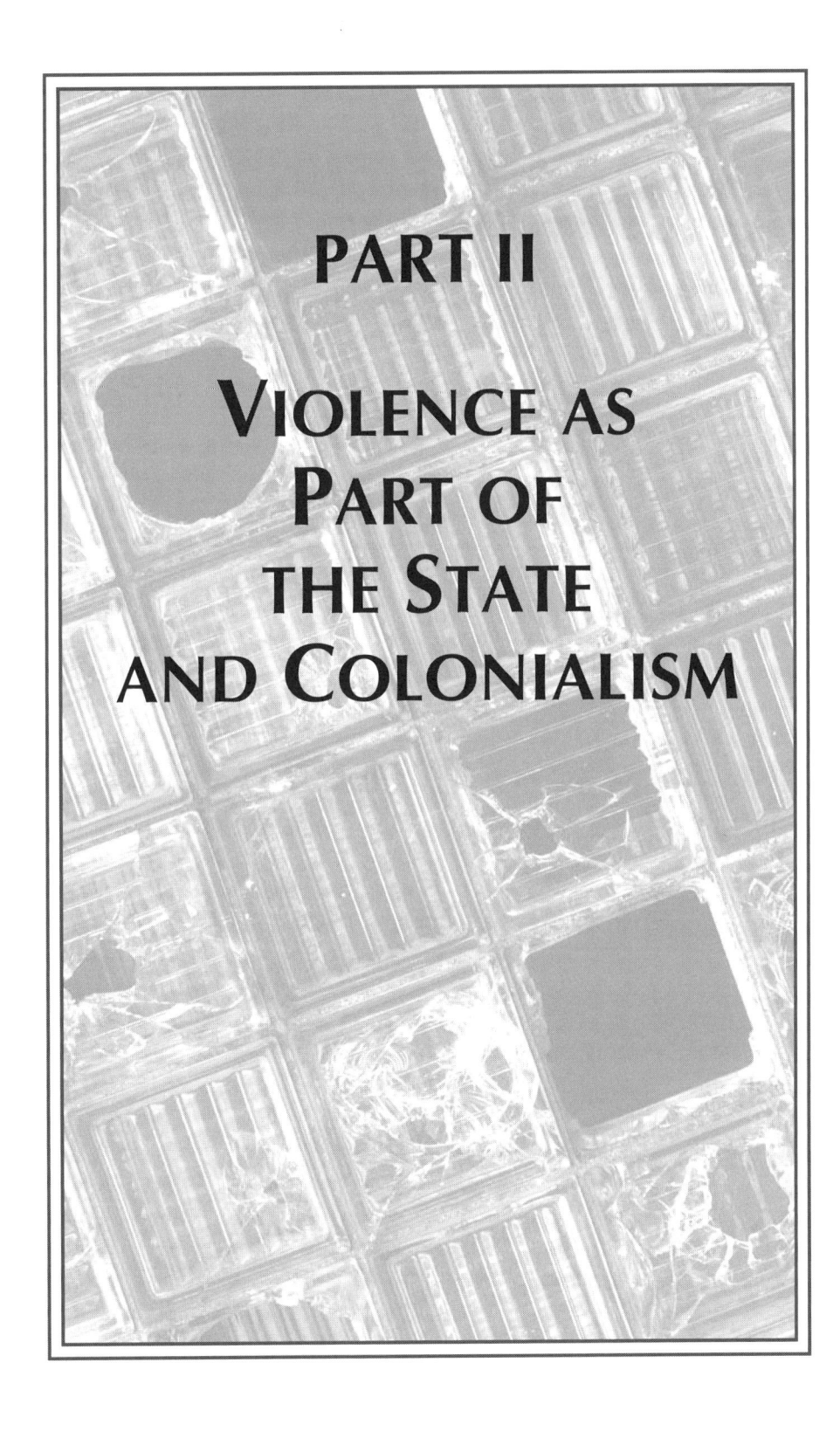

Violence as Part of the State and Colonialism

Making Distance through a Violent Imagination

William Leggett

Groups shift, change, fragment, expand, and migrate; space remains.
—James Boon (1977)
The Anthropological Romance of Bali: 1597–1972

The map thus collates on the same plane heterogeneous places, some *received* from a tradition and others *produced* by observation.
—Michel de Certeau (1984)
The Practice of Everyday Life

If terror thrives on the production of epistemic murk and metamorphosis, it nevertheless requires the hermeneutic violence that creates feeble fictions in the guise of realism, objectivity, and the like, flattening, contradicting and systemizing chaos.
—Michael Taussig (1987)
Shamanism, Colonialism, and the Wild Man: A Study in Terror and Healing

INTRODUCTION

In this essay I explore the violent underpinnings of a body of knowledge that produces social distance between populations seemingly divided by time and space despite their shared occupation of the same office block within the same city. The ethnographic space involved, a transnational corporate office in the heart of Jakarta, Indonesia, is the type of space in which many of us (by "us," I mean the typical) expect to find ourselves at some point during our lives. Yet sociocultural interactions in these offices are still poorly understood. History has been moving in fits and starts of late. The political, environmental, social, and cultural calamities that rang in the twenty-first century—each identifiable through a one-word, celebrity-like moniker (Katrina, Iraq, 9/11)—

Written especially for *Ruminations in Violence*.

continue to shift the ground beneath our feet. These tectonic shifts are doing much to undermine long-standing borders and, in the process, they are upsetting the fragile structures of identity around which borders are constructed. Fissures in the social landscape are opening up, and people are responding through violence, retrenchment, and retreat.

At the same time, and certainly not unrelated, global economic processes persist in expanding capitalist networks that effectively dismantle borders. In other words, as there are fractures there are also links. Sometimes these links correspond to those developed during the age of empire. Southeast Asia continues to be a source of cheap labor and raw materials, for example. And significant segments of the continent of Africa continue to be divvied up among world powers, both national and corporate, in the extraction of oil, gold, and human bodies.

But there are also new links being established that don't always follow those established during the colonial period. At present, for example, Japanese auto executives are at work negotiating, and in the process most certainly reconfiguring, business and labor practices in Nashville, Tennessee. At the same time Congolese traders are doing something similar within the second economy of Paris, France. India and Barbados, among others, have captured enough of the information-processing industry to have a say in the policies, procedures, and pay related to this thriving industry.

Simply put, we are—more of us, at any rate—coming and going into and out of places with which we may or may not be familiar and are encountering a variety of peoples we probably do not know very well. Human bodies are hurtling across the planet into new spaces and new assemblages at an accelerating pace, and with consequences we have yet to fully appreciate. How we as a global population negotiate these encounters will have a profound influence on how well we live within the shrinking confines of the twenty-first century.

Transnational corporate offices represent unique spaces of social interaction made possible through global economic processes of production, distribution, and consumption. While they are spaces wholly created through the processes of global capitalism, they are also interesting cultural spaces in which new identities are being constructed and negotiated. This essay explores how one workforce occupying such an office (of a company to which I assign the fictitious name of BCB) at the end of the twentieth century relied heavily on a fictional or imagined past in the ordering of their transnational present. The fictional past deployed in this office caused employee interactions to be couched in a field of terror, based on a (mis)reading of Indonesia's colonial history that reinforced Western notions of the "Other" and segregated the corporate workforce along lines of race and nationality.

WELCOME TO JAKARTA

This essay is primarily based on my ethnographic interactions with the employees of "BCB"—a Western-owned transnational corporation with representative offices, research facilities, factories, and retail outlets in and around Jakarta, Indonesia (as well as around the world). In order to understand the architecture of the social space that comprises BCB, one must also seek to understand the composition of the larger social space within which the company resides. The BCB office which is the focus of this essay is located within Indonesia's capital city of Jakarta—a city richly layered with the strata of classical, colonial, national, and transnational encounter (Sklair 1991; Berland 1992; Lefebvre 1979, 1984; de Certeau 1984). A city of migrants, domestic and international, Jakarta might be described as coherent in the way of a Rauschenberg "combine"—a style of three-dimensional art that brings together painting, sculpture, collage, and found objects in the making of something entirely new, strange, and somehow, simultaneously, familiar. Much like the best of Rauschenberg's work, the fragments of architectural and social difference abutting one another along Jakarta's busy and overcrowded streets provoke in the city traveler a simultaneous sense of tension and harmony. For there is an eerie, if not entirely comfortable, familiarity tucked within Jakarta's inimitable landscape.

The usual visual juxtaposition evoked in the travel literature for Jakarta (and most other primate cities of the so-called "Third World"), illustrated through the requisite photographic trope of glass-and-steel skyscrapers bearing down on dilapidated shanties, does little justice to a landscape constructed through the hands of numerous, often migratory, sometimes imperial, self-interested actors. Jakarta's streets are colored as much by the aesthetics of ethnic identity, colonial nostalgia, and a national desire for the public displays of modernity as they are by the dramatic class divisions evoked through the trope of skyscraper and shanty. The popular divisions in the landscape are tangible in roof lines and road signs, in the names on storefronts, as well as in the aromas of cooking, and the wary or welcoming looks on people's faces; so much so that even the uninitiated city traveler is quickly aware of boundaries being crossed.

When postmodernist political and literary critic Jameson considered the concept of hyperspace, he could have had Jakarta in mind (Jameson, 1991). Hyperspaces, according to Jameson, challenge "the capacities of the individual human body to locate itself, to organize its immediate surroundings perceptually, and cognitively to map its position in a mappable external world" (ibid., 44) When, for example, an American traveler enters one of Jakarta's many shopping malls or Western-style restaurants he or she might feel, if only for a moment, a sense of transportation from the strange to the familiar (an experience felt in reverse, I discovered, for some older and more rural Indonesians for whom an escalator within a shopping mall was something to approach with curiosity and trepidation). But the sensation is temporary. The juxtaposition of a Jeffersonian-style steak house—next to the Starbucks that is adjacent to a Planet Hollywood—has an almost Disney-esque sense of "imagineering" of home for our imaginary traveler; a space familiar yet somehow artificial and out of place.

Conversely, when Ati, an Indonesian national with enviable engineering skills and a quiet yet determined sense of self-confidence, first came to work at the offices of BCB, she noticed quickly and to her surprise that her normal attire, including a colorful *sari* and simple *tudung*, were out of place. "The dress is very casual," she told me. "And the office is casual too. It is all about sports here . . . I don't play *basketball*." From Ati's desk, looking over stacks of shoeboxes and generic-blue partition walls, one could see a glossy framed poster of an NBA basketball player leaning hands-on-knees at the free-throw line of an unusually dark and ominous court, his bald head bent down between muscular shoulders while sweat drips profusely into an exaggeratedly large pool on the floor. For Ati this poster, along with the "casual" clothing of her coworkers, reinforced the sensation that she was crossing a border every time she walked through the doors of BCB.

What these two contrasting scenarios illustrate is that Jakarta is a place of layers and juxtapositions that speak to the longevity of global projects at work upon its terrain. These layers do much to confound the modern-day resident as choices must be made on a daily basis about language, dialect, clothing style, food choice, and many other arenas of life—all within a fairly small body of land (more than 10 million people live within the approximately 411 miles of Jakarta). As such, Jakarta proves an inviting (if challenging) space for ethnographic investigation into the creative processes through which social actors negotiate identity and construct meaningful places out of the spaces in which they work and live.

I argue that for many Southeast Asians employed within diverse sectors of the transnational economy, there was a desire—perhaps even a need—to draw upon historical (not to say accurate) images of self and other *and* of the spaces they inhabited, in order to negotiate a social world so culturally variegated as to sometimes feel overwhelming. The historical "imagination" was deployed in order to understand and organize the seemingly chaotic spaces in which these individuals worked and lived. I believe that this historical imagination is derived from a colonial body of knowledge built upon a foundation of terror—a product of the uncertainty experienced when one feels dislocated from the social networks and institutions within which a sense of self was constructed and confirmed.

THE COLONIAL IMAGINATION

During three years of ethnographic research conducted within transnational corporate office spaces throughout Southeast Asia, I witnessed the consistent expression of an historical discourse—which I refer to as the *colonial imagination*—that has greatly impacted the words and actions of those who negotiate the transnational corporate work spaces that now permeate our economic and social worlds. Within these corporate social spaces I found the colonial imagination to be a central component in the ongoing struggle to make sense of the strange, the unfamiliar, and the unexpected aspects of working and living within the dynamic networks of our global economy.

By colonial imagination I mean a manufactured presentation of place and person, through which spatial (geographic) relations are temporally understood (Fabian 1983; Harvey 2001). As Taussig (1987, 21) has stated, "all societies live by fictions taken as real" (see also Ludden 1993). The perpetuation of transnational encounters brought about by global economic processes has allowed for the broadcast of a particular fiction through the travels of Western workers into non-Western, often post-colonial spaces. These spaces—far from arbitrary to the global economy and saturated with the history of Western expansion and domination—are especially susceptible to geographic mappings that deny contemporaneousness. In other words, despite the fact that individuals from different backgrounds continue to work side by side in the same office, there persists a perception that one segment of this workforce is more-or-less a remnant of an imagined colonial past. Simply put, through the colonial imagination an image of Indonesia was evoked by some Western expatriates that highlighted images of "backwardness" (at best) and "savagery" (in the more brutal statements) within an untamed landscape awaiting the civilizing hand of Western man (and, it should be noted, the majority of expatriates I came to know in Indonesia were male).

The presence of the colonial imagination pervasively impacts the verbal terrain of corporate discourses and the physical terrain of corporate office spaces. How colonial references effectively slip into a late-twentieth century transnational socioeconomic context reveals much about the strategies people use in the exercise of power, in the social mapping of space, and in the negotiation of identities within global work spaces.

Through the deployment of a colonial body of knowledge to describe their Indonesian co-workers, some expatriates were in effect constructing a mythical discourse out of historical encounters framed by fear and/or desire (Dirks 1993, 280).[1] The colonial imagery deployed by Western-born expatriates at BCB took a variety of forms—from racist comments that referenced monkeys, jungles, cannibalism, and uncontrollable violence ("these people are just out of the trees," "every time I get into a taxi I think I'm going to get stabbed"); to explicit stories of sexual conquest involving "wild" and "predatory" women "begging for it," to more material form in the codified and accepted management practices of the corporation.

While the sexualized comments regarding Indonesian women as "ripe" for conquest spoke to a certain desire for the "exotic" that is often present in racial discourses, what I specifically address here is the underlying *terror* that colored many of the expatriate comments about Indonesia and Indonesians

---

[1] I address the sexualized aspects of the colonial imagination in Leggett (2007). This paper explores the cultural practices through which Indonesian workers also deploy the colonial imagination. It focuses in particular on descriptions of expatriate workers that equate transnational executives with past colonizing populations (Dutch and Portuguese). This equation is most apparent in discussion about the rumored (and actual) sexual exploits of expatriates at BCB as well as in discussion of their general lack of morality. Here too the colonial imagination serves to create temporal distance between two populations occupying the same geographic space.

and resulted in a persistent social distance between Western "expatriates" and Indonesian "nationals." To be clear, the colonial imagination informed not just daily racialized and sexualized discourses but, more importantly, structural hierarchies within an increasingly multicultural, transnational corporate terrain (see, for example, Young 1995). As such the colonial imagination served as a form of epistemic violence that resulted in forms of material violence as well.

Epistemic violence, a term best articulated by Gayatri Spivak (1988), refers to processes of knowledge production about "Other" populations in the exercise of power. Epistemic violence occurs when a dominant population systematically describes and defines a subordinate population in such a way that discipline and control of the subordinate group is both effective and justified. *The colonial imagination is a form of epistemic violence* in that it produces such a body of knowledge about an Indonesian workforce seen as inferior to and justifiably under the control of Western executives within BCB. The materialized effects of this knowledge system is manifested in a number of the institutional practices of BCB (including hiring and promotional systems) but is perhaps most clearly illustrated in the racial segregation imposed by the social architecture of the BCB office.

THE SPACE BETWEEN—THE SOCIAL ARCHITECTURE OF BCB

The employees of BCB are part of a global network that expands and contracts, unites and fragments in relation to changes in such things as currency exchange rates, material costs, distribution chains, labor costs, market opportunities, and political stability (Sklair 1991, 8–9; Harvey 2001, 121). Within the offices of BCB, the unsettled landscape created through the economic exigencies of the global economy has come to be understood by many not only through a language of modern capital—with its emphasis on production and consumption, cheap labor, shifting markets, and volatile distribution chains—but also (and perhaps primarily) through the colonial imagination that orders global relations through reference to a past of imperial expansion, cultural encounter, and economic exploitation (Dussel 1998, 13; Taussig 1987; Mignolo 1998, 33–34).

My intent is not to claim that the colonial imagination deployed by the employees of BCB correctly references the "age of empire." For, as Bestor (2004, 16) has noted,

> What is most important about the past is the present-day perception of it. The past becomes relevant to understanding contemporary social life insofar as past practices are evoked or invoked to legitimate (or invalidate) contemporary ones, to create ideological norms that one aspires to emulate (or overthrow), or to craft sets of symbolic meanings and references within (or against) which one can situate one's own contemporary circumstances.

What I claim instead is that at the end of the twentieth century the colonial seemed a particularly apt moment of history to evoke by Western-born (and, though not my focus here, Indonesian) members of the transnational capitalist class working in post-colonial Indonesia.

The representative office of BCB-Jakarta is located on the twenty-second, twenty-third, and twenty-fourth floors of a sleek high-rise along one of the three busy intersecting streets that make up much of Jakarta's central business district known as the "Golden Triangle"—a space in which I spent much time observing the daily operations of a "typical" transnational corporate office. When I first visited BCB in 1997 the office was occupied by approximately thirty expatriates (primarily from the United States but also from Britain, Germany, and Japan) working alongside more than four hundred Indonesian supervisors and support staff. Many of the Indonesian employees I came to know were born and raised in and around Jakarta. Others had moved to Jakarta from Sumatra, Bali, and the far reaches of Indonesia either at the start of their university education or afterwards to find employment in a prestigious global company. Under the expatriate management and director corps, these employees oversaw a complex network of research, manufacturing, distribution, retailing, and public relations issues both within and beyond Indonesia's borders. However, to speak of the Indonesian and expatriate employees as actually working *together* would be, to say the least, misleading.

While the international workforce at BCB shared a common office space, relied on shared communication and research technologies, and operated within a shared and promoted corporate culture, there remained persistent and sharp social and structural divides. In the representative offices of BCB, subjectivity was often negotiated through a binary of "expatriates" and "nationals." Other identity markers—gender, race, nationality, and religion being the most prominent—were, of course, pertinent to social relations and social positions within the office. For the most part, however, these other identifying categories were integrated into the dominant "expatriates–nationals" organizational principle. Even though these two populations shared the same office space, with many overlapping functions, in my experience strikingly little interaction took place between the expatriate and national employees of BCB.

The social partitions constructed through this expatriate–national binary were materially reinforced through the interior design of the BCB office. The individual offices of the various managers and directors (all "expatriates") lined the outer walls of the BCB floor space. These offices, with their floor-to-ceiling windows looking out onto the traffic jams, roofs, and crowded streets of Jakarta, were also fronted on the opposite side with glass walls—in this case covered with Venetian blinds. Within this square of glass sat an open floor plan of connected cubicles that ran throughout the middle of the floor space. Here sat the Indonesian employees of BCB. My first glance from a director's office onto this work space revealed that BCB was an office designed with separation and surveillance in mind. One could look out through the blinds, but one could not necessarily look in.

In observing the representative office of BCB on a typical day, one rarely saw Indonesian nationals venture, unless summoned, into the glass-fronted offices of "expatriate" executives, nor "expatriates" move through the maze of Indonesian "national" occupied cubicles. Entering a superior's office was equated, by many I interviewed, with punishment and extra work. "I don't want to go in there," Ati said one day with what I took as a nervous laugh. "I only go in there when I am in trouble. If he asks to see me it means I will be here all night." And yet, for the office to function, "expatriate" managers and directors had to communicate with "national" supervisors, technicians, material specialists, factory representatives and support staff.

To overcome what appeared to be a social desire to restrict physical encounter, alternate modes of communication were used; the primary one being e-mail. "It's just easier and more efficient," said Matthew, an "expatriate" director. "Also," he noted, "it is good for saving face. When someone on my staff makes a mistake, I've learned it doesn't work to scold him in front of his peers. But through e-mail I can explain exactly what he did wrong, and why." In this particular case, by using the word *scold* in discussing the disciplining of subordinates, Matthew established a relationship between "expatriate" and "national" that corresponded to that between a parent and child, effectively infantilizing his "national" subordinates.

It is perhaps an irony of the modern transnational corporate office that a technology believed to connect distant peoples has become instead a tool in the maintenance of social distance. More important here, however, is the fiction allowed to persist through this technological separation. By avoiding direct contact, the expatriates at BCB were never forced to confront possible challenges to their own presumed superiority. More to the point, through the maintenance of social distance "expatriates" never had to confront their own mistaken preconceptions of a "savage," "violent" and "backward" Indonesian population they viewed as dependent on their assistance for survival in the global economy.

As I spent more and more time at BCB and became comfortable coming and going as I pleased, I became increasingly aware that my comfort was not one shared by "national" staff. Part of their discomfort resulted, it seemed to me, from the interior design of the expatriates' offices. Recall Indonesian employee Ati's reaction to the basketball poster in the BCB offices. The office space had been designed as an American space with images of American landscapes (the Grand Canyon was a particularly popular choice for wall art, though I'm not sure why except to note that it appeared "distinctly" American and difficult to confuse with other places), and American sports heroes. Often there was a set of golf clubs and/or a tennis racket near the door. Frequently there were images of lone outdoorsmen in pursuit of self-accomplishment against a backdrop of nature at its most brutal—whether climbing Mt. Everest or a steep cliff wall, or surfing a giant wave. The image was always one of overcoming (or becoming one) with some great natural phenomenon.[2]

---

[2] There are other issues involved. Elsewhere I have discussed the importance of "drama" in making the mundane performance of office work into a meaningful exercise (see Leggett 2005). This argument is based on a Marxian reading of dislocation from the production process.

Such office décor served a number of purposes in terms of making places out of organizational spaces. Sociologist and philosopher Henri Lefebvre was the first to point out a fundamental connection between the way bodies move through space and the ways that space is perceived. He argued that bodies reproduce themselves in space as they also produce the space they occupy. One could see Lefebvre's point in the way that the corporate offices of expatriates at BCB served as markers of the bodies that occupied them. On the one hand they were very much "national" spaces—reproductions of America in a distant place, and at the same time they were also masculine spaces. This combination of nationality and masculinity had the effect of essentially feminizing Indonesian bodies as they entered the offices. But this was something that rarely happened, for such an encounter could effectively disrupt the implied link between space and body that was intended through the interior design.

Indonesian employees did at times speak to me about their discomfort entering expatriate offices. The language used often pointed to physical effects related to cross-cultural encounters in the space of the "expatriate" office. Elinda said her stomach hurt (*perut sakit*) when she knew she had a meeting in the director's office. Yanis, on the other hand, said his superior looked up as if "shocked" (*terkejut*) to see him standing in the doorway to his office. These descriptions speak clearly to a disruption of space designed and reserved for expatriate occupation. The Indonesian "nationals" became, in these instances, "space invaders" upon their own "national" soil (Puwar 2004).

A Brief History of Social Distance

In his history of technology and nationalism in the Dutch East Indies, Rudolf Mrazek (2002) describes how—through roads, railways, architecture, air conditioning, and other material aspects of modernity—late-colonial Dutch society strived to insulate itself from the unfamiliar cultural and environmental surroundings of their colonial territory. Driving this separation, according to Mrazek (2002, 56), was a threat of "contamination" perceived to occur through dirt, water, air, and—most importantly—through direct contact with "native" Indonesians:

> The threat, especially as modern cities were emerging in the Indies, was in fluidity. In semen and blood untamed ... in water—polluted, dripping, leaking, or flowing unregulated. ... To rule the colony, to become modern there, to stay, meant to confine the flow.

Mrazek persuasively illustrates the degree to which the Dutch inhabitants of the East Indies were willing to go in order to seal themselves off from the messy reality of colonial relations. Their self-imposed quarantine was continuously challenged by the actions of "natives" perceived as "out of place" in spaces of Dutch creation and control. When the colonial population took to the Dutch-built asphalt roads to transport themselves (and their goods) around Java, for example, it was viewed by the Dutch as a hazardous affront to the sterile order created out of the colonial enterprise. Reports from the period describe how "natives" rode in "wild buses and trucks" or "second-hand, and even third-hand [vehicles] in a state of being barely able to hold together" (ibid., 18). The seemingly "primitive" machinery soiled the new Dutch technology of asphalt roads, corrupting the *wegen-hygiene* (road hygiene) of modern design (ibid., 27). Mrazek explores various ways in which the local population and environment seeped into Dutch spaces, "infecting" their civility with an air of the primitive. In response, the Dutch worked ever harder to separate themselves from their surroundings while, simultaneously, manufacturing connections between themselves and the Netherlands. In the process, the social distance between the two populations—"Dutch" and "native"—grew wider, and the presumed differences (cultural and racial) between the two groups became increasingly reified. Although both groups were living in relatively close quarters in the crowded spaces of the Dutch capital of Batavia, social interaction was forcibly kept at a minimum in order to maintain the fiction of a civilized, modern Western society "taming" a violent and backward wilderness.

The point to be made here is that the (intentionally) limited interactions of employees at BCB demonstrates continued evidence of a corporate organizational map bifurcated by a grid of social and temporal distance. To walk from the office of an American expatriate to the cubicle of an Indonesian national was, for many, a trip back in time. It was, therefore, a trip many would just as soon avoid. "I can't talk to him," Richard (a U.S.-born BCB employee) told me. "He doesn't understand me." On the surface this comment about Yanis, an Indonesian-born, Japanese-educated factory supervisor, appears to be about simple and inevitable linguistic obstacles to communication. Yanis, however, is fluent in English (and Japanese). Richard obviously knew this as I had seen the two speak on occasion. Richard's comments, however, point to an issue more complicated than the existence of a language barrier. In conversations with numerous expatriates at BCB I became aware of a shared *technological discourse* in which individuals emphasized the need to speak a *specialized language* often viewed as "too technical" for their Indonesian peers to understand. This emphasis on technological language marked more than differences in education. In fact, this technological discourse was used as a marker of modernity and, as such, a temporal marker of difference. I suspect Richard believed Yanis "didn't understand" him because the language he used was of a present to which Yanis was not yet part.

Cultural anthropologist Johannes Fabian (1983, 30–31) makes the critical point that "for human communication to occur, coevalness has to be *created*."[3] Communication, in other words, is about *sharing time*. Richard was in

---

[3] Coevalness, according to Fabian, expressed the need to steer between such closely related notions as *sinchronic, simultaneous,* and *contemporary*. Synchronic refers to events occurring at the same physical time; *contemporary* asserts co-occurrence in . . . typological time. Coeval . . . covers both.

effect denying Yanis's presence in the same temporal plane as himself. Through such linguistic practices, the shared spaces of BCB were temporally divided, indicating that the transnational economy has yet to overcome a long and prolific colonial history founded upon the denial of coevalness. The result is an office within an office—an internal colony if you will—in which the Indonesian employees are positioned much like migrant labor within the agricultural economy of the United States at the beginning of the twentieth century. They are viewed as necessary but temporary residents—sojourners in the land of their birth.

TERROR AND THE COLONIAL IMAGINATION

How do we account for this production of social distance in transnational spaces seemingly primed for social encounter? As I have implied throughout this paper, I believe the social distance I witnessed at BCB was constructed upon a foundation of terror. If we take terror as a product of ignorance, of being dislocated from our usual social networks and geographic contexts, then we can see terror as foundational in the creation of "American" places in non-American spaces. Michael Taussig views terror as a by-product of what he calls *epistemic murk*, a term that conjures up the chaos of uncertainty and dislocation that derives from travel into the unknown:

> If terror thrives on the production of epistemic murk and metamorphosis, it nevertheless requires the hermeneutic violence that creates feeble fictions in the guise of realism, objectivity, and the like, flattening, contradicting and systemizing chaos (132).

Through the concept of epistemic murk Taussig points to the unruliness of a situation in which little makes sense and categories cannot be pinned down. It is in this lack of order, a lack of recognizable categories, that terror comes to the forefront. Terror, according to Taussig, makes a "mockery of sense-making" (1987, 132). My point, however, is that terror is *central* to sense-making in that it takes the place of, and often is given the name of, reason or logic within the post-colonial spaces of the transnational economy. The order that has been imposed upon a disorderly capitalist enterprise is built, fundamentally, on a foundation of terror. The categories seemed old and outdated—native turned national, colonial turned expatriate—but they were the ones around which many in the expatriate community organized their experiences. As expatriates, the employees of BCB transposed a colonial cultural order onto a transnational economic enterprise. An expatriate's journey, beginning in the elevator and ending in the corner office, became an errand through the "national" wilderness of office cubicles in between. It was a journey more often than not avoided by skirting along the edges of the office space. Simply put, fear of the unknown served to maintain a distance that, in turn, provided the colonial imagination a space to persist.

Conclusion

My concern in this essay has been with how Western members of the transnational capitalist class impose a shared knowledge system onto the lived experience of working in Jakarta. It is a system of knowledge that, I argue, finds its efficacy by imposing a capitalist order that simultaneously reproduces while pretending to overcome colonial terror. In telling a story of Jakarta's shifting terrain, I have used a transnational corporate office space to illustrate the power of a rather limited Western imagery in the production and negotiation of a landscape simultaneously modern and primordial. I introduced the notion of the colonial imagination to point to the immediacy with which certain presumably colonial images are called upon, not only in circumstances of uncertainty and terror but also within the mundane encounters of daily life.

As previously stated, the ethnographic space addressed here, the transnational corporate office, is destined to be the kind of space in which more and more of us find ourselves during our work lives. BCB is not, strictly speaking, a space of Indonesian culture, nor is it a space of Western or American culture. Transnational corporate offices represent unique spaces of social interaction made possible through global economic processes of production, distribution, and consumption. They are spaces wholly created through the processes of global capitalism. What is intriguing (and disturbing), from an anthropological perspective, is how those occupying these offices rely heavily on a fictional past in the ordering of the transnational present.

References

Berland, Jody. 1992. "Angels Dancing: Cultural Technologies and the Production of Space." In *Cultural Studies*. Lawrence Grossberg, Cary Nelson, Paula Treichler, eds. 38–55. New York: Routledge.

Bestor, Theodore C. 2004. *Tsukiji: The Fish Market at the Center of the World*. Berkeley: University of California Press.

Boon, James. 1977. *The Anthropological Romance of Bali: 1597–1972*. Cambridge: Cambridge University Press.

———. 1990. *Affinities and Extremes: Crisscrossing the Bittersweet Ethnology of East Indies History, Hindu-Balinese Culture, and Indo-European Allure*. Chicago: University of Chicago Press.

De Certeau, Michael. 1984. *The Practice of Everyday Life*. Berkeley: University of California Press.

Dirks, Nicholas B. 1993. "Colonial Histories and Native Informants: Biography of an Archive." In *Orientalism and the Postcolonial Predicament: Perspectives on South Asia*. Carol Breckenridge and Peter van der Veer, eds. Philadelphia: University of Pennsylvania Press.

Dussel, Enrique. 1998. "Beyond Eurocentrism: The World-System and the Limits of Modernity." In *The Cultures of Globalization*. Fredric Jameson and Masao Miyoshi, eds. 3–31. Durham: Duke University Press.

Fabian, Johannes. 1983. *Time and the Other: How Anthropology Makes Its Other*. New York: Columbia University Press.

Harvey, David. 2001. *Spaces of Capital: Towards a Critical Geography*. New York: Routledge.

Jameson, Fredric. 1991. *Postmodernism: Or, The Cultural Logic of Late Capitalism.* Durham, NC: Duke University Press.

Lefebvre, Henri. 1979. "Space: Social Product and Use Value." In *Critical Sociology.* J. W. Freidberg, ed. New York: Irving Publishers.

_____. 1984. *Everyday Life in the Modern World.* Translated by S. Rabinovitch. New Brunswick: Transaction Books.

Leggett, William H. 2005. "Terror and the Colonial Imagination at Work in the Transnational Corporate Spaces of Jakarta, Indonesia." *Identities: Global Studies in Culture and Power* 12(2). Routledge: Taylor and Francis Group.

_____. (2007). "Expatriate Ethnoscapes: Place-Making in the Transnational Corporate Spaces of Jakarta, Indonesia." In *Ethnic Landscapes in an Urban World. Research in Urban Sociology. Volume 8.*

Ray Hutchison and Jerome Krase, eds. Oxford: Elsevier Research in Urban Sociology Series.

Ludden, David. 1993. "Orientalist Empiricism: Transformations of Colonial Knowledge." In *Orientalism and the Postcolonial Predicament: Perspectives on South Asia.* Carol A. Breckenridge and Peter van der Veer, eds. Philadelphia: University of Pennsylvania Press.

Mignolo, Walter D. 1998. "Globalization, Civilization Processes, and the Relocation of Languages and Cultures." In *The Cultures of Globalization.* Fredric Jameson and Masao Miyoshi, eds. 32–53. Durham: Duke University Press.

_____. 2002. "The Many Faces of Cosmo-polis: Border Thinking and Critical Cosmopolitanism." In *Cosmopolitanism.* Carol A. Breckenridge, Sheldon Pollock, Homi K. Bhabha, and Dipesh Chakrabarty, eds. 157–187. Durham: Duke University Press.

Mrazek, Rudolf. 2002. *Engineers of Happy Land: Technology and Nationalism in a Colony.* Princeton: Princeton University Press.

Puwar, Nirmal. 2004. *Space Invaders: Race, Gender and Bodies Out of Place.* New York: Berg.

Sklair, Leslie. 1991. *Sociology of the Global System* (2nd ed.). New York: Prentice Hall/Harvester Wheatsheaf.

Spivak, Gayatri Chakravorty. 1988. "Can the Subaltern Speak?" In *Marxism and the Interpretation of Culture.* Cary Nelson and Lawrence Grossberg, eds. 271–313. Basingstoke: Macmillan Education.

Taussig, Michael. 1987. *Shamanism, Colonialism, and the Wild Man: A Study in Terror and Healing.* Chicago: University of Chicago Press.

Young, Robert. 1995. *Colonial Desire: Hybridity in Theory, Culture and Race.* New York: Routledge.

Ethnic Riots in a Small Balkan Town
Understanding Hate and Violence in Macedonia

Robert Hislope

> In other places, there is no gap between real prejudice and the readiness to act on that prejudice. Here the gap is very big, and in this gap is where politics is found.
>
> —*Ljubomir Frckovski*[1]

This essay focuses on the role of ethnic animosities in generating conflict. I argue that interethnic antipathies are real, critical factors that often accurately characterize multiethnic societies. Thus, I take issue with the trendy "constructivist" and "instrumentalist" positions adopted by many scholars today, which not only deny a causal role for emotional factors like hatred but also bring an intellectual suspicion to the concept of ethnicity itself. To many constructivists/instrumentalists, ethnicity is an artificial construction having no basis in reality. In the case under investigation in this study—the Republic of Macedonia—this position is without empirical support. The opposite error is advanced by the doctrine of primordialism, which frames ethnic animosities as ancient in origin and incapable of being extinguished once ignited. Constructivist and instrumentalist thinkers have offered sharp and convincing criticisms of the "ancient animosities thesis," but this does not mean they have offered a compelling alternative.

Written especially for *Ruminations in Violence*.

---

[1] Personal interview with Ljubomir Frckovski, former Macedonian interior minister, foreign minister, and joint author of the 1991 Macedonian constitution (November 21, 2000), Skopje, Macedonia.

In contrast to the extremes of primordialism and constructivism/instrumentalism,[2] I offer an argument that contains two parts: (1) in some societies, ethnic hatreds are quite palpable and do shape the pattern of political dynamics; but (2) such hatreds are insufficient to spark violence. As the opening quotation by Ljubomir Frckovski notes, it is one thing to express hatred or resentment and quite another to act on this disposition. Therefore, a major component of this discussion is to specify exactly what types of factors bridge the gap between *expressive* hatred and *actionable* hatred, and what types of factors and conditions make that gap wider.

Macedonia, the test case for these propositions, achieved independence in 1991. Post-communist Macedonian and Albanian elites never had to convince their respective communities to dislike each other, because interethnic animosity is part of the social fabric—a point that will be discussed later on. The intriguing story, however, behind the evidence of widespread interethnic antipathies is the fact that Macedonia remained relatively peaceful for the first decade of its independence, which suggests that primordial-like societies (those with hard ethnic boundaries, interethnic animosities, ethnic distance) are not inherently prone to implosion.

War did eventually come to Macedonia in 2001 in the form of an external, spillover effect from the fighting in Kosovo and southern Serbia. But this was certainly a low-scale conflict with a small death toll[3] and was successfully mitigated within six months by international diplomatic intervention. The interesting element about the conflict—for our purposes —is that it spawned two episodes of ethnic rioting in the southern town of Bitola. In section two of this essay, I analyze the riots in Bitola and contrast them with the relatively peaceful conditions in the northern Macedonian town of Kumanovo. The major difference between the two cases is this: In Bitola, the anger and grievances of the Macedonian community spilled over into direct action because it was in a state of mourning over the death of several young, local soldiers killed by Albanian guerillas on the war front. Interethnic animosities are a crucial element in the riots, for without the community-level anger and grief it is difficult to imagine how the riots could have been triggered. However, by the same token, it took the encouragement of local elites and institutions to transfer expressive hatred into actionable hatred. In contrast, local Macedonian and Albanian elites in Kumanovo successfully worked over time to ensure that latent animosities would remain just that: latent.

---

[2] For excellent theoretical analyses of the three competing paradigms of comparative ethnic studies, see Motyl (1999); Fearon and Laitin (2000); Brubakers and Laitin (1998).

[3] Balalovska, Silj, and Zucconi (2002); Rusi (2001); The Macedonian government has yet to release an official figure of the casualties. Early estimates were 200+, but it is likely higher. Eighty thousand Albanian refugees sought temporary shelter in Kosovo.

Portrait of an Ethnically Divided Society

Macedonia is the very exemplar of an ethnically divided society. The two principal ethnic groups, ethnic Macedonians (64.18%, or 1,297,981) and ethnic Albanians (25.17%, or 509, 083) are fractured on just about every key trait of group identity: culture, language, religion, and family structure. Apart from this central bipolar division, Macedonia contains a potpourri of ethnic groups from the region, including Turks (77,959; 3.85%), Roma (53,879; 2.66%) Serbs (35, 939; 1.78%), Vlachs (9,695; 0.48%), Bosniaks (17,108; 0.84%), and "others" (20, 993; 1.04%).[4]

On top of Macedonia's ethnic diversity and cultural distance is a whole layer of mutual frustrations and antipathies. Ten years of post-communist politics witnessed considerable tension over cultural issues like flags, language, and education. A casual racism permeates Macedonian society. On the Macedonian side, racism shows up in the endlessly cruel jokes about "*Shiptari*" (derogatory term for Albanians), in the traditional media associations of Albanians with criminals and terrorists, and in contempt for Albanian cultural traditions. Essentially, Macedonians express a cultural hierarchy in which they are portrayed as "advanced" and Albanians are portrayed as "backward."[5] Albanians who are more modernized and open to friendship with Macedonians are typically referred to as *Albanci*. In this case, the term *Shiptar* is reserved for imagined migrants from Kosovo, villagers, and criminals. Albanians draw similar distinctions. Macedonians who are accepted by Albanians are said to be "like an Albanian." This delineates decent Macedonians from those who are nationalistic and chauvinistic.[6]

Polling data confirm Macedonia's deep divisions.[7] One of the most graphic manifestations of this is what I term the "seesaw" character of public opinion. If Albanians see *black*, so to speak, Macedonians surely see *white*. This is apparent across many different issue dimensions. Table 1 expresses this phenomenon well.

Macedonian and Albanian views on minority rights are diametrically opposed. The Macedonian community was overwhelmingly against granting the kinds of rights Albanians were nearly uniformly demanding. This same pattern of positions on ethnic rights was replicated in surveys conducted by the United National Development Program (UNDP) in June and October of 2000. When the focus shifts from internal Macedonian politics to security issues in the Balkan region, the ethnic divide is preserved. Thus, Mace-

---

[4] State Statistical Office (2003).
[5] Horowitz (1985).
[6] Naegele (2001a).
[7] The surveys examined in this essay are all from U.S. State Department-commissioned studies from 1998 to January 2001, and United Nations Development Program "early warning reports" from October 2000 to March 2001. I thank Anna Sweeny and Dina Smeltz at the U.S. State Department and Albana Gjuzi at UNDP for providing copies of the surveys. Nationally representative samples of 1,000 plus adults aged 18 and over were drawn by both organizations.

Table 1 Rights for Ethnic Albanians in Macedonia

"Recently, various politicians have suggested amending the constitution of Macedonia, mostly to make political structures more representative of Macedonia's various ethnic groups. For each of these following amendments, please tell me whether you would support or oppose."

		Macedonians	Albanians
Creating a vice-presidency, which would be held by an ethnic Albanian	support	5%	93%
	oppose	93%	3%
Legalizing universities which teach using minority languages	support	2%	82%
	oppose	96%	14%
Giving the Albanian language legal status equal to that of the Macedonian language for official contracts and business, such as in courts and in the parliament	support	—	93%
	oppose	98%	4%
Giving greater authority to municipal governments	support	24%	91%
	oppose	74%	3%

Office of Research, Department of State (May 9, 2000), p. 4. Poll was conducted March 19–20, 2000.

donians cited Kosovo (81.6%) and Albania (45.4%) as the two most serious regional threats to the state of Macedonia. Albanians, in contrast, chose Serbia (75.5%) and Montenegro (33.6%) as the principal destabilizing forces in the region.

Both groups traditionally have a low opinion of the other. For example, in a 1998 U.S. State Department survey, 77% of the Macedonian respondents held an unfavorable view of Albanians. Among Albanians, 43% indicated an unfavorable view of Macedonians. Interestingly, negative views of one another do not preclude market transactions. Survey data as well as personal testimony suggest that private business contacts between the two communities are largely unhindered by ethnic prejudice.[8]

Making money is one thing; making love is quite another. Albanians and Macedonians are psychologically unprepared to accept intermarriage between their two communities. Seventy-six percent of those polled by the UNDP in 2001 agreed with the statement, "Most citizens of Macedonia are not ready to marry outside their ethnic group." In sum, there is very little evidence of affective and dense social networks between Albanians and Macedonians. In fact, both before and after the 2001 conflict a trend towards the ethnicization of public space was evident in both Skopje and Tetovo (the center of Albanian political life).[9] As journalist Kim Mehmeti bemoaned in 1992,

---

[8] UNDP (2000, p. 15), Office of Research, Department of State, (June 4, 2001, p. 3); personal interview with former economics minister, Jane Miljovski (Skopje, November 21, 2000). This point was also made by several small-scale entrepreneurs who were ethnic Macedonians.

[9] Petruseva (2001); Borden (2001); Pritchard (2001); Icevska (2001).

58   Part II: Violence as Part of the State and Colonialism

> We have lived together for more than four decades, but only side by side, without feeling any need to know each other better and to become closer to each other.... It would have been sufficient if each Albanian in Macedonia had just two or three Macedonian friends, or if two or three Macedonians had one common Albanian friend. This might have maintained some degree of normal communication between those who happened to share the same place and the same fate.[10]

In political terms also, ethnicity matters in Macedonia. During the first multiethnic coalition government between Macedonians and Albanians (1992–1998),[11] several crises confronted the government, including the lack of international recognition, economic turmoil caused by an international embargo on Serbia (Macedonia's main trading partner) and punitive trade sanctions from Greece over the name of the new republic, secessionist conspiracies by Albanian extremists, several episodes of interethnic violence, and a failed assassination attempt on President Kiro Gligorov in 1995. Macedonia's second multiethnic coalition (1998–2002)[12] endured both the spillover of 200,000 Kosovo refugees in 1999 and the 2001 conflict. Macedonia's relative domestic peace during these severe challenges attests to the virtues of interethnic political accommodation, for the political parties of each community were able to find common interests in sharing power. The general lesson is that primordial-like societies (as defined above) are not inherently unstable.

When Serbian armed forces led by Slobodan Milosevic were forced by NATO to extricate themselves from Kosovo in 1999, an important shift in the regional distribution of power took place. Suddenly, Albanian nationalism was the main threat to peace and stability in the region. The international effort to disarm and reintegrate the Kosovo Liberation Army (KLA) into postwar Kosovo was unsuccessful, and remnants of this organization regrouped to spread insurrection—first to southern Serbia in January 2000, in the form of the Liberation Movement of Presevo, Medvedja, and Bujanovac (UCPMB); and then to Macedonia in February 2001, in the form of the Albanian insurrectionary group, the National Liberation Army (NLA).[13] Thus, the primary cause of Macedonia's conflict was a spillover effect from Kosovo.[14]

Overall, Macedonian society does not have a web of interlocking relations that cut across ethnic divisions and instill obligations based on family, friendship, and common interests. As a result, there are no horizontal mechanisms that inspire feelings and behavior based on the realization of a common destiny. The cleavage lines that separate the ethnic groups are firm and deep. Con-

---

[10] Mehmeti (1992), p. 12.
[11] The Macedonian Social Democratic Party was joined in coalition with the Albanian Party for Democratic Prosperity.
[12] The Internal Macedonian Revolutionary Organization–Democratic Party for Macedonian National Unity was joined by the Democratic Party of Albanians.
[13] I am using the English acronyms for the NLA and the KLA, since their Albanian initials are the same (UCK).
[14] Hislope (2003); Hislope (2002); Liotta and Jebb (2004); Vankoska (2003).

sequently, ethnic cleavages structure the political system, shaping the modes of political organization (i.e., the monopolization of all political expression by ethnic parties) and the issues that dominate the political agenda. The system is afforded no relief from the pressure of politicized ethnicity. In all of these ways and more, ethnicity matters in Macedonia. It is instructive to compare two ethnically divided cities in Macedonia, one which experienced ethnic rioting during the course of the 2001 conflict and one which did not. The objective of this section is to determine how expressive antipathies became actionable.

A TALE OF TWO CITIES: KUMANOVO AND BITOLA

The region of Kumanovo, northeast of Skopje, was an important recruiting center for the NLA in the 2001 conflict and was also the site of a second front that opened in early May of that year. Despite its proximity to the theater of war, the inhabitants of Kumanovo avoided a direct confrontation. On the opposite, southern, side of the country is the town of Bitola. Two episodes of ethnic rioting occurred there, one in late April/early May, and the other in early June. These two contrasting cases offer important insights into the nature of the relationship between ethnic animosities and violence.

Kumanovo

Constituting the second largest urban enclave in Macedonia (behind Skopje), Kumanovo lies twenty miles northeast of the capital. Situated in Skopje's Black Mountain (*Skopska Crna Gora*) range, Kumanovo sits on a traditional crossroad that links Skopje, Nis (Serbia), and Sofia. It is also the beginning of an arc of Albanian-populated areas that move westward and then southward, ringing Macedonia's borders with southern Serbia, Kosovo, and Albania. The city of Kumanovo is multiethnic, with sizable communities of Serbs (9,035; 8.75%) and Roma (4,256; 4.12%) adding to the Macedonian-Albanian mosaic. The town itself has over 100,000 inhabitants. Albanians comprise 26% of that number. However, if we consider the surrounding villages and countryside dwellings, many of which are nearly 100% Albanian, the Albanian population comprises 37% of the total.[15]

The Albanians of the Kumanovo district have several grievances, which made them a fertile recruitment base for the NLA. Most notably, inhabitants of the border villages with southern Serbia were never issued citizenship documents. During Yugoslavia's existence the border zones between republics, particularly in these mountainous terrains, were never defined or carefully monitored. Albanians could thus reasonably wonder, with the fracturing of Yugoslavia along republican lines, to which future state they belonged. The Macedonian state, permanently paranoid about the illegal (i.e., unwanted) influx of Albanians from Kosovo, demanded from these villagers documentation of their residence in Macedonia during the communist period—docu-

---

[15] State Statistical Office (2003); UNDP, *Territorial Division*.

ments which the villagers, due to their remote location and the institutional ineffectiveness of the Macedonian bureaucracy, never received. In this way, ten years of "democracy" passed in Macedonia with scores and scores of border Albanians disenfranchised.[16]

Among such disaffected people, the NLA found a ready base for mobilization. The rural areas in the district, such as Lipkovo, were believed to be locations for NLA military training and exercises. NLA fighters even declared "liberated zones" in the Lipkovo area in May. Much of these rural areas lie adjacent to the Presevo Valley, where Albanian guerrillas of southern Serbia conducted an unsuccessful bid for secession from Serbia in 2000. Moreover, many Kumanovo Albanians eagerly joined the KLA in 1999 and gained valuable combat experience.[17] This whole cross-border region, therefore, became a stronghold of pan-Albanian nationalism and paramilitary networks.

The town of Kumanovo too, has long been a delicate interethnic mixture. The Second World War opened in Macedonia in Kumanovo, and relations among the various communities were stained by that experience. Ethnic rivalry has often spilled into nationalist quarrels and fights. According to analyst Nexhat Aqifi, "inter-ethnic relations have long been Kumanovo's biggest challenge. The town has always been tense, with Serbs and ethnic Macedonians often in conflict with Albanians."[18] When fighting came to this area in early May, many feared the city would become a "second Vukovar." Indeed, one could say that deteriorating conditions in the countryside made the outbreak of violence in the city a safe bet. The most intense fighting of the war occurred in the Kumanovo countryside. Many villages were heavily shelled, and there are widespread, credible reports of Albanian villagers being severely abused by the police.[19] Furthermore, the NLA cut off the water supply to the city between the 6th and 14th of June, and Albanian villagers flocked to Kumanovo in search of refuge once the shelling began.[20] All of this caused obvious hardship and tensions.

Nonetheless, the city did not implode. Credit is due to the town's mayor, Slobodan Kovacevski, and Albanian local leaders, all of whom worked tirelessly to ensure confidence and to maintain open, honest communication channels. Kovacevski regularly contacted all the local mayors in the district, urging them to calm the population and promote peaceful relations. He asked local party leaders to refrain from protest rallies, he convinced the police to stop wearing facial masks during patrols, and he ensured that NGO relief convoys could reach besieged villages. Feriz Dervishi, the Albanian chair of Kumanovo's interethnic commission, sums up the contribution of the mayor in the following way:

---

[16] Naegele (2001e); Balalovska (2002), p. 26.
[17] Naegele (2001f); Ordanoski (2001); Latifi (2001).
[18] Aqifi (2001).
[19] Steele (2001).
[20] Petruseva (2001).

Thanks to the actions since 15 March of Mayor Slobodan Kovacevski, we have succeeded in ensuring that interethnic relations in Kumanovo have not been damaged, even though the situation has escalated in the Lipkovo villages. Kumanovo has remained relatively calm and interethnic relations have not been violated.[21]

In this respect, therefore, one can conclude that the concerted efforts of capable elites were sufficient to dampen otherwise high-conflict conditions for violence.

Bitola

The city of Bitola lies in the southwestern part of the country, about 105 miles from Skopje. Macedonian citizens perpetrated two rounds of anti-Albanian rioting in 2001. The first episode began the evening of April 30 and continued until the evening of May 1. The second riot occurred on June 6 and lasted for four hours. In the first event, a few hundred rioters burned and looted 59 shops and businesses and 10 kiosks. In the second, at least 1,000 Macedonians (some estimates reach as high as 3,000) gathered to destroy 50 Albanian and Turkish (or, more generally, Muslim) shops, 20 homes, and one mosque. Some Muslims were beaten. Anti-Albanian graffiti was spray-painted on building after building, most of it calling for "Death to the Shiptars," "Pure Bitola," and "Get Out Albanians."[22] Speaking in the aftermath of the May disturbance, the Albanian leader Arben Xhaferi decried it as the equivalent of "Kristallnacht."[23]

Bitola—or Monastir, as it is called by the Albanians—is an important cultural landmark in Albanian history. The city of Bitola lies in the southwestern part of the country, about 105 miles from Skopje. Between 1908 and 1909, Albanian intellectuals gathered to debate the codification of the Albanian language and settled on the Latin script (over the Greek and Arabic, which were also used at the time). The polyethnic character of Bitola changed over time. Between 1953 and 1980, Belgrade and Ankara had a special arrangement that encouraged Turkish migration. During this period approximately 30,000 Turks emigrated, with many Albanians joining the exodus. The town has also experienced a steady population decline due to poor economic conditions. Bitola's economic activity is naturally oriented towards Greece, as Florina is only 20 kilometers away (whereas Skopje is 180 kilometers). Thus, the five-year (1992–1997) Greek boycott on Macedonia took a destructive toll on Bitola livelihoods. Furthermore, the city was hit hard by a corrupt pyramid investment scheme that floundered in 1996.[24]

---

[21] Naegele (2001d); Latifi (2001); Ford (2001).
[22] I visited Bitola and Prilep (also the scene of a riot) in November 2002 and saw many burned-out businesses, shops, and a demolished mosque (in Prilep). In Prilep, I interviewed a local Turk, whose shop was destroyed. At an adjacent building, the words "UCK" [NLA] were spray-painted on the window. The author thanks Zoran Ilievski and family for the tour of Bitola, and Dane Taleski for leading the investigation in Prilep.
[23] Human Rights Watch (2001); Naegele (2001b,f).
[24] International Crisis Group (2001).

There are five separate threads that weave together the rioting of May and June: (1) the source of Macedonian outrage, (2) the role played by relatives of the deceased, (3) the irresponsibility of the media and the use of rumor, (4) the passivity of the police, and (5) the encouragement of elites. The precipitating events for both riots occurred not in Bitola, but in the Sar mountain range above Tetovo, 170 kilometers from the city. Each time, angry Macedonians assembled because the NLA ambushed and killed soldiers who came from the Bitola area. In May, NLA forces gunned down four Bitola policemen on active duty in the army; in June, NLA units killed three Bitola natives.

When Macedonians reacted to these triggering events, they unleashed a furious revenge, not only on local Albanians but on Turks as well. The transferal of retribution from Albanians to Turks may lead one to question the nexus between precipitants and targets, but there is a logic to this displacement. According to the 2002 census, Albanians in the district numbered only 2,522 (2.92%) of the population, which makes them the third largest ethnicity, behind Macedonians (77,470; 90%) and Roma (2,594; 3%). Turks are the fourth largest ethnic group in Bitola, numbering 1,580 (1.83%).[25] By selecting Turks as a substitute target for Albanians, Macedonians not only were acting out traditional antipathies that stretch back to Ottoman rule but also were broadening the boundaries of the immediate adversary to include the more encompassing category of "Muslim." Consequently, there occurred what Horowitz labels a "cumulation" effect, or the "conjunction of direct and displaced aggression."[26]

A second common element of the riots is that they occurred in the aftermath of funeral ceremonies, when relatives of the deceased organized friends and neighbors to join in demonstrations. The siblings and friends of those murdered were at the forefront of the May rioting, according to local eyewitnesses. In the June rampage, a brother of one of the victims organized a protest among taxi drivers that quickly snowballed into mob action.[27]

A third thread that facilitated the rioting was the activity of the media. When the Macedonian soldiers were killed on April 28, a privately owned local television station (Tera TV) reported that the Albanians of Bitola were celebrating the deaths by discharging guns in the air. When individual rioters were later questioned, they cited the television report as one of the reasons for their behavior. Also revealed on television was the state coroner's report, which documented in detail the disfiguration of the soldiers' bodies. Reportedly, NLA guerrillas mutilated the fingers, eyes, and scalps of the victims.[28] The editor of *Fakti* (an Albanian newspaper), Lirim Dulovi, holds such media reports directly responsible for the subsequent carnage. He described the media's role as follows:

---

[25] State Statistical Office.
[26] Horowitz (2001), pp. 137–8.
[27] Naegele (2001b,c).
[28] Naegele (2001c); Taylor (2001).

> The Macedonian language media were put in position to create hatred, I underline this—hatred, and to urge violence against the non-Macedonian population. . . . I shall remind you that what happened in Bitola was inspired by the murder of eight soldiers near Vejce. . . . After the funeral ceremony of the soldiers, the article developed by Mende Mladenovski and presented at Tera TV included details that could be qualified as urging racial hatred. In the article, [Tito] Petkovski [nationalist Macedonian politician] said that while the soldiers were buried, the Albanians from the city were celebrating their death. After this article, the city was set on fire and ethnic cleansing of the non-Macedonian population begun. . . . So, this was simply manipulating with the public.[29]

A fourth thread concerns the reluctance of the police to intervene. Human Rights Watch, which published a study on the riots, concluded that local policemen not only passively stood by but also, in some cases, actively participated in the mayhem. In June, the police did not even attempt to enforce their own declared curfew of 10 PM, and instead waited until 1 AM to clamp down on the vandals. Albanian eyewitnesses, including those whose shops were destroyed, claim to have seen a few policemen either directly participating in the rioting or preventing Albanians from attempting to put out fires. In May, the only significant action of the police over two nights was to protect the home of Albanian deputy Health Minister Muarem Nexhipi. In June, not even his home was spared. According to a local Albanian television reporter, the minister's home was burned "in the presence of Macedonian police who were just spectators."[30]

The fifth thread centers on the role of elites. Vladimir Milchin, director of the Open Society Institute branch in Skopje, is a major proponent of this thesis. In an article published in *Utrinski vesnik* on 3 May, Milchin raised the spectre that dark forces were at work in Bitola:

> There is something smelly in this dim story, something that stinks much more than the burnt shops in the bazaar in Bitola. Power and money are the agents of movement of this "death game." Someone is encouraging enmity to incite voluntary or violent ethnic cleansing.[31]

Milchin observes that hard-line interior minister Ljube Boskovski was in Bitola on the day of the funeral and stayed until the next day.[32] This rather suspicious appearance too neatly coincided with the subsequent passivity of the police, who even disobeyed the mayor's demand to impose order. The June event also involved a prominent personality who, by virtue of his position, provided holy cover for sinister deeds. At the funeral service, Orthodox Bishop Petar presented an incendiary speech, in which Albanian political party leaders were accused of being collaborators with those who murdered the young men.[33]

---

[29] Dulovi (2001).
[30] Human Rights Watch (2001); Naegele (2001b,c).
[31] Milchin (2001).
[32] Personal interview with Vladimir Milchin, June 21, 2002, Skopje.
[33] ICG (2001).

Police collusion, likely at Boskovski's request but impossible to confirm, undoubtedly made possible the extent of destruction. More questionable, however, are the various conspiracy theories that have arisen in connection with the Bitola events. For example, some commentators have attempted to assign complete responsibility to hooligans bused in from Skopje.[34] However, such reports contradict the claims of residents who insist that locals alone perpetrated the violence.[35] Much is also made about the fact that wealthy Albanian homes were targeted, which presumably indicates the planned nature of the riots. Perhaps a better explanation is that local Macedonians had no trouble identifying the property of prominent Albanians simply because in small, parochial settings, people grow up knowing "who's who." The looting of homes, therefore, represented a criminal opportunity as well as a way to punish Albanians for the misdeeds of the NLA.

Conclusion

Traditional antipathies become salient when a community experiences a traumatic, precipitating event, and such antipathies predetermine the targets for retribution. Moreover, triggering events such as ethnically motivated crimes reciprocally confirm and validate long-standing prejudices and suspicions. But other factors need to be present in order to facilitate the transposition of hatred from attitude to behavior. The Bitola riots were sustained by the local power structure but not jump-started by them. For that, we must look to the close relatives and friends of the victims. Macedonian politicians could not have successfully mobilized riots in the absence of the macabre slayings of Macedonian soldiers. The killings were a triggering event that prompted a visceral reaction in the Macedonian community. As Milchin acknowledges, conditions in Bitola make it "a town which is easily pushed into being involved in events like a pogrom."[36]

Like Bitola, Kumanovo is a town widely recognized to contain fragile interethnic relations. However, diligent elites in that town worked overtime to prevent any type of conflagration as the war commenced in the surrounding countryside. But this brief comparison demonstrates another crucial difference between Bitola and Kumanovo, namely, the presence of a precipitating event in the former and its absence in the latter. Traumatizing events such as interethnic rapes, murders, and mutilations trigger powerful emotions in a community and represent a fundamental factor that can tip the balance from expressive to actionable hatred.

---

[34] ICG 2001; Alusevski 2001.
[35] Personal interview with Zoran Ilievski and Ljubcho Ilievski, Bitola residents, (November 22, 2002).
[36] Naegele (2001c).

References

Alusevski, Sime. (2001). "Bitola Spirit Crushed," *Balkan Crisis Report*, 253 (June 6). Retrieved February 14, 2007, at <www.iwpr.net>.

Aqifi, Nexhat. (2001). "Kumanovo Braced for War," *Balkan Crisis Report*, 244 (May 6).

Balalovska, Kristina, Alessandro Silj, and Mario Zucconi. (2002). *Minority Politics in Southeast Europe: Crisis in Macedonia* (Rome: Ethnobarometer).

Borden, Anthony. (September, 2001). "A Bridge Across the Vardar," *Balkan Crisis Report*, 282.

Brubaker, Rogers and David D. Laitin. (1998). "Ethnic and Nationalist Violence," *Annual Review of Sociology*, 24: 423–452.

Dulovi, Lirim. (2001). "The Media and the Conflict in Macedonia," *Lobi* (December 4).

Fearon, James D. and David D. Laitin. (Autumn, 2000). "Violence and the Social Construction of Identity," *International Organization*, 54 (4): 845–877.

Ford, Peter. (2001). "Part of the Balkans that Has Not Exploded," *Christian Science Monitor* (July 11).

Hislope, Robert. (May/June 2004). "Crime and Honor in a Weak State: Paramilitary Forces and Violence in Macedonia," *Problems of Post-Communism*, 51 (3): 18–26.

———. (January, 2003). "Between a Bad Peace and a Good War," *Ethnic and Racial Studies*, 26 (1): 129–151.

———. (May/June 2002)."Organized Crime in a Disorganized State: How Corruption Contributed to Macedonia's Mini-War," *Problems of Post-Communism*, 49 (3): 33–41.

Horowitz, Donald L. (2001). *The Deadly Ethnic Riot* (Berkeley: University of California Press).

———. (1985). *Ethnic Groups in Conflict* (Berkeley: University of California Press).

Human Rights Watch. (2001). "Rioters Burn Albanian Homes in Bitola" (New York, June 8). Retrieved February 19, 2007, at <www.hrw.org/press/2001/06/Bitola0608.htm>.

Icevska, Gordana Stojanovska. (2001). "Skopke 'Spirit' Threatened," *Balkan Crisis Report* (April 5).

International Crisis Group. (2001)."Macedonia: The Last Chance for Peace," p.113. Report issued June 20, 2001(Skopje/Brussels: Author).

Latifi, Veton. (2001.) "Kumanovo Holds Together," *Balkan Crisis Report*, 268 (August 3).

———. (2001)."Ghosts of Vukovar Haunt Kumanovo," *Balkan Crisis Report*, 231 (March 30).

Liotta, Peter H. and C. R. Jebb. (2004). *Mapping Macedonia: Idea and Identity* (Westport, CT: Praeger).

Mehmeti, Kim. (November–December 1992). "More Sinning than Sinned Against," *East European Reporter*, 5: 12.

Milchin, Vladimir. (2001). "Here Comes the Plague," *Utrinski vesnik* (May 3).

Motyl, Alexander J. (1999). *Revolutions, Nations, Empires: Conceptual Limits and Theoretical Possibilities* (New York: Columbia University Press).

Naegele, Jolyon (2001a). "How the Nation's Albanians and Slavs Perceive One Another (Part 2)," *Radio Free Europe/Radio Liberty* (June 28, 2001). Retrieved February 21, 2007, at <www.rferl.org>.

———. (2001b). "Violence Returns to Bitola," *Radio Free Europe/Radio Liberty* (June 7).

———. (2001c). "Questions Linger, Rumors Abound in Torching of Bitola's Albanian Businesses," *Radio Free Europe/Radio Liberty* (May 30).

———. (2001d). "Kumanovo, So Far, Avoiding Interethnic Conflict," *Radio Free Europe/Radio Liberty* (May 18, 2001).

———. (2001e). "War Comes To A Village," *Radio Free Europe/Radio Liberty* (May 16, 2001).

———. (2001f). "Anti-Albanian Riots Put Conflict On New Level," *Radio Free Europe/Radio Liberty* (May 2, 2001).

Ordanoski, Saso. (2001). "NLA Violence Sabotages Talks," *Balkan Crisis Report*, 243 (May 2).

Petruseva, Ana. (2001). "Step-by-Step Towards Division," *Balkan Crisis Report*, 271 (August 14).

———. (2001). "Thirsting for a Return to Normality," *Balkan Crisis Report*, 256 (June 15).

Pritchard, Ellie. (2001). "Macedonia: Tetovo Riven by Ethnic Hatred," *Balkan Crisis Report*, 306 (December 21).

Rusi, Iso. (2001). "How Many Victims Did the War Have?" *Lobi*, 44 (December 17).

State Statistical Office. (2003). *Census of Population, Households, and Dwellings in the Republic of Macedonia, 2002* (Skopje Republic of Macedonia, December 1).

Steele, Jonathan. (2001). "Macedonian Police Beat Fleeing Albanians," *The Guardian* [London], June 2: 17.

Taylor, Scott. (2001). "On the Edge of an Abyss," *The Ottawa Citizen*, May 12,: B1.

United Nations Development Program. (2001). *Territorial Division of FRY Macedonia into 34 Municipalities* (Skopje: Country Office FYR Macedonia), Retrieved April 19, 2001; Web link no longer available.

United Nations Development Program. (2000–2001). "Early Warning Report." Report nos. 1 (October 2000), 2 (November 2000), 3 (December 2000/January 2001), 4 (February/March 2001), Skopje: Author.

U.S. State Department. (2001) survey data from 1998 to January 2001. Office of Research.

Vankovska, Biljana. (2003). *Current Perspectives on Macedonia: The Struggle for Peace, Democracy and Security*, four part series The Heinrich Boll Foundation., Retrieved February 21, 2007, at < www.boell.de/asp/frameset_en.html>.

Acknowledgments

Research for this paper was made possible by grants from National Research Council (2000), the Open Society Institute in Macedonia (2002), Union College (2003), and invaluable insights and support from Prof. Gjorge Ivanov and my friends in Skopje at the Institute for Democracy, Solidarity, and Civil Society (Nenad Markovic, Ivan Damjanovski, Dane Taleski, Vladimir Bozinovski, Ivica Bocevski, and Zoran Ilievski). I also thank Vladimir Milchin of the Open Society Institute (Macedonia), Silva Kantareva, and Michele Angrist. A very special thanks to Ann-Marie Rajhmundhani.

The Afro Feast of Saint Francis of Assisi in Quibdó and Its Narratives of Amendment

Daniel Mosquera

Since the early twentieth century the feast honoring St. Francis of Assisi in Quibdó (the capital city of the state of Chocó, Colombia) has emerged as the most prominent cultural event of the year for the local population. Its origins date to the seventeenth century under Franciscan evangelization of indigenous peoples, but its afro-descendent character does not become evident until the late nineteenth century.[1] Those who have written about the feast confirm that the people, having gradually wrested it away from church authority, turned it into an event with deep, ethnic, cultural, and political overtones. One of the popular sayings during the feast is that San Pacho—the familiar name by which the feast is locally known—is for those who delight in it (*"San Pacho es pa'l que lo goce"*). Whereas the feast remains an event of gratification in the popular imagination, it also critiques and exposes local and national corruption, the historical indifference at the hands of the state and, more intensely in recent years, the realities of displacement in the face of armed aggression. This essay examines this apparent incongruity by focusing on two aspects of local memory present in the feast in its modern guise: chronic disregard of *Chocoanos* by the Colombian political establishment, and the violence made possible by this indifference as armed pressure sets in to secure territorial control and Chocó's natural resources.

Written especially for *Ruminations on Violence*. Portions of this essay include quotations and photographs from "Re-constituting Chocó: The Feast of San Pacho and the Afro Question in Colombia" (*JLACS*, 13, 2 [2004]: 171–194), reprinted with permission from Carfax Publishing (Taylor & Francis Ltd.). The essay is also based in part on written histories and analyses, and on interviews and video archives from the 2002, 2003, and 2005 feasts.

---

[1] The term "afro-descendent," used throughout the essay, offers a more inclusive, less theoretical notion when referring to peoples of African ancestry, without suggesting a national "hybrid" status that erases historical tensions from the term.

Examining how the feast chronicles this systematic insensitivity through contestation and critique can help the reader to understand why the region—not the communities that inhabit it—is significant within what is today referred to in Colombia and the world as "the armed conflict."

In this complex array of pressures, the feast emerges as a cultural and political catalyst. It is an instrument used to chronicle these processes and how they have affected the afro-descendent communities. Ultimately, the feast expresses a desire for change. It gives a partial glimpse of how people who experience segregation and violence as a matter of daily life can still maintain local histories and shape a sense of self. The analysis that follows relies on recorded or archival material from the 2002, 2003 and 2005 feasts.

A Brief Backdrop

Located on the Pacific rim of Colombia, the state of Chocó is a lush, diverse, forest-rich area comprised of a majority of afro-descendent peoples. Like its capital, Quibdó, Chocó for the most part remains remote from national consciousness—at least until a new massacre or displacement emerges in the media with new images of violence and of people's flight from it. Many of these people settle, perhaps briefly, in modern cities or their peripheries (where most Colombian displaced peoples often end up), making their displacement tangible to the crowds accustomed to watching it on the news. Before the arrival of Spaniards, indigenous communities (today Emberas, Waunanas, and Tules) inhabited the territory. Although exploited intensely within the Spanish imperial system for over two hundred years, during its colonial history Chocó remained largely unsettled by Spaniards and *criollos* (people of Spanish extraction born in the Spanish colonies of Latin America), most of whom directed mining operations and controlled transportation and food production either from settled capitals elsewhere or by staying in Chocó for short periods of time. By 1810, there were few resident merchants and virtually no farming and colonization, such as had occurred in many other parts of the larger republic (Sharp 1976, 193). Until the end of slavery in 1851 Indians and African slaves faced compulsory labor in mines, centered early on the extraction of gold. The region witnessed the brisk decimation of indigenous communities; their gradual replacement by African slaves; and the passage of evangelists, fortune hunters, and European or criollo travelers.

After slavery was abolished, a system of inequity persisted in various legal, semi-legal, and informal ways, the vestiges of which still inform Colombian social realities today. Because of its river channel to the Atlantic coast, throughout the eighteenth and nineteenth centuries Chocó also had a direct link to Kingston, Jamaica, with which it maintained commercial and cultural relations. Syrian and Lebanese families also settled in the region in the late nineteenth century. As a result, it is not surprising to find surnames like Maluk, Halaby, or Thomson in the phone books of Quibdó or the existence of *quibes* (Arabic lamb patties) and dumplings in the local cuisine.

In 1906 Chocó stopped being the "exploited yard" of the southern state of Cauca and became a separate district—an *intendencia* (having limited status)—and subsequently a full state (or *departamento*) in 1947. In a land deal at the turn of the century that still haunts the region, Chocó lost part of its territory to the state of Antioquia. This situation has been alluded to in many *disfraces*—parade floats during feast of San Pacho, which feature a theaterlike, life-size arrangement on top, manipulated internally by one or more persons as the float moves along the streets. In photo 1, for instance, an *antioqueño* (a person born in the state of Antioquia, a wealthy, industrial state bordering Chocó on the eastern side) is seen pulling a part of Chocó away from the region in the upper part of the disfraz.[2]

Even though the Colombian Constitution was rewritten in 1991 to restore cultural and territorial autonomies to indigenous and black communities (and amended two years later to correct some oversights regarding afro-descendent rights), today both populations still see their peoples, cultures, and territories threatened by violence, uncertain legislation, and outwardly coordinated economic interests.[3]

Photo 1: 2005 Roma neighborhood *disfraz: Al caído, caele: abandonados y de ñapa fumigados* (smack the fallen [the equivalent of "hit them when they're down" or "adding insult to injury"]: abandoned, and what's left is fumigated) [*Abandonados* and *fumigados* refer to lands vacated by intimidated local landowners and to the pesticide threat referenced in footnote 3].

With a rising black political leadership throughout the twentieth century, most of Chocó's politicians belong to afro-descendent political elites who

---

[2] The banana industry that ships much of its product to the United States and Europe, formerly owned by the United Fruit Company, now Chiquita Brand International, is partially located in this area. In 2004, Chiquita revealed that it had, through Banamex (its subsidiary in Colombia), paid "terrorist" organizations for their help, once it realized paramilitary and guerrilla groups had been so-designated by the State Department ("Chiquita admits payments to terror groups." *The Seattle Times.* Wednesday, May 12, 2004).

[3] Today, Chocó's natural forests and biodiversity are beset by the onslaught of a new environmental threat, accompanied also by armed aggression: commercial plantations of oil palm or African palm trees. These agro-business projects are promoted by multinational corporations alleged to be relying on paramilitary assistance to intimidate local landowners (sometimes resulting in "abandoned" land—see photo 1) and enforce palm production. The current president, Alvaro Uribe, sanctioned this business incursion, which has been widely documented and continues to be debated. Wikipedia or Google entries on palm oil or *palma Africana* will direct readers to the debates and illustrate the complexity of the arguments. The threat posed by agro-business, pesticides, and "mono-cultivation" to the biodiversity of *Chocoanos* has been a repeated topic of the feasts.

subscribe, for the most part, to two-party national conservative or liberal ideologies. Much pride is expressed in the fact, however, that most institutional and political leaders in Chocó are afro-descendent and that one of two national senators is an Embera Indian from Chocó. There has been a small but tangible generational flux of white *antioqueños* (who have settled and made a living in the region's cities and towns over the years). Most are men, and many have created mixed-race families with local women and have come to own most of the businesses there. Why this is the case is a thorny issue for locals and difficult to examine historically. Surely, the lack of capital and the disconnection of Quibdó from modern urban centers like Bogotá, Medellín, and Cali have played a role. Historical racism toward the afro-descendent population is also a significant contributor, as are the predicaments befallen communities unable to meet the demands of a modernity on which they hardly deliberated. Nonetheless, a more cohesive sense of ethnic identity has ripened over the years and, especially with the new constitutional recognition, heralded a more dynamic type of socio-political standing for the afro-descendent people (Wade 1993, 356).[4] Today this new position faces its most formidable obstacle in the form of armed conflict, since it involves territorial control and the ownership and extraction of natural resources.

Attention sparked by the new autonomies and coalitions derived from the 1991 Constitution has also increased, as local and international activists, social scientists, and cultural analysts document ethnic and diasporic realities and the violence that besets them. In spite of being another enclave of the African diaspora and sharing much of Afro-Caribbean culture, Chocó is neither an island nor is it recognized as part of the Caribbean basin. A continued displacement, a much publicized massacre of rural blacks at the hands of guerrillas in the district of Bojayá in 2002[5] (of the 119 dead in its town of Bellavista, 46 were children), and ongoing bullying tactics of native communities all contribute to continued conflict in the region without an end in sight. Power struggles over water channels to both oceans (Pacific and Atlantic) have also resulted in armed aggression, as paramilitaries and guerrillas, both involved in illicit drug and arms trafficking, vie for their control (*The Guardian* 2005). The resulting displacement of local communities repeatedly has been a topic of San Pacho as well as of national and international media outlets.

The Feast

San Pacho is the most important of a series of saint and Virgin feasts dotting the region's Catholic year and connecting, through rivers, the afro-descendent towns and cities of the north Pacific region. Officially, it begins on September 3 with the *alborada* (or dawning), an initiation day when the saint and the

---

[4] For a better understanding of blackness and multiculturalism in Colombia, see Wade (1993) and Agudelo (2005).
[5] See photo 5 for the Cristo Rey neighborhood disfraz commemorating this event.

organizing committees are blessed in the church, accompanied by a musical procession through the city. Villa Rivera (1989, p. 25) explains that this opening is a synthesis of similar smaller alboradas in each of the neighborhoods between August 20 and September 2. On September 19, members of the central committee and some old-time regulars go out to announce the feast (a process called *pregón*), demanding that everyone enjoy it and respect each other as a matter of law. On September 20 the 12 participating neighborhoods brandish their flags, borrowing from local, national, and international symbols, which colorful *cachés* (choreographies in which the participants wear colorful costumes) and *chirimía* music groups escort through the city. Rogerio Velásquez (p. 22) describes *chirimía* as street music of multitudes, present also in Chocó's political events, pageants, and other celebrations as well as in what is known as "afro masses," liturgies where afrodescendent regional musical and cultural traditions compose the mass (Lizcano, 2005). The feast serves as the creative platform where all musicians exhibit their craft, whose topics might also restate the thematic concerns of the disfraces or floats. Occasionally, some cachés are themselves theatrical representations of local memory exploring such topics such as slavery, relations with antioqueños, or an imagined Africanness (photo 2).[6]

Photo 2: 2005 caché sponsored by a local business: *Y sigue la esclavitud* (and the slavery continues).

Between September 21 and October 2 the twelve neighborhoods that participate officially in the celebrations put together parades, each on an assigned day. Each pageant is made up of the flag, a disfraz, a caché led by the neighborhood committee and their friends, succeeding groups each accompanied by *chirimía* musicians, and ending with a procession (mostly of young people) that contracts and expands at the rhythm of *chirimía* music in a dancing ritual called *rebulú*. This danced procession circles the city through all of the respective neighborhoods, pausing every half a block to display the inventive contraption of the disfraz, which holds one or several craftsmen

---

[6] To augment the author's literal translations, in some instances the publisher has attempted to provide more idiomatic meanings to facilitate readers' understanding. These additional translations appear in brackets.

inside the device in order to make it function (photos 3–10). The artistic range is broad and oftentimes novel, as each neighborhood committee chooses a topic to re-create, gathers the money for the project, and hires one of the available local artists to build it. Local businesses and national companies—the most prominent of which sell liquor—help to fund these projects. Money also comes from organized neighborhood events such as bingos, parties, and raffles.

After approximately five hours the pageant is over, and each neighborhood holds a *verbena* (or night dance party), exhibiting the neighborhood effigy of the saint near the committee president's house. The entire quarter is closed off to moving vehicles and resembles a street fair, with food made and sold on site, drinks, and music concerts. During the festivity many of the residents cook regional dishes and welcome friends to their houses for food and high spirits. Two large tents sponsored by liquor companies are erected in central streets animated by local DJs and national and local bands. *Chirimía* groups enliven some of the private parties as well. On October 3 all of the disfraces come out for one last parade around the city, accompanied by chirimía and selected cachés, giving the judges one more chance to look before they decide on the winner. At 3 AM the following morning there is a walked mass, following the same neighborhood circuit of the parades and stopping to sing the locally composed Saint Francis anthem before each neighborhood altarpiece. The main effigy of the saint comes out of the church around noon on the same day. The festivities end on October 5, when the saint effigies are once again safely ensconced in their respective altars, where they remain until the next feast. Soon after, other neighborhoods not officially included in the feast have their own celebrations that extend the spirit of San Pacho well into December. In fact, the winning disfraz gets one more chance at a pageant on December 31, before the end of the year.

There is a saying impugning the feast as 40 days of revelry and only one of reflection. It alludes to the many days of carnal celebration, dancing and drinking and the sole day at the end of the feast, October 4, when the saint leaves the church for the yearly procession. Upon closer observation, it becomes evident that only a small part of the population is present during most mass celebrations (one every evening for each neighborhood). A throng of people emerges only for the walked mass and, more important, on St. Francis's day in the afternoon of October 4, when the arches or *arcos* (allegorical *tableaux vivant*, or moving pictures, that present a figure of the mediating saint, not unlike archetypal images of the Virgin Mary in many other Catholic traditions [photos 11–13]) are displayed in each neighborhood and the saint is brought before each of them.

Some consultants from my fieldwork in 2005 implied that people should reevaluate the history concerning the impact carnival traditions had on the religious celebration. Saint Francis is present everywhere in the feast, but not every use of the saint connotes him as an exclusively pious icon. After all, the

Mosquera The Afro Feast of Saint Francis of Assisi in Quibdó 73

Photo 3: 2002 César Conto neighborhood disfraz, *Indiferencia ante una agonía* (indifference in the face of agony).

Photo 4: 2002 Pandeyuca neighborhood disfraz: *Chocó exprimido por los dos lados* (Chocó, squeezed from both sides). The device on this disfraz resembles the grinding device to extract juice out of sugar cane. The "two sides" doing the squeezing are the soldier and the politician (only the soldier is visible in this photo).

Photo 5: 2003 Cristo Rey neighborhood disfraz, *Bojayá después de un año. La doble tragedia* (Bojayá, a year later. The double tragedy). A year after the massacre, people attempted to return to their homes only to find conditions too dangerous, and they were forced to leave again. The "double tragedy" refers to this double displacement, and the state is unwilling to provide the safety the people need.

Photo 6: 2005 Pandeyuca neighborhood disfraz: *No a la privatización de las universidades públicas* (no to the privatization of public universities).

historical Francis was himself both a *bon vivant* and a stoic, spiritual man.[7] Once afro-descendents took control of the feast it changed its identity, from a strictly religious celebration into a spectacle partially reminiscent of carnival "through theatricality, pantomime and parody" (Friedemann and Horner 1995, p. 116). As Wade has thoughtfully summed up, "The [feast is] a vehicle for political protest, for the Chocoanos' view of themselves as a social and racial unit in the nation's political economy" (p. 126).

The feast is divided into stages, all of which string together its religious and secular expressions. Often, discussions about the utility of the feast or its length enter public debate among locals but, it seems, these discussions are already accounted for as part of the feast itself. Those with whom I consulted remembered instances in which specific disfraz themes or specific feasts resulted in concrete, positive changes for the population. If anything the theme of the feast, while alluding to former feasts, changes every year. In spite of the history of aggression and neglect that has plagued the region, through the vehicle of the pageant the people continue to express their needs: education, sustainable agriculture and environmental policies, reliable and affordable services such as drinking water and electricity, honest politicians, the protection of children, and, above all, the freedom to pursue these needs without fear of reprisal and bloodshed.

The committee in charge of deciding which disfraz deserved a prize during the 2002 San Pacho feast opted for Kennedy's, a neighborhood whose rendition literally revisited the massacre of Bojayá (photo 7). It used pyrotechnics mimicking the blast of missiles, with guns pointing from the sides, and had blood funneled into the building. Indirectly, it exposed the fragility of the church and the state as the two founding institutions unable to ward off the violence unleashed by the Colombian armed conflict. This dramatization also implied that the rule of law consecrated in the constitutional reforms of 1991–1993 had lost a sociopolitical bearing beyond its metropolitan identity. It called attention to the fact that both the church's and state's political capital was in short supply in rural areas and had not gained further legitimacy. To the committee members, this representation effectively epitomized the local sentiment of outrage and vulnerability in the face of a reality that multiplied tenfold

---

[7] I was reminded of Saint Francis's love for merriment even as he became a religious man by a locally well-known committee member, Vladimiro Garcés (personal interview, September, 30, 2005).

an already existing history of displacement and abandonment. It also criticized a political system they felt was complicit both directly and indirectly in this situation.[8] The El Silencio neighborhood presented a variation on the same theme, with pyrotechnics and a cracked church front with a homemade missile flying into it. On that day, there was a caché of women dressed in black with children wrapped in body bags carrying a coffin, also a reference to the massacre of Bojayá.

With hundreds of refugees sitting inside the city stadium, Bojayá was no longer a simple town eight hours up river north of Quibdó. It became one more scattered, extra-territorialized, afro-descendant collective whose claim to land and cultural autonomy had suddenly evaporated. This massacre, condemned and analyzed in the international press, was used in 2002 in different ways as a referent by other neighborhoods in their own processions. One of them even incorporated a caché of displaced peoples in one of the processions (photo 8). This group merely took its place between *chirimía* groups by dressing in rags and carrying furniture, tables, mattresses and other household belongings on their backs. This episode was of particular significance, for it multiplied the layers of self-parody and innovation embodying the event. This spectacle reverberated with other images that presented the massacre as mediated by various actors and spectacles.

Photo 7: Kennedy neighborhood disfraz: *¿Por qué somos así?* (Why are we this way?) [roughly the equivalent of "How has it come to this?"] September 27, 2002. Reproduced with permission from the local newspaper *Chocó 7 Dias*.

While this was taking place, the float carrying the disfraz from the César Conto neighborhood just a block ahead had a complex interpretation of the same event (photos 3, 9). This float featured a black man chained prone on a tilted surface, who would from time to time move as if struggling to free himself. Another black man dressed in a suit and tie and carrying a briefcase—the metropolitan attire of a politician—stands next to him and moves his shoulders up and down in a shrugging motion, expressing both indifference and resignation. His dress seems incongruous and contrived. The two men

---

[8] It is believed that government military forces anticipated the attack and might have been able to prevent it (*Revista Semana*, 2005).

76 Part II: Violence as Part of the State and Colonialism

are separated (or connected) by a television screen. Above the television screen a sign reads "*La indiferencia ante una agonía*" (literally, indifference before [in the face of] agony). A constructed figure of a child sits before the two men and the television screen, watching a rotating collection of images as the procession moves through the streets. One of the images is of the massacre of Bojayá (photo 9), a cartoonlike rendering that concentrates its iconographic appeal on the military boats, missiles, the explosion, and the mindless execution of civilians. This news clip is interspersed with clips of other news about soccer, the overpriced sale and inconsistent provision of electricity, and other images about celebrity popular culture. In photo 3 a real child spectator stands behind the child-marionette—watching him watch, as if focused intently on the multiple realities and the drama of destitution.

The politician in this drama is afro-descendent, but the institutional culture he represents is not. The television screen becomes a superficial, though ubiquitous, representational space unable to mediate in a critical fashion between national and local histories. After decades of broadcasting displacements, persecutions, and massacres between news about beauty pageants and soccer games, the TV screen merely serializes local histories as a daily sedative.

The massacre of Bojayá was also used in 2003 to direct attention to the precarious situation of displaced peoples trying to return to their ancestral lands (photos 5, 10). Continuing in 2004 ("a year later," see photo 5) and still

Photo 8: A caché representing displaced peoples.

Photo 9: Massacre of Bojayá as seen on the TV screen in the César Conto disfraz.

today, people from Bojayá are caught in the crossfire between paramilitaries and guerrillas and continue to experience the agony and uncertainty caused by this situation (*Agence France Press* 2005; *El Tiempo* 2005). References to displaced peoples appeared again in 2005 disfraces. These references directly and indirectly re-created a consciousness of self-preservation (see, for example, photo 1, alluding to fumigation programs instituted under Plan Colombia; and photo 10, one of several attempts of displaced people to return to their lands that was covered by the media). It persists as a reminder that the survival of local autonomies cannot be guaranteed by a state whose constitutional identity is weakened by its own history of discrimination and violence.

Photo 10: Filmed return of villagers to Bojayá in October of 2002. Reproduced with permission from *Cocomacia*, Consejo Comunitario Mayor de la Asociación Campesina Integral del Atrato.

How the participants internalize and interpret these complex critiques is difficult to assess. The disfraces weave together parables (some more literal than others) of neglect and displacement—a series of animated dramas that express political alternatives, denounce local and metropolitan hypocrisies, and advance utopian expressions. A study of the disfraces created between 1979 and 1987 suggests that topics related to state-sponsored marginalization, economic isolation and racism continue, alongside critiques of local and regional politics, to preoccupy the black population (Villa Rivera 1989, p. 31). Floats from the 2002, 2003, and 2005 celebrations confirm this assessment. A longing for a sustainable, autonomous lifestyle that is not severed from national political decisions is implicit in many of the disfraces and carries over to the final iconic stage, the *auto sacramental* or arco on October 4 (these representations are also called *misterios*).

When the effigy of the saint makes its circuit through the city on October 4, each neighborhood prepares an arco hidden from view until the effigy arrives before it. At that point the arco is unveiled. The arcos on the day of Saint Francis offer a tangible and logical conclusion to, and continuity between, the twelve disfraces and the political cachés. Their thematic orientation provides a direct link between the problems the population faces and the hunger for a better life and for justice. The population transfers the weight of their problems onto the saint. A healing and captivating force to the afro-descendent population, the saint and amends the wrongs committed.

Locally, there is no mystery in the origin of the story of the saint— it is manifest in the most popular and least formal published history of the feast that circulates among *Chocoanos*—Ana Gilma de Ayala's *Reseña histórica* (re-edited every year since 1997). Read by all elementary school children as well as by adults, her book begins with a chronological hagiography of St. Francis of Assisi in Italy. In the introduction of the book, St. Francis is recognized as a multi-dimensional figure immersed in and imbued by *Chocoanos*: "He is immersed in(to) *Chocoanos* and we consider him a travel companion, a friend in lived and felt tragedies, a protector; this has always driven us to see him here (*'creerlo siempre allí'*) and that is why we call him San Pacho" (Ayala 2002).

The pictures of arcos included here exemplify the devotional stature of Saint Francis, whose significance is both religious and political. The stories narrated in the dramatic representations of the arcos go well beyond the mere expression of a longing. They also constitute historical accounts that are both testimonial and analytic. In other words, they become part of the process of writing the history of the region and the nation. In the world of interconnections and free trade agreements of modern societies, a world increasingly troubled by the decline of natural resources, the once-remote Chocó is increasingly viewed with an opportunistic eye by developed societies. Olga Arbeláez (1999) explained that in Colombia, Chocó no longer represents just another region with minimal investment per capita in education, health and infrastructure, "but also a site of a brutal violence not known in the modern history of the region" fueled by a variety of armed groups claiming control of land or natural resources and by national and multinational interests in the region:

> A wave of violence has been unleashed against Chocó's inhabitants during the past 10 years, but especially soon after the Colombian govern-

Photo 11: 2002 arco, in which guerrillas and paramilitaries give up their arms and military garb.

Photo 12: 2005 arco, *construyamos paz* (let's build peace).

ment announced plans to construct an Inter-oceanic channel in the region that would, potentially, open up the area for further exploitation of natural resources: This catapulted the interest of national and international corporations on the potential use of strategic resources in the region, both biological and in mining. . . . Ironically, the same constitutional changes that recognized the presence of blacks and indigenous communities as legitimate and autonomous in the country have become responsible for the new wave of violence visiting the region (p. 29).

Analyzing and documenting violence in Colombia are part of a recognized literary and intellectual tradition within the country and abroad. The feast, we can surmise, is to an extent part of this tradition. After all, Colombia is a country with the third largest (after Sudan and Congo) number of displaced nationals due to armed aggression (Human Rights Watch 2005). Not coincidentally, it is also the nation receiving the third largest amount of U.S. financial support.[9] In photo 1, the indiscriminate fumigation promoted by Plan Colombia under U.S. pressure to eradicate coca and poppy plantations is criticized; and in photo 6, the push to privatize education is denounced as damaging to society in general. These representations critically address political decisions taken in Colombia but influenced by policies and decisions made in Washington, DC.

Photo 13: 2002 arco in which the saint prevents the explosion of a homemade missile and redeems a man dressed in military garb.

Today Chocó has an indigenous (Embera) senator, a black governor, and other afro-descendent representatives in Congress. A bill proposed by one of them in 2005 asked that the feast of San Pacho be given national patrimony, given that other national feasts (such as the Carnival of Barranquilla and others) enjoys such a status. The bill passed in Congress, but current president Alvaro Uribe vetoed it, arguing vaguely that some aspects of the proposal

---

[9] Americans familiar with U.S. aid to other countries will have already heard of *Plan Colombia*. According to the U.S. State Department (2006), the $7.5 billion Plan is meant to promote "the peace process, combating the narcotics industry, reviving the Colombian economy, and strengthening the democratic pillars of Colombian society." The Plan has, above all, been used to fund the military establishment and controversial fumigation programs whose effectiveness has yet to be seen. In Colombia, Chocó is one of several regions attracting constant military incursions from guerrillas, paramilitary groups often linked to the Colombian army, and the Colombian army itself.

were inadequate (Birri 2005). The passing of this law would have resulted in granting special funds and recognition to the feast and to the people who organize it. Although the feast had more exposure in the national media in 2005 than ever before, Chocó was once again ignored by the central government. Since colonial times, the region has been an economic frontier linked to national and international markets as a source of raw materials, and as a space where labor forces mobilize around their extraction at very low costs. Plagued by a history of transience and exploitation, Chocó is further destabilized by forced migrations, renewed evangelization, trenchant racism and clientelistic politics, and systematic neglect by the state and by centralized political and cultural forces. After the constitutional changes in 1991–1993, the search for a multicultural national identity in Colombia today cannot evade the question of Afro-descendant autonomies and cannot dispense with regional ethnicities through the concept of unity.

The feast of San Pacho serves as a constant reminder of the nation's failure to correct past and present wrongs. Alongside the reciprocity established between devotees and saint, there lies the demand for a sovereign space to resolve personal and collective local strategies of development that balance social, cultural, and economic needs. More importantly, the feast has been used to wrest the location and production of afro-descendent history from the national media channels and metropolitan discourses by appealing to spaces and practices created within popular religion. It is a testimony to a historical and sociopolitical abrogation of the symbolic authority of church and state. To an outsider, the feast might seem futile as a sociopolitical mechanism to transform society and to empower local autonomies in light of such a dramatic history. After analyzing the feast for several years and speaking with many *chocoanos* it is clear, however, that the feast has a concrete, lasting effect on how people perceive their identities, in relation to each other as well as to the rest of the nation. Equally important, it emboldens the local population to speak out in light of and against historical aggression and violence. As such, the feast is much more than just a mere religious or social ritual. It is a testimony that is both ephemeral and permanent, part of the regional memory for generations to come.

References

Agence France Presse. 2005. "More than 2,000 Afro-Colombians displaced by violence." May 8. Retrieved June 2006 from LexisNexis.

Agudelo, Carlos. 2005. *Retos del multiculturalismo en Colombia: Política y poblaciones negras* [Blackness and race mixture: The dynamics of racial identity in Colombia]. Medellín: La Carreta Editores.

Ayala, Ana Gilma. 2002. *Reseña histórica de la fiesta de San Francisco de Asís*. Quibdó: Talleres Gráficos Publiartes Buenoss.

Arbeláez, O. 1999. "Oídos del mundo oí: Representaciones de la identidad negra e indígena en la tradición oral del Chocó Colombia." *Afro-Hispanic Review*, Fall: 22–31.

Birri, Francisco. 2005. Personal interview with subject (a Colombian Senator), October 6.

"Chiquita admits payments to terror groups." *The Seattle Times*, Wednesday May 12, 2004. Retrieved May 2006 at http://seattletimes.nwsource.com/html/nationworld/2001926458_chiquita12.html.

Friedemann, N. and J. Horner. 1995. *Fiestas, celebraciones y ritos de Colombia*. Bogotá: Villegas Editores.

The Guardian. 2005. "Price of Cocaine Paid with Blood." February 15, 2005. Retrieved June 20, 2006, at http://www.guardian.co.uk/colombia/story/0,,1411917,00.html.

Human Rights Watch. 2005. *Statistics on Colombia*, retrieved June 2006 at http://hrw.org/doc/?t=americas&c=colomb.

Lizcano, José Oscar. 2005. Personal interview with subject (a Claetian Father), October 1.

Mosquera, Daniel. 2004. "Re-constituting Chocó: The Feast of San Pacho and the Afro Question in Colombia." *JLACS*, 13, 2: 171–194.

Revista Semana 2005. "Tragedia anunciada ¿Porqué no se pudo reaccionar a tiempo para proteger a la población de Bellavista?" May 13. Retrieved May 2005 at http://semana.terra.com.co/wf_InfoArticuloArchivado.aspx?IdArt=20953.

Sharp, W. F. 1976. *Slavery on the Spanish Frontier: The Colombian Chocó 1680–1810*. Norman: University of Oklahoma Press.

El Tiempo. 2005. "Habitantes de Bojayá recordaron la tragedia que hace tres años sembró el dolor y la muerte." May 2. Retrieved June 2006 at http://eltiempo.terra.com.co/coar/DER_HUMANOS/derechoshumanos/ARTICULO-WEB-_NOTA_INTERIOR-2056639.html.

U.S. State Department. 2006. *Support Plan for Colombia*. Retrieved May 2006 at http://www.state.gov/p/wha/rt/plncol/.

Velásquez, R.M. 1960. "La fiesta de San Francisco de Asís en Quibdó." *Revista Colombiana de Folclor*, 2/4: 15–37.

Villa Rivera, W. 1989. "San Francisco de Asís o la poética de la calle." *Boletín Cultural y Bibliográfico*. Bogotá: Biblioteca Luis Ángel Arango: 23–37.

Wade, Peter. 1993. *Blackness and Race Mixture: The Dynamics of Racial Identity in Colombia*. Baltimore: Johns Hopkins University Press.

PART III

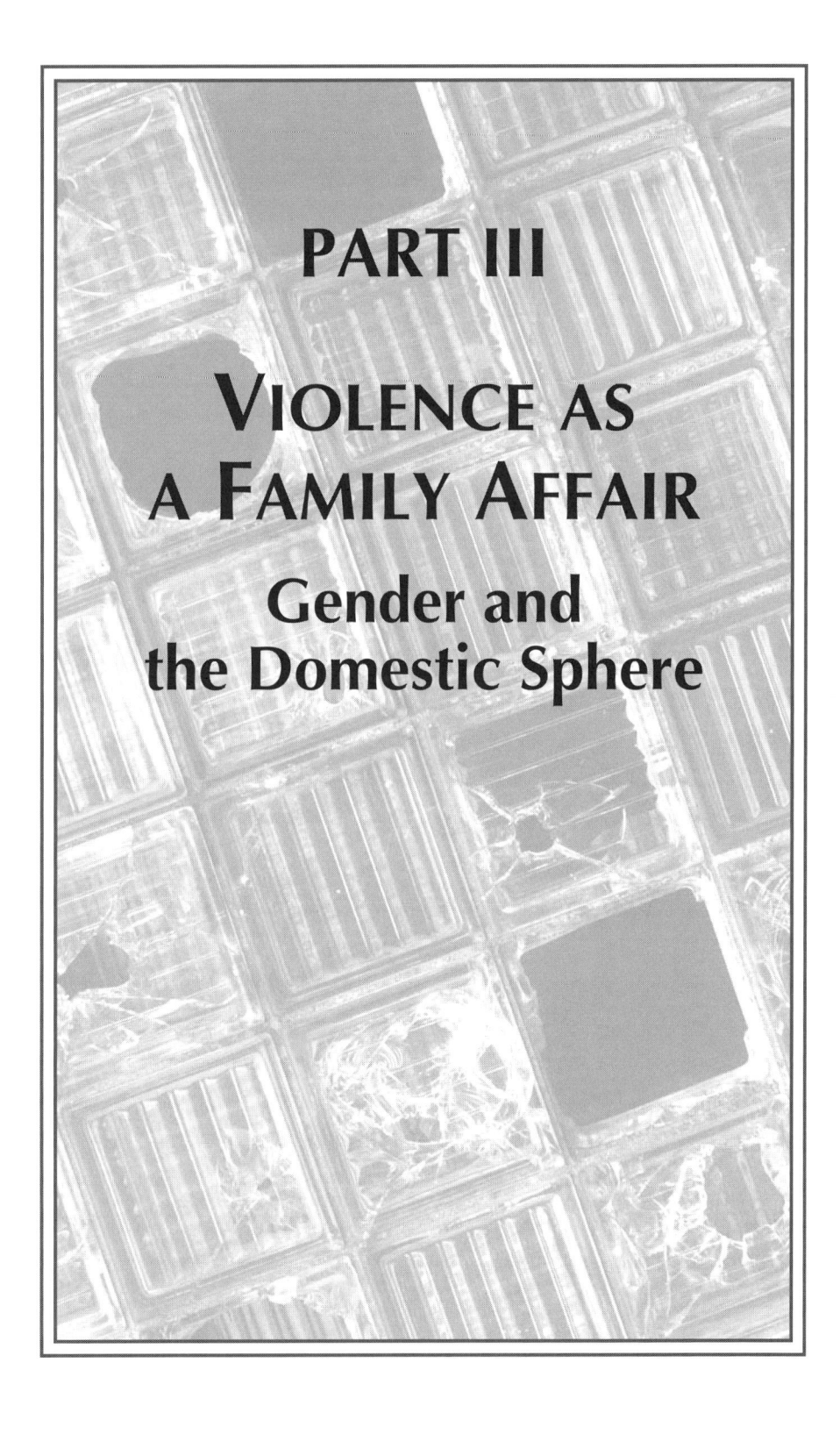

VIOLENCE AS A FAMILY AFFAIR

Gender and the Domestic Sphere

6

The Moral Imagination of Colombian Youth
Displacement, Survival, Paramilitarism and Peacemaking

Victoria Sanford

> I stood in the courtyard with the other young recruits of my unit, strangers all; in the gloom of initial anonymity, what comes to the fore is coarseness, otherness; that is how it was for us; the only human bond we had was our uncertain future....
>
> —Milan Kundera

DISPLACEMENT AND CHILD SOLDIERS[1]

Recent studies have shown the disproportionate impact of war on children. Between 1985 and 1995, armed conflicts in different parts of the world were responsible for the deaths of two million children, left one million children orphans, six million children injured, and 12 million displaced and left homeless. In 1996 alone, more than 300,000 children were soldiers and combatants in wars around the world Machel (1996). In Colombia, there are an estimated 16,000 child soldiers today (Paez 2003). Each day, violence in Colombia forces some 1,000 civilians to flee their homes (Osorio Perez, forthcoming). Some 2,900,000 Colombians have been internally displaced since 1985 (CODHES 2004) and Bogotá alone is home to more than 400,000 displaced people (WCRWC 2002). Women and children represent fully 80 percent of the total displaced population and children alone com-

---

Written especially for *Ruminations in Violence*.

[1] This section draws on Victoria Sanford, "The Moral Imagination of Survival: Displacement and Child Soldiers in Guatemala and Colombia" in Siobhan McEvoy, Ed., *Troublemakers or Peacemakers? Youth and Post-Accord Peace Building.* South Bend: University of Notre Dame Press, 2006.

prise more than 54 percent (Profamilia 2001:123). If these percentages have remained roughly constant since 1985, that means that more than half of displaced Colombians or nearly 1.5 million people were displaced as children. In other words, the majority of displaced people are/were children at risk of forced recruitment.

The ever-increasing numbers of internally displaced Colombians presents a humanitarian crisis of epic proportions. While much has been written about displacement, in-depth comparative studies of child soldiers and child peacemakers remain scarce. In the literature on displacement in Colombia, there are numerous studies about the basic needs of the displaced (Fajardo-Montana 2001), their uncertain legal status (CCJ 1999a, b; Tassara 1999), and the disproportionate affect of displacement on women and children (Young 2002). Often times, the conditions of displacement are explained in tandem with the lives of refugees or the internally displaced (Osorio & Lozano 1995; Hernandez-Hoyos 2000; HRW 1994a; ICG 2003; Peacaut 2001) or studies provide a history of displacement within particular regional studies of La Violencia (Roldan 2002; Ramirez 2001).[2]

Most literature on child soldiers emerged in the fields of law, medicine and psychology based on the reflections and efforts of human rights advocates and service providers working in zones of conflict and post-war reconstruction in Africa. Thus, the trauma and medical needs of child soldiers have been empirically documented (Machel 1996; McBeth 2002; Castelo-Branco 1997; Pearn 2003; Somasundaram 2002; Maier 1998; Kearns 2003). Additionally, abuse and trauma of child soldiers has been explored to establish the need for rehabilitation and/or reintegration programs specific to the needs of child soldiers (Thompson 1999; Chaudhry 2001; Rakita 1999; Alfredson 2001; de Silva et al. 2001; Bracken 1996; Menkhaus 1999; Skinner 1999).

The Rights of the Child (Ramgoolie 2001; Heppner 2002; de Berry 2001), human rights (Maslen 2000; Von Arnim 2000), international humanitarian law (Cohne 1994; Rone 1994; Human Rights Watch 1994b, 1995), the Optional Protocol on the Involvement of Children in Armed Conflict (Ahmad 1999; American Academy of Pediatrics 2000; Dennis 2000), and the ILO Convention on Child Labor (Halsan 2001; Dennis 1999; Amnesty International 1999, 2000; Fernando 2001) have provided legal frameworks for the international community to condemn the use of child soldiers and establish legal protections for children (Kalshoven 1995; Abbott 2002; Campbell 1999).

In her work in Mozambique, Thompson (1999) suggests that the conditions of child soldiers "erase" analytical categories of military, civilian and child. Transformation in kinship and family situations in Sierra Leone (Zack-Williams 2001) and the cultural meaning of the category of youth in Mozambique (West 2000) have been explored in relation to the phenomenon of child soldiers. Millard (2001) challenges the primarily legal approach to the issue of

---

[2] My articles on peace communities (2003c, 2004) and child soldiers in Guatemala and Colombia (2006) are the first scholarly studies on the topic.

child soldiers, suggesting that it limits our understanding and policy options. De Berry (2001) identifies state crisis and local influences as the two contexts for the emergence of child soldiers in Uganda. De Waal (1996) notes that child soldiers are part of the war aims of armed actors in Africa that tend to be local and specific bands who integrate commerce and violence to sustain and enrich themselves. This research in Africa resonates with the findings of Lovell and Cummings (2001) on children in Northern Ireland. They argue that children do not merely react to conflict but also interpret the meaning of conflict to themselves, their families and communities. They suggest the need for research on families and communities to achieve successful interventions for children. Likewise, De Berry (2001) suggests the need to develop a community-based approach to the problem of child soldiers, and Wessells (2002:254) calls for "research on the anthropological factors that affect child recruitment and prevention strategies."

This essay builds on the existing literature on displacement and contributes to emerging literature on child soldiers by seeking to understand the role of internally displaced Colombians and forcibly recruited youth and children within the complex and violent web of internal armed conflict. Moreover, I include the efforts of Colombian youth who have organized themselves to resist forced recruitment and seek to make peace in the midst of war.

THE MORAL IMAGINATION OF SURVIVAL

In Colombia, following several years of marginal life on the urban peripheries after being displaced from their villages by paramilitary violence, some 12,000 Colombian peasants negotiated the return to their land (in the middle of the war zone) as *peace communities* in 1999 (Sanford 2003b, 2004). Peace communities have sought to rebuild community life as neutral, unarmed civilians. Moreover, they have sought to build interdependent utopian communities based on citizen participation, mutual respect, and collective survival. After years of struggle, the peace communities have been recognized by the Colombian government and by the United Nations as civilians with the right to rebuild their lives. These peace communities continue to struggle for their survival in Colombia's ongoing war.

Given the large numbers of displaced people living in desperate circumstances of misery, how and why have these communities sought not only reconstruction but also a better, more peaceable way of life in the midst of war? While living in war is not unique, efforts to build utopian communities in war zones represent a highly creative response by seemingly powerless peasants to the violence that crashes unbidden upon them. In an era of lawlessness, they reassert their rights as citizens. This essay explores how the practices of creative peacemaking and reconstitution of citizenship represent a new kind of political power grounded in community integrity and moral courage. This power is not of a violent nature but rather is power derived from the *moral imagination*—power that creates new realities and new possibilities by pushing the frontiers of the possible in the midst of the war zone, power that supports Hannah Arendt's (1973) belief that violence can destroy power but not create it.

If we can learn how the lives and survival of the displaced become part of the violence, then perhaps we will be better able to understand how and why displaced communities can also organize to generate spaces for peace and democratic participation in the midst of war. How have seemingly utopian Colombian peace communities survived in war zones, and what are their prospects for the future? How do children and youth become a part of these peacemaking projects, and how does this participation transform their visions of their own future? I consider these questions by exploring the experiences of displacement and forced recruitment in Colombia. I begin with the experiences of surviving displacement in peace communities, followed by an account of forced recruitment as told by a Colombian paramilitary youth, and I offer an analysis of memories of trauma. I end by documenting the efforts of today's Colombian youth who seek to avoid forced recruitment and work for peace amid the ongoing conflict in their country.

COLOMBIAN PEACE COMMUNITIES[3]

In her work on displacement, Hannah Arendt wrote: "The first loss which the rightless suffered was the loss of their homes, and this meant the loss of the entire social texture into which they were born and in which they established for themselves a distinct place in the world" (Arendt 1973:293). And displacement is driven by violence. In the Uraba-Choco region of Colombia, Joselito was one of 45,000 people displaced by paramilitaries in the late 1990s. Recalling the time when he fled his community in 1997, he said,

> Helicopters were bombing and paramilitaries were firing machine guns. To go to the river to cut bananas was to risk one's life. They burned our village and we lost all our rice. When the army would come, they would say, "Don't be afraid of us, have fear of those who come after," meaning the paramilitaries. They had no respect for our lives. We had to leave.

According to those who have been displaced, these displacement operations are joint maneuvers between the paramilitaries and the army. The army frequently uses planes and helicopters to bomb civilian areas, forcing the inhabitants to flee while paramilitaries carry out ground maneuvers, destruction of physical community, threats and assassination of those deemed by paramilitary lists as "subversive" or potentially so, and sometimes full-scale massacres.[4] Yulian, a paramilitary soldier who had recently returned from combat, confirmed these survivor testimonies. Specifically about massacres, he told

---

[3] This section draws on Victoria Sanford, "Contesting Displacement in Colombia: Citizenship and State Sovereignty at the Margins" in *Anthropology in the Margins of the State*, edited by Veena Das and Deborah Poole, Santa Fe: School of American Research, 2004.

[4] Author interviews 2000 and 2001.

me, "Human rights are a problem. Now we can't massacre everyone, we have to kill them one by one, one by one."[5]

Hannah Arendt (1973:279) suggested that the term "displaced persons" was expressly invented for the liquidation of the category of statelessness that paved the way for the loss of the rights of citizenship, creating a category of the persecuted as rightless people. Significantly, she stated, "The more the number of rightless people increased, the greater became the temptation to pay less attention to the deeds of the persecuting governments than to the status of the persecuted" (294). Moreover, she pointed out that this shift from the deeds of the government to the needs of the displaced constituted an innocence, "in the sense of complete lack of responsibility" which "was the mark of their rightlessness as [much as] it was the seal of their political status" (295)," because as rightless people, she wrote, "their freedom of opinion is a fool's freedom, for nothing they think matters" (296). Joselito became a peace community leader because, as he explained to me,

> When one is displaced, one loses the feeling of being Colombian, a citizen with rights and responsibilities. After many community meetings of the displaced, we decided to return together in 1999. We decided to live in the middle of the conflict because if we waited for it to end, we would never return to our lands. We opted for pure nonviolence. They should respect the decision of the people. If they want to fight with each other, they can—but not on our land and we won't fight with them. As the peace communities, we have a life of peace, not violence. Our goal is to support peace, not war.

In this way, peace communities reassert their rights, rebuild community structures, and transform the isolation of displacement. Colombian peace communities constitute new domains of social justice, citizenship and conflict resolution. This is not, however, to suggest that these constitutive processes of the peace communities are not affected by the violence of the armed actors that surround them.

THE (PARA)MILITARIZATION OF YOUTH IN COLOMBIA

It is perhaps among the youth within the communities of displaced people and their efforts to avoid or seek out recruitment by armed actors that one encounters both the moral imagination and the iniquitous monotony of survival. It is most often through displacement that violence and criminality appear, to these children, to be their only opportunities. Displaced children live without power in a world of armed power. In this section, I offer the testimony of a 19-year-old paramilitary to provide an opportunity for understanding child experiences in armed conflict. The testimony presented here challenges us to overcome the tendency to simply categorize these children as

---

[5] Author interview August 7, 2001. This interview with paramilitary youth was organized clandestinely. "Yulian" is a pseudonym. The interview was granted on condition of anonymity.

victims, on the one hand, and as a danger to citizen security on the other. In both international humanitarian aid as well as popular images found in the media, these children are displayed as victims of war structures that have destroyed their lives. Yet, if in order to survive the child becomes a soldier, combatant or paramilitary, this same child is no longer viewed as a victim but rather as a dangerous delinquent because he or she no longer fits within the framework of the innocent child which society continues to maintain, despite all realities to the contrary.

The narrative of the experience of Yulian, a paramilitary youth in Colombia, resonates with those of the forcibly recruited youth in Colombia and other parts of the world (Sanford 2003c). Thus, his testimony transcends the experiential location in Colombia and becomes a site of contestation, challenging forced recruitment of youth and demanding recognition of the rights of the child and international humanitarian law. Moreover, understanding the experiences of Yulian provides an opportunity for international humanitarian aid programs to develop alternatives to violence for children now living in internal armed conflicts.

My field research in Colombia indicates that displaced and orphaned children generally have four options: (1) join the army; (2) join the paramilitaries; (3) join the guerrilla; or, (4) rural-to-urban flight. Moreover, those children who displace from rural villages under siege to urban barrios must frequently displace from one urban site to another in order to escape recruitment by urban armed actors.[6] Many people are afraid of these (displaced rural) urban youth. Authorities treat them like criminals, and they are often targets of paramilitary "social cleansing." One way to escape this social cleansing is to join the ranks of the paramilitaries. This was the case of 19-year-old Yulian, who lived in the paramilitary-controlled Barrio Obrero in Apartado; a barrio founded by displaced people in the early 1990s. He told me,

> I lived each day in fear that the paramilitaries would grab me and accuse me of a crime I hadn't committed. I had no opportunities until one day a friend of mine said, "Come on, let's go join them." As soon as we got there, they gave us camouflage uniforms, rifles, new guns and other equipment. Those who had no army training went into training. We had been in the army so we went right into operations, which means we went to the mountains to fight the enemy. Who is the enemy? In vulgar terms, the guerrilla. We are enemies. We are in conflict. We are also on the margin of the law.
>
> We were taken by helicopter and we began to look for the guerrilla. We started looking in every way among the campesinos. The campesinos help the guerrilla, so sometimes we have to grab them. Grab them means kill them. They have to respect us because we wear the symbol that says, AUC: Autodefensas Unidas de Colombia. When we kill a campesino, it is because there are really few displaced people. What there are among

---

[6] Author interview, May 31, 2003.

the displaced are a lot of guerrilla infiltrators who are very astute and intelligent. Once, some campesinos told some others that we had arrived in their community. We didn't want the guerrilla to know we were there. So, we had to kill them with machetes and chop them up piece by piece and bury them. Human rights are a problem because we can't grab 30 people and kill them all at once because that would be a massacre.

But we don't kill anyone without authorization. Because I have a family, sometimes it was painful for me when we got to a town and the civilians would be praying. But I am just a patroller and surely when a commander tells a patroller, "Kill this civilian," I really cannot ask him why. No, I simply have to do what he tells me to do. Because one goes there to kill or one is killed, right?

I am on leave right now, but if a patron here (in Apartadó) comes to me and says, "Let's go do a little work, we have to grab someone," I go do it because I am part of the organization. Sometimes in a week, we have to kill five people. Maybe on one day, we kill two. If the police and the prosecutor aren't doing much, we kill more. It all depends on what we are ordered to do. We have to follow orders. This is a war without end. If you make a mistake, you pay with your life.[7]

MEMORIES OF TRAUMA

Yulian's testimony chronicles displacement, the witnessing of atrocities, and survival. It also communicates profound feelings of powerlessness in an unpredictable world of terror mixed with nostalgia for the elusive power that comes with carrying a gun. Though Yulian gives his testimony just ten days after returning from paramilitary actions, the sensations of fear, self-doubt, betrayal, and self-hate as well as the desires for individual and community liberation and transformation remain palpable in his memories. It was an overwhelming sense of rightlessness associated with direct or indirect displacement that led to his recruitment. I want to heed Arendt's caution about the slippery slope implicit in focusing on the status of the rightless and refocus the lens of analysis on the deeds of those responsible for forced recruitment, because the deeds of those responsible can also be read as the constitution of available options for youth living in armed conflict.

Further, I suggest that the constitution of available options for youth living in armed conflict can be traced to the original traumas preceding forced recruitment, which are recounted in testimonies. In Colombia, driven to paramilitarism by fear and poverty, Yulian sees no exit from the violence of the paramilitaries to which he has now tied his survival—however reluctantly, even as his experience in the paramilitaries is mediated with memories of fear and hatred. At the time of the testimony, Yulian struggled with what it meant to be a paramilitary while living a disjointed existence, disarticulated from his community of origin and struggling to survive at the margins of the state; and this disjointed disarticulation was itself a product of trauma pre-

---

[7] Author interview, August 7, 2001.

ceding Yulian's recruitment. My meeting with Yulian was clandestine and anonymous, so I do not know his fate.

Writing on the available options for youth in the Putumayo region, Maria Clemencia Ramirez (forthcoming) writes:

> The paramilitaries have recruited youth in the towns to their intelligence-gathering operations, which consist of reporting the identities of other town youth who have been recruited to the intelligence operations of the guerrillas. The latter are also known as *milicianos*. Youth participate in one or the other of the groups for personal reasons, e.g., to avenge the death of a brother or at the urging of a family member, or simply to find work, given the poverty and unemployment in the region.

The experience of forced recruitment, even when remembered as consensual, is layered upon that of original displacement—what Arendt referred to as the "loss of social texture." Forced recruitment was not the first trauma in Yulian's testimony. Rather, survival of selective and massive violence, marginalization, poverty, and displacement marked Yulian for recruitment by any of the armed groups. For Yulian and other displaced youth, this displacement or loss of social texture represents the displacement of individual and community life boundaries. This displacement of boundaries in turn defines new fields of subjectivity and memory.

Pierre Janet wrote that memory "is an action," but that when an individual is unable to liquidate an experience through the action of recounting it, the experience is retained as a "fixed idea" lacking incorporation into "chapters of our personal history." The experience, then, "cannot be said to have a 'memory' . . . it is only for convenience that we speak of it as 'traumatic memory'" (Herman 1992:37). Further, Janet believed that the successful assimilation or liquidation of traumatic experience produces a "feeling of triumph" (41). Judith Herman suggests that those who have not liquidated their "traumatic memory" express it through "post-traumatic play," which she describes as "uncanny" in its reenactments of original trauma. She writes, "Even when they are consciously chosen, they have a feeling of involuntariness . . . they have a driven, tenacious quality" which resonates with Freud's naming of "this recurrent intrusion of traumatic experience" as "repetition compulsion," which is no less than "an attempt to master the traumatic event"(41) Whether recruited through coercion or consent, child soldiers and combatants attempt to master previous traumas in the violent acts of everyday armed life. At the same time, the new layer of trauma produced in the everyday life of the child soldier or combatant demands consideration.

Few would dispute Herman's assertion that traumatic experiences "destroy the victim's fundamental assumptions about the safety of the world, the positive value of self, and the meaningful order of creation" (51) What is of particular interest to us in analyzing the case of forcibly recruited youth is our own underlying assumptions about traumatic events and where on the continuum of life experience we choose to locate these violent events. Forcibly recruited youth face double trauma—the trauma of the violence that preceded and made them vulnerable to forced recruitment as well as the trauma of witnessing and participating in violence—whether as soldiers, paramilitaries, or combatants. While forced recruitment may be the public trauma of structural violence, forcibly recruited youth first share their private traumas leading up to their recruitment.

Whether our focus is on prevention of forced recruitment or post-war reintegration, the experience of child soldiers behooves us to pay close attention to how the fractured subject position of Yulian also reflects the formation of agency and survival in structures of terror (Das 2000:222). Here, I am suggesting that experiences of armed action are remembered within the framework of preceding structural traumas (in Arendt's words, the "deeds of those responsible") that impacted their lives long before they ever held a gun. Weapons and their accompanying power are remembered with nostalgia because their use was a "post-traumatic play," where unresolved traumas and powerlessness were violently reenacted as a "spontaneous, unsuccessful attempt at healing" pre-recruitment trauma (Herman 1992:41). Thus, whether we set our sights on preventing recruitment in situations of armed conflict or reintegration in post-conflict civil society, we must problematize the pre-recruitment traumas of displacement.

CHILD PEACEMAKERS

Still, there are children who seek to make peace in the very same communities in which other children have been recruited. In Colombian peace communities, youth have organized to reject recruitment by all the armed actors. Alvin is a peace community youth leader. He decided to focus his energies on youth organizing against forced recruitment because, in his words, "A weapon resolves nothing." He explains: "Weapons destroy the soul. I have seen this happen since my childhood." Indeed, in her work on violence in Putumayo, Ramirez (forthcoming:4) found a "permanent wariness" in the youth because "no one can trust another, though he or she may have once been a well-known classmate. No one can know 'what that person might be into . . . you don't know who he or she might be.'" Thus the youth quickly learn to be "tight-lipped" and not look at others. In this way, "the young accommodate themselves to the specter of daily violence."

In the peace communities, rather than passive accommodation the youth have organized to resist recruitment. When I asked Alvin how the youth were able to organize themselves, he said,

> One of the principle sources of support for us, for the youth, is the example of the process of the peace communities. We are nonviolent. We don't support what the armed actors are doing. We have developed a way of life without weapons. We have shown the Colombian government and also the world that we are capable of building peace. For this, we have become the target of the armed actors. Our future is something that we

have to build for ourselves. Many times youth take up weapons because they are unaware that it is not really in their interest, nor their family's or community's interest. We have to teach one another how to live together in peace. We want the children in our communities to grow up with positive feelings about the future and a commitment to the community so that they can be leaders in the community, not obstacles to the community peace process.[8]

When I asked Alvin and others how the international community could support the youth, Alvin said, "I know that when people come to visit us from outside, they leave with a weight of pain because it is inhuman what is taking place here. But we need very simple things to develop ourselves. The most basic and most needed is education and recreation." Others agreed:

"Yes, we always aspire to have an education."

"Training to improve our skills."

"Musical instruments for the youth because our communities lost our instruments when we were displaced."

"Soccer uniforms so that we can exercise and have soccer tournaments amongst the communities."

From 2001 to 2002, a series of violent attacks against youth leaders culminated with the assassination of Edwin Ortega, who represented the youth of peace communities internationally and was an outspoken advocate of the right of youth to resist forced recruitment.[9] Rather than abandon their organizing project, peace community youth gathered on October 22, 2002 to restructure their organization, because "It is only through our organization that we have the possibility of a future. Alone, only weapons await us." The restructuring included two key points: First, leadership training would no longer identify and train youth leaders; rather, all youth would be trained and viewed as leaders. Further, all intercommunity meetings would involve groups of youth leaders rather than one single representative from each community. As one youth explained to me, "If we are all leaders, we remove the individual targets from our backs."[10] The second key point was to establish an international commission to begin a new dialogue with the armed actors. The youth presented these proposals to the general assembly of the peace communities at their meeting on October 23, 2002.

Both of these proposals were received favorably by the General Assembly of the peace communities. During the discussion of the youth proposal, Celsa, a mother who lost her son to paramilitary violence, said, "We have to recognize that we must support our youth. If we look beyond the barrel of the gun, it is our youth pointing the guns at us. We have to stand with our youth to support them. We must unite with them to stop the armed actors from tak-

---

[8] Author interview July 15, 2001.
[9] It is because of the brutal assassination of Edwin Ortega and other youth leaders that I use pseudonyms and deliberately do not identify the specific peace communities of quoted youth leaders.
[10] Author interview October 22, 2002.

ing them."[11] Since November of 2002, a Negotiating Commission (*Comision Negociadora*) has been traveling to all the communities of the Lower Atrato. The peace communities celebrated their sixth anniversary in October 2003 with a General Assembly of peace communities followed by an international anniversary celebration. A central focus of both the assembly and celebration was the right of youth to organize for peace. "We are here because we want a positive future," explained Luis. "We refuse to be targets of the armed actors. We refuse to carry their guns. We want our right to peace respected."[12]

It is not only in the peace communities that youth organize to provide a respite from the violence that engulfs them. Yolanda, a youth organizer in Barrancabermeja, told me, "Our work is difficult. We open a space here so that youth have a place to distract themselves from the violence that surrounds us. We have hope that this violence will end. We struggle for life."[13]

Conclusion

While testimonies and interviews from child soldiers indicate the connection between displacement and forced recruitment, the experiences of the peace communities demonstrate that apparently powerless peasants can organize to survive and assert their rights in the midst of war. These collective survival strategies generate local spaces for peace and democratic participation despite the ongoing armed conflict. The survival of these seemingly utopian community efforts deserve both the attention and support of the international community because they represent the survival of civil society in increasingly restricted political spheres. Moreover, the resilience of these peace communities offers an opportunity for the greater civil society of Colombia to learn from these experiments about the long-term strengthening of citizen participation. The value of this participation is evident in the enthusiastic participation of youth in the peace communities. In contrast to the youth who have been forcibly recruited, the youth of the peace communities have hope for their futures and see a role for themselves in shaping the life of their community. The international community should heed the call of the youth for support for education, soccer and music. It should honor Celsa's plea that "we must support our youth."

Testimonies of child soldiers and peace activists prove that youth do not merely respond to conflict—they also interpret the meaning of conflict. These lived experiences rupture the binary stereotype of innocent victim or dangerous delinquent and challenge us to recognize these children as active participants in shaping their own lives, who develop survival strategies for themselves, their families, and communities.

In this way, youth peacemakers reassert their rights, rebuild community structures, and transform the isolation of displacement and everyday life in

---

[11] Author's notes, Asamblea General Oct 23, 2002.
[12] Author interview October 17, 2003.
[13] Author interview October 12, 2000.

the war zone. These youth peacemakers, like the peace communities, constitute new domains of social justice, citizenship, and conflict resolution. Moreover, these constitutive processes: (1) connect the individual to the nation-state and international community; (2) rebuild the social fabric damaged by displacement; and (3) construct new modes of agency and citizen participation, which is necessary for peaceful resolution to the internal armed conflict as well as post-war reconstruction. These transformations are not grounded in determinism or utopia outside of power. Rather, as Hardt and Negri (2000:66) suggest, the "actual activity of the multitude—its creation, production and power"—is a "radical counterpower" in the present. This counterpower is evident in the everyday life and moral imagination of the peace communities and the youth peacemakers.

Acknowledgments

This essay is dedicated to the survivors and their children. The essay would not have been possible without the kindness, generosity, and trust of Yulian, Joselito, Alvin, Luis, and other friends I am unable to name because of ongoing conflict in Colombia. I thank Raul Figueroa Sarti for his unconditional support and Valentina Figueroa Sanford for reaffirming the joy of life each day. Shannon Speed, Monique Skidmore, Carolyn Nordstrom, Roberta Culbertson, Joanne Rappaport, and Philippe Bourgois provided useful comments and insights as I collected these testimonies and sought to process their meaning. I thank Derek Pardue for his patience and support. This research was supported by grants from the Shaler Adams Foundation, a Rockefeller grant from the Virginia Foundation for the Humanities and a grant from the United States Institute for Peace. A leave from Lehman College allowed me to make the most of these grant opportunities. The opinions, findings, and conclusions or recommendations expressed in this chapter are mine alone and do not necessarily reflect the views of any of these funders.

References

Abbott, Beth. 2000. "Child Soldiers: The Use of Children as Instruments of War," *Suffolk Transnational Law Review* 23, 2 (Summer):499–537.
Ahmad, Khabir. 1999. "UN Resolves to Protect Children against Wars," *The Lancet*, 354, 9 (Sept. 11, 1999):929.
Alfredson, Lisa. 2001. "Sexual Exploitation of Child Soldiers," *Child Soldiers Newsletter* (December):1.
American Academy of Pediatrics. 2000. "An Accord on Child Soldiers," *Pediatrics* (May) 105, 5:1045.
Amnesty International (AI). 1999. Children's Rights: The Future Starts Here. London: AI.
———. 2000. Amnesty International Report on Colombia 2000. London: AI.
Archdiocese of Bogota and CODHES. 2001. *Rostros Invisibles del Desplazamientos en Bogota*. Bogota: CODHES.
Arendt, Hannah. 1973. *The Origins of Totalitarianism*. New York: Harcourt Brace.
Bracken, Patrick. 1996. "The Rehabilitation of Child Soldiers: Defining Needs and Appropriate Responses," *Medicine, Conflict and Survival* 12 (April/June):1362–1369.
Braun, Herbert. 1994. *Our Guerrillas, Our Sidewalks: A Journey into the Violence of Colombia*. Niwot: University of Colorado Press.
Campbell, Scott. 1999. *Democratic Republic of Congo: The Casualties of War—Civilians, Rule of Law and Democratic Freedoms*. New York: Human Rights Watch.

Castello-Branco, V. 1997. "Child Soldiers: the Experience of the Mozambican Association for Public Health," *Development in Practice* 7,4 (Nov):494–7.

Chaudhry, Samena. 2001. "Rehabilitating Sudan's Child Soldiers," *British Medical Journal* (June):179.

CODHES. 2004. Vecinos en el borde de la crisis. *CODHES Informa Boletín informativo de la Consultoría para los Derechos Humanos y el Desplazamiento*, No. 49. Bogotá, April 21.

Cohne, Illene. 1994. *Child Soldiers: The Role of Children in Armed Conflict*. Geneva: Clarendon Press.

Colombian Commission of Jurists (CCJ). 1993a. *Espacios internacionales para la justicia colombiana*, vols.II & III. Bogota:CCJ.

———. 1993b. *Nordeste Antioquia y Magdalena Medio*. Bogota: CCJ.

———. 1994a. *Arauca*. Bogota: CCJ.

———. 1994b. *Uraba*. Bogota: CCJ.

———. 1994c. *El caso Caballero y Santana—Colombia en la Corte Interamericana*. Bogota: CCJ.

———. 1994d. *Derechos humanos en Colombia, 2 informe de la Commission Inter-American de Derechos Humanos*. Bogota: CCJ.

———. 1999a. *Derechos humanos en Colombia*. Bogota: CCJ.

———. 1999b. *Follow-up to Recommendations of the Representative of the Secretary General of the United Nations for Internal Displacements 1996–1999*. Bogota: Support Group for Displaced Peoples Organizations (GAD).

———. 2000. *Panorama de derechos humanos y derecho humanitario en Colombia Informe de avance sobre 2000*. Bogota: CCJ.

Das, Veena. 2000. "The Act of Witnessing: Violence, Poisonous Knowledge and Subjectivity." In Veena Das and Arthur Kleinman, eds., *Violence and Subjectivity*. Berkeley: University of California Press.

De Berry, Jo. 2001. "Child Soldiers and the Convention on the Rights of the Child," *Annals of the Academy of Political and Social Science* 575, 1 (May 2001):92–105.

Dennis, Michael. 2000. "Newly Adopted Protocols to the Convention on the Rights of the Child," *American Journal of International Law* 94, 4 (October):789–796.

———. 1999. "The ILO Convention and the Worst Forms of Child Labor," *American Journal of International Law* 93, 4 (October):943–948.

De Silva, Harendra. 2001. "Conscription of Children in Armed Conflict—A Form of Child Abuse," *Child Abuse Review* 10, 2 (March–April):125–134.

De Waal, Alex. 1996. "Contemporary Warfare in Africa: Changing Context, Changing Strategies," *IDS Bulletin* 27, 3 (July):6–16.

Fajardo Montaña, Dario. 2001. "Los Circuitos de los Desplazamientos Forzados en Colombia." In Martha Segura Naranjo, ed., *Exodo, Patrimonio e Identidad*, 68–75. Bogota: Museo Nacional de Colombia.

Fernando, Jude, ed. 2001. Children's Rights—Special Issue, *Annals of the American Academy of Political and Social Science* 575 (May):8–224.

Halsan, A. 2001. "Underage and under fire: An enquiry into the use of child soldiers 1994–98," *Childhood* 8, 3 (August):340–362.

Hardt, Michael and Antonio Negri. 2000. *Empire*. Cambridge: Harvard University Press.

Heppner, Kevin. 2002. *"My gun was as tall as me": Child Soldiers in Burma*. New York: Human Rights Watch.

Herman, Judith. 1992. *Trauma and Recovery*. New York: Basic Books.

Hernandez Hoyos, Diana. 1999. *Derecho Internacional Humanitario*. Bogota: Ediciones Juridicas Gustavon Ibanez.

Human Rights Watch (HRW). 1990. *The Drug War in Colombia.* New York: HRW.
———. 1992. *Political Murder and Reform in Colombia.* New York: HRW.
———. 1993. *State of War: Political Violence and Counterinsurgency in Colombia.* New York: HRW.
———. 1994a. *Generation under Fire: Children and Violence in Colombia.* New York: HRW.
———. 1994b. *Easy Prey: Child Soldiers in Liberia.* New York: HRW.
———. 1995. *Children of Sudan: Slaves, Street Children and Child Soldiers.* New York: HRW.
———. 1996. *Colombia's Killer Networks: The Military-Paramilitary Partnership and the United States.* New York: HRW.
———. 1998. *War without Quarter: Colombia and International Humanitarian Law.* New York: HRW.
———. 2000. *Colombia: The Ties that Bind: Colombia and Military-Paramilitary Links.* New York: HRW.
International Crisis Group (ICG). 2003. *Colombia's Humanitarian Crisis.* Brussels: ICG.
Kalshoven, Frits. 1995. "Child Soldiers: The Role of Children in Armed Conflicts," *American Journal of International Law* 89, 4 (October):849–852.
Keairns, Yvonne. 2003. *The Voices of Girl Child Soldiers—Colombia.* New York: Quaker United Nations Office.
Kundera, Milan. 1982. *The Joke.* New York: HarperCollins, p. 39.
Lovell, Erin and E. Mark Cummings. 2001. *Conflict, Conflict Resolution and the Children of Northern Ireland: Towards Understanding the Impact on Children and Families.* Notre Dame: Kroc Institute Working Papers Series.
Machel, Graciela. 1996. *Impact of Armed Conflict on Children.* New York: United Nations.
Maier, K. 1998. "The Universal Soldier," *Yale Review* 86, 1 (January):70–93.
———. 2002. "Inquiry," *Journal of Children and Poverty.* 8, 1 (March):67.
Maslen, S and S. Islamshah. 2000. "Revolution not Evolution: Protecting the rights of children in armed conflicts in the new millennium," *Development* 43, 1 (March):28.
McBeth, John. 2002. "Children of War," *Far Eastern Economic Review* 165, 17 (May):44–45.
Menkhaus, Ken. 1999. "Children of War," *New Routes* 4, 4:4–7.
Millard, Ananda. 2001. "Children in Armed Conflict: Transcending Legal Responses," *Security Dialogue* 32, 2 (June):187–200.
Osorio Perez, Flor Edilma. Forthcoming. "De Las Rupturas al Incierto Recomenzar: Lecciones de Persistencia de Desplazados por la Guerra en Colombia," in Victoria Sanford, ed., *Markings: Violence and Everyday Life in Colombia.*
Osorio Perez, Flor Edilma and Fabio Lozano. 1995. *Desplazamiento rural: Violencia y Pobres.* Bogota: Consejeria Presidencial de Derechos Humanos.
Paez, Erika. 2003. "Child Soldiers in Colombia, South America." *Enabling Education Network* 7:1–2.
Pearn, J. 2003. "Children and War," *Journal of Pediatrics and Child Health* 39, 3 (April):166.
Pecaut, Daniel. 2001. *Guerra contra la sociedad.* Bogota: Espasa e Hoy.
Profamilia. 2001. *Salud Sexual y Reproductiva en Zonas Marginales, Situacion de las Mujeres Desplazadas.* Bogota: Profamilia.
Rakita, Sara. 1999. *Forgotten Children of War: Sierra Leonean Refugee Children in Guinea.* New York: Human Rights Watch.
Ramgoolie, Monique. 2001. "Prosecution of Sierra Leone's Child Soldiers: What Message is the UN Trying to Send?" *Journal of Public Affairs* 12 (Spring):145–162.

Ramirez, Maria Clemencia. Forthcoming. "Paradoxes of the Coca Economy: Community Organizations and Citizen Participation in the Midst of Political Violence," in Victoria Sanford, ed., *Markings: Violence and Everyday Life in Colombia*. Piscataway, NJ: Rutgers University Press.

———. 2001. *Entre el estado y la guerrilla: Identidad y ciudadania en el movimiento de los campesinos cocaleros del Putumayo*. Bogota: Instituto Colombiano de Antropologia e Historia.

Rappaport, Joanne. 1987. *The Politics of Memory—Native Historical Interpretation in the Colombian Andes*. Cambridge: Cambridge University Press.

Roldan, Mary. 2002. *Blood and Fire—La Violencia in Antioquia*. Durham: Duke University Press.

Rone, Jemera. 1994. *The Lost Boys: Child Soldiers and Unaccompanied Boys in Southern Sudan*. New York: Human Rights Watch.

Sanford, Victoria. 2004. "Contesting Displacement in Colombia: Citizenship and State Sovereignty at the Margins," in Das, Veena and Deborah Poole, eds., *Anthropology in the Margins of the State*. Santa Fe: School of American Research.

———. 2003a. *Buried Secrets: Truth and Human Rights in Guatemala*. New York: Palgrave Macmillan.

———. 2003b. "Peacebuilding in the War Zone: the Case of Colombian Peace Communities," *International Journal of Peacekeeping*, 10, 2.

———. 2003c. "Colombian Paramilitaries and the Legacy of Central American Death Squads, Contras and Civil Patrols," *Social Justice—A Journal of Crime, Conflict and World Order*, 30, 3.

———. 1997. *Mothers, Widows and Guerrilleras: Anonymous Conversations with Survivors of State Terror*. Uppsala: Peace and Life Institute.

———. In Press. "The Moral Imagination of Survival: Displacement and Child Soldiers in Guatemala and Colombia," in McEvoy, Siobhan, ed., *The Next Generation: Youth and Peacebuilding*. Notre Dame: University of Notre Dame Press.

Skinner, Elliott. 1999. "Child Soldiers in Africa: A Disaster for Future Families," *International Journal on World Peace* 16, 2 (June):7–22.

Somasundaram, Daya. 2002. "Child Soldiers: Understanding the Context," *British Medical Journal* 324, 73 (May):1268–1272.

Tassara, Carlos and Dalia Maria Jimenez Castrillon, Luigi Grando, et al., eds. 1999. *El desplazamiento por la violencia en Colombia*. Bogota: UNHCR.

Thompson, Carol. 1999. "Beyond Civil Society: Child Soldiers as Citizens in Mozambique," *Review of African Political Economy* 26, 80 (June):191–206.

Von Armin, Gabriele, ed. 2000. *Yearbook of Human Rights, 2000*. Frankfurt: Suhrkamp Taschenbuch.

Wessels, Michael. 2002. "Recruitment of Children in Sub-Saharan Africa: An Ecological Analysis," *Comparative Social Research* 20:237–254.

West, Harry. 2000. "Girls with Guns: Narrating the Experience of War of FRELIMO's 'Female Detachment,'" *Anthropological Quarterly* 73, 4 (October):180.

Women's Commission for Refugee Women and Children (WCRWC). 2002. *Unseen Millions: The Catastrophe of Internal Displacement in Colombia—Children and Adolescents at-Risk*. New York: WCRWC.

Young, Wendy. 2002. "The Protection of Refugee Women and Children," *Refugees* (Winter/Spring):37–44.

Zack-Williams, AB. 2001. "Child Soldiers in the Civil War in Sierra Leone," *Review of African Political Economy* 28, 87 (March):73–82.

Family Responsibility for Stopping Violence

David Kaczynski and Linda E. Patrik

We were high school freshmen when news of Kitty Genovese's murder hit the national media. It wasn't so much the crime itself that shocked the nation as the manner in which bystanders had reacted—or, more precisely, had failed to react. A 28-year-old New Yorker from Queens, Kitty was chased into the courtyard of her apartment complex by a knife-wielding maniac who stalked and assaulted her for 32 minutes before administering the final, fatal stab wound. Although 38 witnesses had seen the vicious assault from the safety of their apartment windows, not one had bothered to call the police. Interviewed later, some witnesses said they'd assumed that surely someone else would call the police and probably already had. At least one witness reportedly remarked to the press, "I didn't want to get involved"—a phrase that soon became a newspaper headline that appeared to sum up the tragedy of modern urban life. Another bystander incorrectly assumed that Kitty and her assailant had a relationship, so he decided not to intervene because "it was between the two of them"—a disturbing reflection of society's broader indifference to the scourge of domestic violence.

Thirty-eight human beings had done nothing to protect a helpless woman, although a phone call to the police would have cost them next to nothing. Each individual witness was presumably frozen in separation from the other witnesses and from the shrieking victim. Thirty-eight individual choices added up to a mind-boggling collective failure—one gigantic sin of omission. It seemed as if the universe had played a cruel trick on the witnesses, making each one of them responsible for Kitty's death precisely because so many others could have intervened just as easily to save her.

It was the kind of story that might well stir self-reflection apart from the loud public calumny that was heaped upon the bystanders. For many, the

Written especially for *Ruminations on Violence*.

question "How *could* they?" may have been echoed by the more unsettling private question, "But how would *I* respond?" as people attempted to imagine themselves in the bystanders' shoes. It seemed difficult to know what the bystanders' behavior revealed about the rest of us. In judging them, of course, we enjoyed the advantage of hindsight. Moral judgment emanated from a public conversation that was denied those paralyzed souls staring out of their separate, beehive windows in the dead of night. It was made possible by a conceptual framework that might not have been instantly available to them.

Perhaps the public's later moral judgment—with its gaps of knowledge, insight and empathy—represented an evasion of responsibility in its own right. Certainly, the capacity to blame others has little to do with the capacity to take responsibility. Quite often, in fact, blaming is a substitute for accepting responsibility. Responsibility cannot be accepted or shared by passing it off to others, but perhaps it can be recovered, nurtured, and lived up to in other ways. In a different setting—the family setting—responsibility to stop violence can be shared.

Talking about a brother's violence is not easy, especially when two married people want to keep their relationship intact. Yet in 1995, when the FBI began to release information about a serial bomber that had been withheld for a decade, we began to discuss the possibility that David's brother might be the so-called Unabomber—then the most wanted criminal in America, responsible for three deaths and numerous injuries caused by sixteen bombs over a period of seventeen years. Information began leaking out in tiny newspaper blurbs during the summer of 1995. Neither of us knew much about the Unabomber before then. Investigators speculated that the Unabomber had been born in Chicago, since the early bombs were placed there or sent from there. They also suspected that the bomber had some connection with the University of California at Berkeley, since a bomb had been placed in a graduate student lounge there. Our discussions began with these news bits: Linda pointed out that David's brother (who had been living for more than twenty years as a recluse in a small cabin in Montana) had been born in Chicago and that he had once been a promising young mathematics professor at UC Berkeley.

At first, David didn't believe it was possible that his brother could commit violence. He had no memories of Ted being violent. Linda, on the other hand, felt differently, based on a psychological reading of letters, expressing pent-up rage, that Ted had sent to David over the years. Even though she had never met Ted, she sensed that violence lurked just beneath the surface of his personality.

As a couple, our initial responsibility concerning Ted was surprisingly to one another—namely, the responsibility to allow one another to express suspicions or doubts openly and forthrightly. In seemingly endless discussions, from late summer through the fall of 1995, we explored the various possibilities that Ted was or was not the Unabomber. On most evenings during those months, we spent hours discussing the evidence released by the FBI, David's childhood and adult memories of his brother, and the family's most recent attempts to communicate with Ted. (Ted had cut off nearly all relations and communications with the rest of the family several years earlier.)

We sat down in October to read the Unabomber Manifesto. It sounded like Ted. That was all we had to go on, really. The theories and the language seemed familiar. We forgot about what the FBI believed and we focused on our own disturbing sense that the voice in the Manifesto was similar to Ted's voice. At the time, the FBI seemed to be barking up a wrong tree. They thought the Unabomber was a younger, taller man—a resident of northern California. Their profilers believed that the Unabomber lacked a college or advanced degree, but Ted held a Ph.D. The FBI seemed to be reading the Manifesto as a group statement on behalf of a network of anti-technology terrorists, whereas Ted was always a loner. It seemed apparent to us that if Ted really was the Unabomber, the FBI wasn't likely to find him.

In the summer and early fall, when we were making wild guesses about whether Ted could be the Unabomber, we felt no strong sense of moral responsibility for stopping him. Wild guesses felt like fantasy—not the kind of evidence needed to support a moral argument. But in the late fall, once we began to recognize Ted's voice in the Manifesto, we felt the burden of moral responsibility.

How does a sense of moral responsibility arise? We feel reasonably assured that the bystanders to Kitty Genovese's murder were not indifferent to Kitty's fate because they felt sympathy for her murderer. Their responsibility as bystanders seems rather straightforward—certainly less complex than the kind of responsibility that defines a close family relationship. The responsibility that I have *to* my relative resulting from bonds of love, memory, blood, and familial interdependence might come into conflict with my responsibility *for* my relative if his or her actions are harmful to others. In that case, steps I might take (or choose not to take) in order to protect my relative could result in serious harm to other people.

Yet even this potential conflict does not exhaust the complexities inherent in assuming responsibility *as* a family member, because relationships between individuals in a family are not independent of the larger network of family relationships. How I understand my responsibility to and for a specific relative (a brother) necessarily reflects upon my responsibility to and for other family members (mother and father, spouse, children, other siblings, and so forth). When pressed by real life circumstances—and perhaps only then—we finally see that the supposedly autonomous "I," who in theory has responsibility for making critical moral decisions, is actually a *we*.

Even when the "I" decides something, it decides in its capacity as *we*, usually in collaboration with one or more others who comprise the *we*. In a couple or family, taking responsibility for dealing with a family member's actions involves sharing the deliberation process and the actions taken to support (or defend) a shared condition of being in relationship. In a family setting, we experience a *we* that those atomized bystanders in Queens never knew. It is a far richer *we* than the univocal, coercive and ultimately deficient "we" of public judgment that howled mass media denunciations of those bystanders to Kitty Genovese's murder.

The third stage of responsibility for stopping violence was taking the step that the bystanders in the Kitty Genovese case never took: the step of taking action. All of our actions in late fall came from a sense of shared moral responsibility. Especially if the FBI was looking in the wrong direction, we as members of Ted's family had to step in and do something if he was indeed the Unabomber. We had to stop his violence. But first we needed to know if he actually was the Unabomber, and so we took action to find out. In our case, it was joint action.

Instead of just talking about the Unabomber and discussing the evidence for and against Ted being the Unabomber, we went to work. We compared the writing style in the Manifesto with the writing style in old letters that David dug up—letters received from Ted years ago. We went to the library and on the Internet to collect all the information we could about the Unabomber. In late November, without revealing our concern about the Unabomber case, we contacted Linda's childhood friend, Susan Swanson, who worked as a private investigator. We simply asked her how to hire someone who could compare two pieces of writing in order to determine if they were written by the same author. At first, Susan thought that Linda was being threatened or blackmailed by one of her former students. Later in December when we finally told Susan that one piece of writing was the Unabomber Manifesto, she guessed the connection to David's brother on her own. An interesting part of this story is that Susan is a life-long family friend—the closest thing to a family member.

As we looked for evidence that might convince us one way or the other, we also had to face the moral implications of what we might find out. As a couple, we debated with one another night after night, sitting on two sofas in the living room. We not only debated the particular details of the Unabomber evidence, but we argued about moral principles in general, principles drawn from our personal views and from classic philosophy—Plato's arguments about injustice, Buddhism's arguments about karma, existentialism's arguments about authenticity and responsibility. As intelligent people, we opened up our relationship to a more intense moral deliberation. We discussed the moral issues as though somebody's life depended upon it. Drawing upon philosophical theories and our own values in nightly discussions—which at this point had stretched over a period of two to three months—we were figuring out how to live our philosophy. But we were committed to living it as a couple, despite our philosophical differences.

How do we weigh loyalty to a brother against the possibility that the brother is a serial killer? How is Ted harming himself, and not just his victims, if he is a murderer? How are the family members of the victims affected by the killings? How do we tell the FBI about our suspicions—suspicions only, not solid evidence—without unleashing government violence or ineptitude against a family member? (The FBI had a lousy public record when it came to arresting dissidents: somebody always got killed—witness Waco and Ruby Ridge.) How do we face the possibility that David and Ted's mother might die from a heart attack or stroke from the shock? If he was the Unabomber, Ted had killed three people. If his mother might die, if Ted or the FBI agents might die when the FBI launched their attack, or if Ted indeed turned out to be the Unabomber and received the death penalty—we considered how we might be responsible for these deaths as well.

The stage of preparing for a moral decision was the fourth step. Beginning in late fall, we weighed the moral implications of various plans for stopping Ted if the evidence continued pointing to him. Our process combined exploration of the options that were open to us with abstract philosophizing about moral values. This process consisted of a dialogue energized by different perspectives, the differences emerging from our uniqueness as individuals but also from the differences in our relationship to Ted and from the emerging differences in our philosophical views on ethics. Everything about us, from our deepest moral values to our childhood memories to our current emotional allegiances, was entered into the dialogue.

Like the first stage of our process—the early stage of giving the other full permission to express all suspicions, wild guesses, doubts, worries—this fourth stage was not bound by any censorship rules. We each said whatever we had to say; we each criticized whatever we disagreed with. There is no way around the fact that a big moral decision can be contentious. Even when there are moral codes such as the Ten Commandments' "Thou shalt not kill," there is no obvious way to make moral decisions that stay true to a moral rule. Dialogue and debate are a necessary means of exploring tough moral territory.

Moral dialogue and debate in a family go beyond the pure abstractions of philosophy to explore the depths of the heart. What we value are not just ethical principles, but people—the people we love. When we attempt to reach a decision that is both morally right and beneficial for loved ones, we try to balance our most profound commitments in life. Without these commitments that forge the heartfelt connections between people, moral values become abstract ideals but not livable guides.

So much is shared in families—memories, celebrations, mourning, to name a few experiences. Most often, parents share responsibility for child rearing, siblings share responsibility for elder care, and even cousins share responsibility for marking important events (births, weddings, graduations, and deaths) within an extended family. Responsibility to stop violence perpetrated by a family member—occurring either within the family or within the wider society—is a naturally shared burden, because of all the connections linking family members to one another and to the perpetrator. Although only one family member may commit the violent act, the other interlinked family members inevitably experience the effects of that person's violence. There is no way for family members to feel unaffected or uninvolved.

Family relationships extend through time as well as space. Unlike the courtyard setting where Kitty Genovese's murder happened unexpectedly and then was over, the couple or family setting contains whole lifetimes of two or more people: years of sharing experiences and memories, decades punctuated by family births, weddings, and deaths; and cross-generational transitions as family members' roles alter when they move away, bring spouses into the family, or grow old. In becoming part of a couple, individuals assume many of the joys and pains of their partners, not just for a day or a week but for many years. As family members, we relate to others in the family for the entire length of our lives. The temporal dimension of a couple's relationship or of family members' relationships means that the future consequences of an act committed by one person will inevitably affect other family members.

Shared responsibility in a couple or family setting arises because family members must live with the effects of one another's actions (or failures to act) for many, many years. If caught, the individual perpetrator of violence reaps the consequences dictated by law for his or her actions. But the partner or other family members of that perpetrator also bear consequences, even if they never committed the violence and never would have condoned it. The consequences faced by family members are emotional turmoil and in some cases social ostracism as well. Sleepless nights, tears, grief, psychosomatic illnesses, and the endless question "Why? Why did he (she) do it?" haunt their lives for many years, if not forever.

Family members do not stay encapsulated in apartments, overlooking the violence committed by their kin. They know the personal childhood history of their relative who, later in life, lashes out in attacks against others. In some cases, family members may have witnessed earlier acts of rage by their relative or may have been victimized themselves. Responsibility for curbing a family member's violence is not a 32-minute choice, but nearly a lifetime of negotiation, fear, and worried strategizing with other family members. A violent relative does not come into existence overnight, even if their violence was unforeseen and even if it occurred undetected for years. To their family members they have often posed a dilemma of understanding, an unmended tear in the fabric of family relations for some time.

When a relative commits violence, the worst nightmare of family members becomes a reality. The family cannot rest; the burden of responsibility calls upon them to deal with what their relative has done or is still doing. They have to respond somehow; they cannot watch from above, as the apartment dwellers could when Kitty Genovese was being killed. They cannot count on others outside the family to intercede, since they alone may see or suspect the truth.

All our lives, we hold a space open for each of our family members—if not a space for regular interactions, then at least a space for important and often formative memories that may stretch all the way back to childhood. The space allotted to one relative, and to one relative alone, does not close up or disappear if and when that relative becomes a violent criminal. Even in cases where siblings see little of each other after they grow to adulthood, the responsibility of brothers and sisters *to* each other, and also *for* each other, is not canceled by their relative independence. The fact that a relative, as an adult, is responsible for his or her own actions does not mean that we bear no responsibility for dealing with these actions at all. Insofar as a relative's actions end up affecting us and other family members, we must endure them in one way or another. Insofar as we can prevent these actions from adversely affecting others, we are bound to do so. The space of a relative's independence is not unlimited, nor is ours. If he or she comes to request help, we cannot turn our backs on them. Likewise, if he or she harms other people, we cannot look the other way.

In this essay we have described moral decision making in a way that focuses less on individual responsibility and more on shared responsibility for moral decisions. We believe that the profound interconnectedness of human beings—an interconnectedness that is often obscured by the individualistic template in Western culture—shapes moral deliberation and moral decision making. This interconnectedness means that moral responsibility cannot be reduced to discrete decisions made by individuals acting alone. The failure of the individualistic model of moral responsibility, revealed in the paralysis of the bystanders to Kitty Genovese's murder, is a failure to connect on a number of levels. Had a sense of connection to the victim and to each other been naturally present, the bystanders would have felt impelled to act. Had they experienced this sense of connection, presumably they would have discovered themselves standing *with* instead of merely standing *by* as the life of another human being was threatened.

Although our own joint decision to turn in a violent family member to the authorities was necessarily reached in private, the consequences of our decision have played out in public. Our decision was eventually exposed (almost violently so) to public scrutiny and discussion when the FBI leaked our role in the investigation, and the media reported that the Unabomber had been "turned in by his own brother." After Ted's arrest, we were surrounded and virtually attacked by the media: they shoved a camera into the car windshield when we tried to bring David's mother to safety at our house; nearly two hundred reporters and photographers set up a 24-hour barricade around our house for several days, making it impossible for us to leave to get food or for friends to come in; a reporter in a speeding car harassed Linda as she tried to drive to work, almost creating a head-on collision.

It is telling that Linda's part in the decision was almost entirely ignored in media reports, all of which drew close boundaries around David's blood relationship with Ted and also around David himself as the presumed lone decision maker. The media's scripted, individualistic template for reporting the story was seemingly immune to the truth about how our decision was actually made. With so many angles to cover (e.g., mystery killer, mental illness, terrorism, death penalty) as well as the background "human interest" story of two brothers, there was little media interest in exploring the actual process of moral decision making in any depth. After some initial ambivalence, the same public "we" (i.e., the media herd) that vilified the bystanders of Kitty Genovese's murder now proclaimed David Kaczynski a hero. Although media accolades came as some relief to a family stigmatized by its connection to the Unabomber, this distortion has also made it difficult for us to publicly explain ourselves or to fully own and justify our moral decision.

Thus, a public accounting represents the fifth stage of our shared process. The story did not end with Ted's trial and sentencing any more than it ended with his arrest. We must both still live with the consequences of our decision. Since the decision was focused on minimizing harm to all, regardless of family ties or proximity, the wider public debate appears fairly settled: *He* (actually *We*) *did the right thing*. But rightness in the moral sense is not really a *thing*. The judgment of "doing the right thing" may focus on a specific decision or act, but doing right ultimately concerns justice, compassion, relationship, and respect for each human life—all of which reflect our human interconnectedness.

The process of doing right cannot be closed and bottled up within a concept of individuality when the driving aspiration is so inclusive. Nor can it be contained in a singular result. For this reason, we continue to reflect on the interdependence of the human community, which stretches through but also far beyond the family. Although family is the cradle of this understanding of interconnectedness, it is only a beginning. Full maturation of this understanding occurs through thoughtful awareness of how others suffer, too often from violence, and of how we all share the consequences of one another's moral decisions. Within the family, we first learn how to be responsible to, for, and with our other family members. Looking beyond the family, we learn how to fathom the great suffering that happens when we do not take joint responsibility for ending violence.

Ted, now serving a life sentence in a federal prison, does not respond to our regular letters, continuing a policy of separation from his family that predated his arrest by several years. In a better world, he would be receiving appropriate treatment for his mental illness—but alas, society has not yet evolved so far. Still, he is alive. Perhaps some day he will recover his grasp of reality and with it his better self. His absence represents a hole in the Kaczynski family and in the hearts of David and his mother. His violence continues to haunt us.

Lives may have been saved by our commitment to each other to "do the right thing." We are closer than ever to each other, and closer, too, to David and Ted's mother Wanda—a brave soul if there ever was one. If we had not given space in our couple relationship to a process of joint ethical deliberation, things might have turned out very differently.

My Dad's Gun Collection

Susan Graham

There is a moment before or just at the first awareness of an occurrence of violence where the brutal outcome can be known or imagined. It's an instant of stillness, suspension, where nothing has yet happened but dread sets in. Some of the film loops, photographs, and sculptures I have made imply this quiet moment or imply possible violence, but they never cross the line into action and so remain innocent. The lacy filigreed gun sculptures I have been making out of sugar or porcelain function in a similar way, as they lay prettily inert in their cases.

These sculptures also embody a basic ambivalence toward guns that is particularly American, though not specific to America. A friend who had grown up in Lebanon during the 1970s looked at one of the small-caliber sugar handguns I'd sculpted and expressed a similar casual view of guns, saying, Oh yes, his mom had one just like that when he was young—he saw her put in her purse whenever she went out at night. I asked him if he knew about the gun, if he knew what kind it was (e.g., revolver or pistol), but he'd been a child when he had seen it and so he simply accepted its presence. It wasn't something she talked about, but with his child's openness he accepted it as something she needed to take with her without worrying about the implications of why she would need a gun. The mixed message sent by a dangerous object like a gun being made of a fragile material like sugar or porcelain is a reflection of my own mixed feelings of desire, nostalgia, and apprehension toward guns.

My Dad's Gun Collection (a work in progress) is a piece I started working on after a few years of making other gun sculptures from sugar and porcelain. After all, it's the memory of seeing one of my dad's guns when I was very young that prompted me to start making guns in the first place. I'd already been working with delicate materials to make sculpture, and the whiteness of the sugar and porcelain is inherent to those materials, lending an ethereal feel to whatever I created. I was thinking about guns in general at the time (shoot-

Written especially for *Ruminations on Violence*.

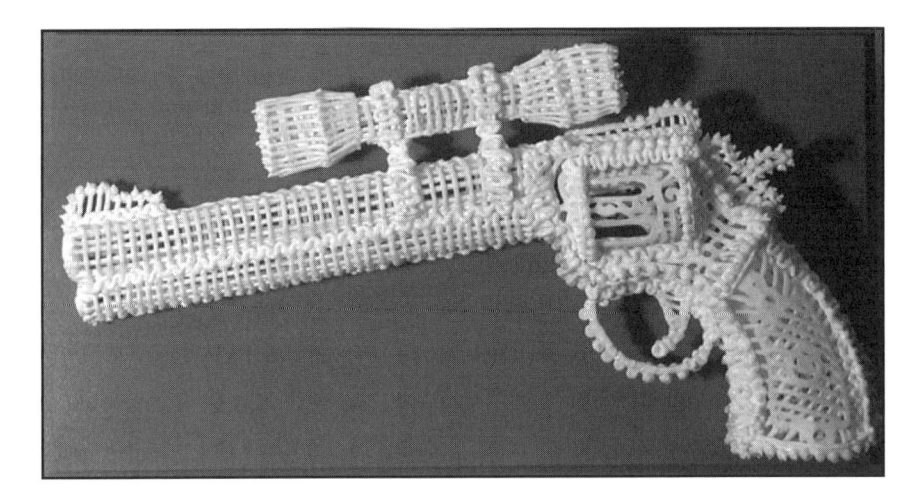

ings were in the news a lot right about then), and I started thinking about my childhood fascination with my dad's guns. The gun sculptures I make are lacy, white, and light—exactly opposite in appearance to the pistol my brother found hidden in Mom and Dad's bedroom one afternoon.

The guns were around, I'd heard a little about them and knew they were dangerous, but I rarely saw one. I knew my father kept hunting rifles, but the more intriguing ones were the handguns that we had been told were very dangerous and that were kept hidden from us children. Despite Dad's good intentions of keeping the handgun tucked away in my parents' bedroom for protection, my younger brother (who confessed as a grown-up to being a snoop and who periodically searched my parents' drawers) found it. I was sitting that afternoon on the couch at the bottom of the stairway, probably watching cartoons on the television, though what I was actually doing escapes me. My brother came walking slowly down the stairs, balancing a pistol in his outstretched hands. It looked huge and heavy in his hands, and the metal was so black that it seemed to absorb the light. He was very young, perhaps four or five years old, and I was two years older. I watched in silent fascination as he descended the stairs, taking each step carefully, and he glanced up at me and said, "Look what I found!" I remember sitting stunned on the couch and calling my mother, and I think the tone of my voice let her know she should come quickly. She came from the kitchen and promptly took the gun away. My brother probably joined me on the couch then to watch cartoons. For years after that the pistol was a topic of conversation between us, and together my brother and I would go to my parents' bedroom and look everywhere for it. The guns were better hidden after that incident, and we never found one again.

Strangely, my brother's knack for finding the guns hidden in my parents' house still lingers. A few years ago we were all home for a summer holiday with our own children and families. My brother happened to open a drawer next to the easy chair in the living room, and there was one of Dad's pistols that he'd forgotten to put away before the grandchildren arrived, lying quietly. Without much fanfare he took it out and asked Dad to put it away, and that was the end of it. We still harbor the acceptance of a gun's presence that we had developed as children.

After I started sculpting the guns I eventually had to broach the topic with my parents, because of course my father especially was quite aware that the gun imagery probably has something to do with his own guns, and he alluded to this—eventually opening the door to more stories being told about the guns (as well as more arguments between us about the politics of gun control in the United States. We can agree on some things, but others seem to set us at opposite ends of the spectrum). I ended up telling my parents how that time when I had seen the forbidden handgun in my brother's hands had stayed with me and was the catalyst for some of my work. My Mom then told us that when we were very young, whenever my Dad went away on business trips she slept with a gun under her pillow for protection. One night she woke up from a nightmare about "robbers," as she called them, and thought she saw someone standing at the end of her bed. As she was reaching for the gun, the image faded as she fully awakened and realized that the impression of an intruder was just the remnants of her dream. She said she never slept with a gun under the pillow again, because we children wandered into her bedroom at night sometimes and she didn't want to wake up confusedly from a deep sleep and reach for the gun when her children were in the room.

I called my father a while ago and asked him to give me a list of the guns he owns, since I wasn't sure how many or what types he had. He sent me a list of 14 in all, and I realized that the collection itself embodies the various meanings and uses guns have in American culture. The rifles and shotguns are mostly for hunting, while the handguns reflect a fear of an intruder or danger on the street and were purchased for protection. One or two guns are probably simply interesting models or collector's items.

I've made nine replicas of the pieces from his collection so far and have displayed them in a case. The whiteness and silence of the sculptures seem to belie the violence implied in their origins. As I work on this essay I continue to indulge my fascination with the guns and the mystery they hold for me as objects that I was never allowed to touch when I was young. The moment of stillness that occurs before an act of violence is reflected in the sculptures themselves, just as it exists in the memory of the gun in my brother's hands— it is drawn out endlessly, allowing for a prolonged contemplation, and in both cases the potentially violent result never comes.

Is Violence against Women about Women or about Violence?

Richard Felson

Suppose a group of men murdered millions of women. Before doing so they shaved their heads, stripped them, and sometimes beat and sexually assaulted them. Would this be an appalling example of sexism? Not necessarily. The Nazis committed these deeds, but they killed millions of men as well. If we ignore their violence against men and look only at that against women, their behavior appears to reflect sexism. Perhaps this same kind of selective focus affects our understanding of violence against women today. Are the offenders sexist or just violent men? Are women victimized because of their gender, or because they make up half the population?

Most sociologists who study violence against women study it separately from violence against men, and they interpret it as a form of sexism. They argue that misogynist men assault women in order to maintain their dominance. They believe that misogynist societies tolerate violence against women, leading offenders to think they can get away with it. They get away with it because victims usually do not report the incidents to the police; when they do, they get blamed, and the offender gets off. The result is an epidemic of violence against women, most of it hidden. This approach, which I call a "gender perspective," is conventional wisdom among sociologists and much of the general public.

Some researchers are beginning to challenge the gender perspective. They take what I call a "violence perspective," arguing that we should rely on theories of violence and crime, not theories of sexism, to explain violence against women. I take this perspective in my book, *Violence and Gender Reexamined,* and my research articles support it. From this point of view, sexism plays at most a trivial role in rape and in physical assault on wives. Typically, men who commit these crimes commit other crimes as well, and their back-

Reprinted with author's consent from *Contexts,* 5(2):21–25. Copyright © 2006 University of California Press Journals/American Anthropological Association. Reprinted by permission.

grounds and attitudes toward women are similar to those of criminals. They are versatile "bad guys"—selfish, not sexist. When they assault women, they do so "behind closed doors" because we stigmatize the behavior—a man should not hit a woman. Traditional values inhibit violence against women rather than encouraging it.

Both sides in this debate would agree about some basic facts regarding gender and violence. They would agree that the typical violent incident involves two men: men are much more likely to commit violent crime than women, and men are much more likely to be the victims. They would also agree that when the victim is a woman, the offender is more likely to be an intimate partner or a family member than when the victim is a man. Finally, they would agree that those who commit sexual assault are almost always men, while their victims are mostly women.

On other issues the two sides disagree. They disagree about whether wives are as likely to hit their husbands as husbands are to hit their wives; they disagree about the motivation of the offenders; and they disagree about whether men who assault women get off easily because society tolerates violence against women. I discuss these issues in turn.

FREQUENCY OF PARTNER VIOLENCE

In the 1970s, Murray Straus and Suzanne Steinmetz created an uproar with survey evidence that wives and husbands hit each other with equal frequency. They faced a protest and even a bomb threat. Straus and Steinmetz acknowledged that husbands are more likely to injure their wives than the reverse; a woman may slap her husband, but a husband is more likely to do serious damage. This point got lost in the battle that followed.

More recent surveys of violent behavior have found the same patterns among both spouses and dating couples. Both women and men use physical force at the same rates. But crime surveys find that women are more likely to be victims because these surveys include more serious forms of violence.

Once the distinction between minor and serious violence is made, the acrimonious debate over frequency becomes unnecessary. The term "battered husbands," despite its media appeal, is a gross exaggeration. We need shelters for women not men. Nevertheless, the finding of gender parity in the overall frequency of spousal violence has important implications. It leads us to wonder why men, who are eight times more likely to commit violence than women, are no more likely than women to hit their spouses. They are bigger and stronger, so there is less risk. What stops them? The violence perspective suggests that violent men are less likely to assault their partners because of the chivalry norm. Even Richard "The Iceman" Kuklinski, who killed more than 200 people during his lifetime, had a chivalrous tendency. He said that hitting his wife was his only regret.

Even if we agree that wives and husbands hit each other with equal frequency but unequal effect, a bone of contention remains. R. P. and R. E.

Dobash, taking a gender perspective, argue that frequency counts are misleading because wives use violence mainly to defend themselves. However, John Archer's analysis of a large number of surveys shows that wives are actually more likely to initiate violence than husbands in domestic assaults. It is still possible, however, that when the violence escalates, women start using violence in self-defense.

Homicide research does show that women are more likely to kill in self-defense than men, but police investigators attribute only 10 percent of homicides committed by wives to self-defense; women kill their husbands for a variety of reasons. In addition, the women who kill their husbands are not usually sweet and innocent. We found that they are just as likely to have criminal records as women who kill in other circumstances. They are no more likely to be motivated by self-defense than other female killers. In general, the evidence suggests that the greater tendency for wives to kill in self-defense reflects the fact that women are generally less violent than men. Most violent wives do not have innocent motives or suffer from "battered wife syndrome"; they kill their husbands for the same diverse reasons that husbands kill their wives.

Domineering Husbands?

A gender perspective implies that men use violence against their wives to maintain their dominance. However, research suggests that husbands are no more controlling than wives, and are perhaps less so. The data are taken from a survey that asked more than 10,000 men and women about their spouse's behavior. It shows, for example, that men are more likely to prevent their wives from working outside the home, but women are more likely to insist on knowing who their husbands are with at all times. Overall, the women are slightly more bossy. However, relatively few husbands or wives engage in any of these domineering behaviors.

Even though husbands are no more domineering than wives, perhaps those who are tend to use violence to get their way, while domineering women use other methods. We found some supporting evidence, but only in troubled marriages. Apparently, in troubled marriages men are more likely to use violence to get their way. However, our findings suggest that the difference has to do with method, not motive. From the violence perspective, size, not sexism, explains their behavior.

My colleague, Mike Johnson, has suggested a compromise position, arguing that sexism and a desire for dominance motivate only those husbands who commit the most serious violence. These "intimate terrorists" commit violence that is more injurious, frequent, and unilateral than the "common couple violence" typically committed by both husbands and wives. However, our research suggests that controlling husbands are not particularly likely to commit serious violence. They have many techniques at their disposal. Some women are certainly terrorized by their husbands, but those husbands may be nasty brutes, not domineering sexists.

RAPE FREQUENCY

An even more heated debate concerns the frequency of rape. One prominent survey carried out by Mary Koss asked American college students about their sexual experiences since age 14. It found that about 9 percent of college women reported that they had engaged in sexual intercourse "because a man threatened or used some degree of physical force (twisting your arm, holding you down, etc.) to make you." But only 27 of the women with this experience thought of these incidents as rape. Scholars with a gender perspective think that these victims buy into "rape myths," blaming themselves or thinking that the term *rape* applies only when the offenders are strangers. Those with a violence perspective suggest that many of these encounters are ambiguous. They note that many of the women attribute these incidents to misunderstandings. In addition, Charlene Muehlenhard finds that three out of four college women report that they had, at least at times, engaged in "token resistance": they said no when they meant yes or maybe. The line between coercion and consent is apparently ambiguous. Because we do not yet know exactly what happens in these incidents, it is impossible to determine the frequency of rape.

RAPE MOTIVES

Gender scholars have suggested that rape is used as a form of male domination and control. In the most influential book ever written on rape, Susan Brownmiller argued that rape is used keep women "in their place" and dependent on their husbands for protection. Anthropologists have found a few tribal societies that use rape to prevent women from observing certain male ritual objects. Because of their intense fear, the women stay away from the objects and, according to the anthropologist who studied them, a group rape had not occurred for 40 years (and perhaps had never occurred).

Whether rape is a form of social control in modern societies is disputed. Evidence shows that women's fear of rape leads them to curb their activities more often than men do. Yet the fact that the fear of rape constrains women's activities does not necessarily mean that the goal of rape is social control, much less that offenders are acting in some way as society's agents. Unlike the Mehinaku, modern societies have severe penalties for rape.

Gender scholars reject sexual motivation for rape, although some recent treatments acknowledge a sexual element. Gender scholars ask why men would use force when other sexual outlets are available. They claim that what the rapist wants instead is to dominate the victim. Studies based on interviews with incarcerated rapists are inconclusive. Nicholas Groth claimed that 65 percent of the 133 rapists he interviewed had a power motive, but others have interpreted his data as implying sexual motivation. Diana Scully reported that some of the rapists she interviewed said they enjoyed the power they had over the victims, but she did no counting.

Other scholars argue that rape is usually sexually motivated. They point to Eugene Kanin's evidence that date rapes typically occur during consensual sexual activity when the man is sexually aroused. He wants intercourse, but she does not want to go that far. Kanin has also found that rapists tend to have high sexual aspirations. They masturbate frequently and spend a lot of time searching for consensual sexual partners. Finally, when rapists are interviewed, they express a preference for attractive victims, and they overwhelmingly choose young women. Only 1.5 percent of rape victims in the United States are over 50.

Young women might be at greater risk than older women because they go out more often. But we found that the average victim of rape committed in conjunction with robbery was seven years younger than the average robbery victim. This suggests that rapists prefer young women, as does the fact that rapes in war zones usually target young women.

The idea that rape is typically sexually motivated is consistent with the feminist argument that men often treat women as sex objects. Much evidence suggests that men often think of women, or at least attractive women, in sexual terms, and that some use underhanded means to influence them to have sexual relations. They seem to think that "all is fair in love and war." The evidence is clear that men are much more likely than women to be indiscriminate and casual in their attitudes toward sexual relations, and that their interest in sex is greater. Evolutionary psychologists argue that the sex difference is biological. Whether biological or learned, sex differences in sexuality lead to conflict between the sexes, according to a violence perspective. Men use a variety of techniques to influence women to have sex, and some of them use force. Young men have sex on their minds, not the domination of women. On a Saturday night they aspire to find a sexual partner, not a woman to boss around.

SEXISM AND VIOLENCE AGAINST WOMEN

Another way to look at motivation is to determine whether men who assault women also have negative attitudes toward women. We need to be clear about whether negative attitudes refer to hatred of women or traditional attitudes about gender roles. While hatred of women goes along with violence toward women, some evidence indicates that traditional men are less likely to assault women. One laboratory study showed that traditional men were less likely to hit women with pillow clubs than were men with more liberal attitudes toward gender roles.

In addition, men who assault their wives and commit rape have attitudes toward women that are similar to those of other male offenders. They tend to commit a variety of crimes, rather than specializing in violence against women. This versatility suggests that men who assault women are criminals, not sexists. Some of them certainly hit their wives but no one else; perhaps they are the domineering sexists. On the other hand, marital conflicts can be intense, so we should not be surprised that husbands who are drunk or have bad tempers sometimes become violent.

Violence against women may be more frequent in societies where women have lower status. Peggy Sanday found this to be true in her study of tribal societies, but no one has found it so in larger, more complex societies. For modern societies, rates of violence against women tend to be high when rates of violence against men are high. Violence is violence. But everywhere, men are much more likely to be victims than are women.

Do Men Get Away with It?

A gender approach implies that men assault women because "they can." Are these offenders more likely to evade the law than other offenders, as the gender perspective suggests? The evidence suggests not. Physical assaults against wives are more likely to be reported to the police than assaults against husbands, even when the offenses are of equal severity. Husbands and wives who engage in minor forms of violence are less likely to be reported than offenders who commit minor violence against strangers, probably because of privacy concerns.

The evidence on sexual assault is more mixed. We have found that sexual assaults are less likely than physical assaults to be reported to the police, particularly if the offender is an acquaintance. However, the criminal justice system does not treat sexual assaults more leniently than physical assaults. Arrest and conviction are just as likely, and the sentences are more severe. No one has examined whether rape victims are assigned more blame than victims of physical assault and other crimes. However, experimental evidence shows that observers assign just as much blame to male victims of rape as to female victims. But they assign the overwhelming amount to offenders—they just think victims can make mistakes.

Scholars who take a gender perspective claim that only women who conform to gender roles are protected from harm. Those who take a violence perspective think it is important to make gender comparisons. For example, a man who dresses like a woman is stigmatized more than a woman who dresses like a man. In general, the evidence on sentencing by the criminal justice system suggests that we respond more harshly to deviant men than deviant women. The tendency to respond more harshly to female promiscuity than male promiscuity—the double standard—appears to be an exception.

Science vs. Social Activism

These controversies in part reflect the policy concerns of social scientists who are also social activists. From a scientific perspective, it is important to be accurate and to use the most general principles possible to understand human behavior. From the social activist's point of view, it is important to emphasize the frequency and seriousness of violence against women in order to build political support and raise money for social programs. Exaggerating the frequency of social problems is standard practice among activists. So is emphasizing dramatic cases, even though most cases are not so serious. It is useful, for example, to claim high frequencies of "wife beating," and to describe victims as "battered wives" or "survivors," even though most violence against women does not involve beatings and is not life-threatening. The media also focus on the worst cases, since they grab attention. Perhaps without these strategies we would not have shelters for battered wives and rape crisis centers—both of them good things. An examination of gender differences in victimization is less conducive to social action on behalf of women.

Social activism and science are clearly at cross purposes when it comes to their perspectives on motive. Those who take a gender perspective worry that judges and jurors might blame victims and treat rapists more leniently if they thought rape was sexually motivated. They believe that the offender might excuse his behavior by saying he was overcome with desire or she somehow enticed him. Alas, no one knows whether beliefs about the offender's motive have these effects. Judges and juries might be just as punitive when they believe rapists are sexually motivated. Moreover, we must understand the offender's real motives if we are to provide effective counseling and treatment.

I am not arguing that we should ignore gender in our response to violence. It may make more sense to arrest and punish violent husbands than violent wives, even when they commit the same offense. Differences in size and strength make violent men more dangerous than violent women. Women are more vulnerable, particularly when they are living with violent men. Equivalent responses to the violence of husbands and wives may not provide women with the protection they need. Of course, if justice is our only goal, then we should ignore gender in the criminal justice system and treat everyone equally. However, equal treatment ignores gender differences in dangerousness and in the need for protection. Special efforts to protect women may be justified.

Ambivalence about special protection for women is not new. After the sinking of the Titanic, one women's group built a monument to honor the men who gave up their lives so that the female passengers might be saved. Other women's groups complained about what they saw as an outdated concept of chivalry. Special protections for women are controversial now (as they were then) because of the image of dependence they imply. The vulnerability of women justifies treating violence against women more seriously than violence against men, even when statistical evidence does not.

Recommended Resources

R. E. Dobash and R. P. Dobash. *Rethinking Violence against Women* (Sage, 1998). A radical feminist approach.

Richard B. Felson. *Violence and Gender Reexamined* (American Psychological Association, 2002). Extensive presentation of the violence perspective.

Richard B. Felson. "Blame Analysis: Accounting for the Behavior of Protected Groups." *American Sociologist* 22 (1991): 5–23. A discussion of the role of ideology in sociology.

Mary P. Koss. *No Safe Haven: Male Violence against Women at Home, at Work, and in the Community* (American Psychological Association, 1994). A moderate feminist approach by a psychologist.

Murray A. Straus. "The Controversy Over Domestic Violence by Women: A Methodological, Theoretical, and Sociology of Science Analysis." In *Violence in Intimate Relationships*, edited by Ximena B. Arriaga and Stuart Oskamp (Sage, 1999). A major participant in the domestic violence controversy presents his side.

LETTER TO THE EDITOR: RESPONSE TO THE FELSON ARTICLE

Is violence against women and men gendered?

Richard B. Felson's recent analysis, "Is violence against women about women or about violence?" (*Contexts,* Spring 2006), misses the mark on deepening our understanding of gender and violence. Felson suggests that feminist explanations of male violence against women are wrong because women are violent too, because women try to control their partners too, and because men who hold traditional gender attitudes are not more likely than egalitarian men to be violent towards women. What Felson misses here is the basic feminist point that all violence occurs in a society systematically structured by gender inequality. Thus, even when women and men behave identically (in perpetrating violence, in trying to control a partner, in reporting violence to the police), the *sameness* of the acts takes on meaning only in the context of the *difference* that gender inequality produces.

As a brief example, Felson concedes that the empirical data repeatedly show that male violence results in higher levels of injury than the same acts of female violence, a finding he attributes to greater male strength and size. His own research finding that, in troubled marriages, men are more likely than women to use violence to get their way, is also attributed to the size difference between husbands and wives: "from the violence perspective, size, not sexism" explains these differences (p. 22). This reading fully misses the fact that size differences are caused by sexism. Men are, on average, larger than their wives or girlfriends because sexist norms about heterosexual pairings encourage tall, strong women to find partners who are even stronger and taller than themselves, and short, small men to find shorter, smaller women.

Felson further claims that the feminist position that men use violence against women to maintain their dominance is wrong because men who hold traditional gender attitudes are less violent towards women than egalitarian men. Here he again misses the crucial point that these data take on meaning only when viewed in the context of systematic gender inequality within society. Traditional men may be less violent because they do not feel that their dominance is called into question. Recent studies show that traditional men are more likely than other men to be violent towards female partners when their masculine authority is called into question by women who don't share their traditional gender attitudes or by their inability to live up to social norms of male providership (Anderson 1997; Atkinson, Greenstein, and Lang 2005; Demaris, Benson, Fox, Hill, and Wyk 2003).

Finally, his argument that gender is irrelevant because we observe similar levels of violence perpetration among heterosexual men and women suggests that gender must similarly be irrelevant in male-to-male or female-to-female violence, despite theory and research that explore the ways in which masculinity (e.g., Franklin 2004) and femininity (e.g., Brown 2003; Miller & White 2004) are practiced and enacted in same-sex violence.

With respect to sexual violence, Felson temporarily abandons his argument on gender parity while maintaining his assertion that sexism is "trivial" in rape. Although he does mention statistics about rape and sexual assault which downplay the incidence and impact of sexual assault for women, he neglects to report any statistics on the frequency of sexual assault by sex of victim. His claim of statistical equivalence in the perpetration and experience of partner violence is cited as indication of gender parity, and therefore an absence of sexism, but the lack of such equivalence in the perpetration or experience of sexual violence is somehow insufficient evidence of sexism's role in rape. Furthermore, his discussion of the debate about power versus sexual desire as motivation for rape contributes to the misconception that somehow power and sexuality are dichotomous, and that power and dominance only occur in the context of violence.

Felson concludes his analysis by suggesting that the motivations of activists (i.e., feminist scholars) serve to obscure the "reality" of the relationship—or lack thereof—between gender and violence posited by scientists (i.e., Felson), as though his own perspective is somehow value-free and apolitical. Felson's final acknowledgement that "the vulnerability of women justifies treating violence against women more seriously than violence against men, even when statistical evidence does not" (p. 25) suggests the striking position that although gender inequality (the cause of women's vulnerability) matters in the real-world context, statistical evidence can, indeed should, be read outside of this real-world context. Where were we led astray in learning that, as social scientists, we should use statistical evidence to illuminate rather than obfuscate real-world social processes?

Kristin L. Anderson
Associate Professor of Sociology
Western Washington University

Jill Cermele
Associate Professor of Psychology
Drew University

References

Anderson, Kristin L. 1997. "Gender, Status and Domestic Violence: An Integration of Feminist and Family Violence Approaches." *Journal of Marriage and the Family* 59:655–669.

Atkinson, Makine P., Theodore N. Greenstein, and Molly Monahan Lang. 2005. "For Women, Breadwinnning can be Dangerous: Gendered Resource Theory and Wife Abuse." *Journal of Marriage and Family* 67:1137–1149.

Brown, Lyn Mikel. 2003. *Girlfighting: Betrayal and Rejection Among Girls*. New York: NYU Press.

DeMaris, Alfred, Michael L. Benson, Greer L. Fox, Terrence Hill, and Judy Van Wyk. 2003. "Distal and Proximal Factors in Domestic Violence: A Test of an Integrated Model." *Journal of Marriage and Family* 65:652–667.

Franklin, Karen 2004. "Enacting Masculinity: Antigay Violence and Group Rape as Participatory Theater." *Sexuality Research and Social Policy* 1: 25–40.

Miller, Jody, and Norman. A. White. 2004. "Situational Effects of Gender Inequality on Girls' Participation in Violence." In Christine Alder and Anne Worrall (Eds.) *Girls' Violence: Myths and Realities*. New York: State University of New York Press.

Impacting the Cycle of Violence One Child at a Time

Carole Merill-Mazurek

The YWCA of Schenectady has been operating an NYS-licensed domestic violence program for 30 years. The long tenure of YWCA services in Schenectady County and our experiential knowledge of domestic abuse have made us experts in the indicators, trauma, frequency, and lethality of domestic violence and its affect on children. In this article, I provide a statistical context of local domestic violence and describe one method we at YWCA have adopted to address this issue: participatory education.

According to the 2003 United Way, Schenectady County Community Profile (http://www.uwschdy.org), from 1995 to 2005, Schenectady County experienced a 48 percent increase in the number of reports of domestic violence made to County law enforcement agencies (from 1,571 to 3,046). Community resources are maximized as Schenectady County struggles to deal with this serious social problem.

Domestic violence in Schenectady County has been escalating at an alarming rate for the past three years, and the domestic violence shelter has been operating at or near maximum capacity for the past several years. In 2005, the YWCA sheltered 336 women and 280 children (with hundreds of victims turned away because of lack of space); served 4037 nonresidential clients (including incarcerated women); and conducted workshops for 2427 students in elementary, middle, and high school.

The Schenectady County School System is especially impacted by the increase of family dysfunction as a result of domestic violence. The increase in the county rate of domestic violence has challenged the school district to protect and assist the children and women who have been victimized by abuse. The YWCA has been working collaboratively with the Schenectady County School Districts since 1998; together we have implemented preventative and direct services to assist domestic violence victims and their families.

Written especially for *Ruminations in Violence*.

Young lives are shattered by the impact of domestic violence. Children often die at the hands of an abuser; others are seriously injured, and in all cases these children suffer severe emotional and psychological trauma. Domestic violence has several negative effects on a child. It severely compromises her or his ability to excel in school, to acquire the social skills necessary to communicate, and to express feelings adequately. As a result of the abuse, the dysfunction within the home is a major stress on children, as frequently exhibited by their physical injuries, illnesses, depression, anxiety, poor communication skills and passive or aggressive behavior patterns. A child in an abusive situation is further stressed by the safety measures that need to be taken by the non-offending parent, such as seeking safe shelter, changing schools, and obtaining orders of custody and protection, with the added stress of being uncertain of future safety. Due to the chaos during an acute domestic-abuse occurrence, children do not know what to do to keep themselves safe and frequently feel responsible for the fighting and/or the protection of younger siblings. A perpetrator frequently inhibits the victim's access to a support system, which limits options to escape the abuse and further exacerbates the inertia and fear experienced by children.

The workshops developed through Schenectady County's domestic violence program are designed to tap into the strengths young children possess; educators use techniques to engage the children's innate creative skills and communication abilities to impart preventative and safety information. Using puppets in conjunction with energetic, interactive group participation enables abused children to utilize creativity and offers them a healthy outlet for self-expression. Children who were involved in the program in third grade were excited to learn that they would be able to experience it again in fourth grade.

Information learned in the workshops boosts a child's ability to be more self-sufficient in communicating his or her own feelings and needs, in addition to understanding the feelings and needs of others. The workshops teach concrete concepts that explain how to attend to a child's immediate safety if a family altercation takes place. They also help a frightened child to feel comfortable reaching out to a trusted adult about her or his situation.

Currently, the domestic abuse educator provides workshops to first through fourth graders in Schenectady County School District. Multi-media student presentations and interactive workshops provide information on physical and emotional abuse, domestic violence, family and social dynamics, communication skills, and safety issues. These presentations and workshops occur inside the classroom and consist of two forty-five minute sessions. The domestic abuse educator conducts the workshop, with the classroom teacher in attendance. The two 45-minute sessions per classroom incorporate audio, visual, and "hands on" learning. Overall, students and teachers have greeted us warmly. Children respond well to our puppets (Sally and Alex) that are used in role-play and interactive situations. The children love the puppets' color, softness, and familiarity as a childhood toy and vie for the opportunity to actively participate in doing role-plays with Sally and

Alex. Teachers have stated that even some of the children who are normally quiet and/or have behavior problems have eagerly participated.

Children enrolled in the program continue to disclose about domestic violence, which indicates that the YWCA's violence prevention program is effective. The YWCA worked with the Schenectady School District to set guidelines for student disclosure and parent referrals, confidentiality, and sensitivity. Intervention procedures are still in place and have been shared with other school districts.

By providing violence prevention and safety in consecutive years (grades 1–4), students will learn through repetition how to improve their relationships through better communication and conflict resolution skills. As a result, students will learn that violence is always unacceptable and that good behavior leads to feeling better about themselves, and they will learn how to establish and maintain friendships. They will also learn how to remain as safe as possible if domestic abuse occurs and to confide in an adult for added intervention and support. Educators will design workshops for first and second grades to complement children's learning and processing abilities at this age. Educators will provide all teachers and parents with flyers that can be posted in the room so that teachers can reinforce the ideas they learned from our program throughout the year.

The main ideas emphasize child safety and violence prevention. Educators have developed surveys that are given to teachers at the beginning of the school year to indicate the level of conflict and violence that occurred in their class during the past year. At the end of the year, the same survey is given to teachers to indicate changes in classroom behavior as a result of our program intervention.

PART IV

NARRATING VIOLENCE

11

Journal Entries

Leahanna Klement

August 13, 2004 (8 months after the November incident)

Dear Journal,
    When I'm happy, what happened doesn't seem to matter as much. I don't feel that constricting pain, the sadness, and worst of all, the following emptiness and desolation. I block it out just like I did in the beginning. Only now, it isn't because of shock. It is because no one can truly help me, not even myself, so there is no real point in lamenting.
    And yet none of it matters because those who matter most to me do not understand. They don't see that I am only strong when I'm happy. They don't understand that one unnecessary negative comment or truth can send me reeling into a mini-depression.
    One joke about rape and girls wanting it. Like the other night—I'm with my closest friends, the ones I know actually care about me. And John starts tickling Shannon and she screams out, while giggling uncontrollably "Rape!" And he says "It's not rape if you like it." I freeze. I can feel myself staring off into space but I can't snap out of it. The first question my boyfriend asked me after I told him what happened: "Are you sure you didn't want it?" I screamed to myself, "It's a joke, no big deal, let it go!" But my whole chest feels clenched and all I can think about is that night. Not to mention the hatred I feel for those who don't get it.
    One comment about how girls who dress and act a certain way get what's coming to them. You wouldn't believe how many people want to know what I was wearing. I wan to hit them every time because I know what their question implies and I can barely control my anger. They say, "What were you wearing?" What they mean is "You probably looked slutty and led some guy on." Further translation: "It's your fault." I see the rage any time one even suggests this. I hate having to explain myself. And you know what?

Written especially for *Ruminations in Violence*.

I was wearing jeans, with a zip up hooded jacket, and my hair in a bun. I bet it was the scandalous hoodie zip-up jacket that made them do it, right?

Because of the hurt I've experienced I'm not even strong enough to deal with these little things. And I hate myself for it. No matter how angry I am with people who cause those flashbacks I hate myself even more. I hate being weak. I hate how I can never explain how part of me has died. I hate that I cannot take a joke any more. I hate that I cry at everything now, simply because the slightest negative comment can push me over the edge.

• • •

>Did you all know, I died once?
>Yes, I was killed
>One night
>In early November
>Under a moon lit sky

>True, my body remains
>And here I stand before you
>But what you see now
>Is a mere shadow of who I once was.

>Each day
>I walk
>Do you hear the fear in my footsteps?
>The echoing patter as my breath quickens?
>I pass familiar faces
>That think they recognize me
>But is that possible when
>I do not even know myself anymore?

>Each night
>I look at myself in the mirror
>And I see the empty eyes
>Of my slain soul

>I no longer shed tears
>Like I used to
>Be able to
>Because
>A Shadow
>Cannot cry.

>Sometime I think
>If I could just make people see
>Maybe then I could see myself again

But if I showed you the place
You would not believe
That the woman you think you see
Was silenced there.

Yes, it's true
What you see now
Is a shadow
Of who I once was
Or maybe a shell
Full of nothingness

And now
When someone thinks
They hear me speak
It's really just that hollow echo
Of puffs of wind
Blowing in an empty soul.

12

Uberlinda

Graciela Monteagudo

In the mid-1990s, suffering the consequences of the International Monetary Fund-sponsored destruction of the economy, Argentinean women (and men) took over bridges and highways, built barricades, and made public what the government knew but refused to acknowledge: brutal poverty and high unemployment rates with no safety nets.

Argentina's doors were opened to the International Monetary Fund (IMF) during the military dictatorship of the 1970s and 1980s. Thirty thousand activists "disappeared" during those years as the military dictatorship detained, tortured, and killed those who opposed them so that there would be no resistance to the economic policies that were sponsored by the United States and other developed nations and were implemented by the IMF.

Throughout the two presidencies of Carlos Menem (1989–1999) the country's resources were sold at wholesale prices to multinational corporations. The state of Argentina owned the oil fields, the production of electricity, natural gas, drinking-water systems, the railroads, the telecommunication services, a TV channel, two national airlines, and the postal service, among other key resources. The multinational corporations that bought these corporations immediately downsized their personnel, in some cases leaving 95 percent of them jobless.

The IMF structural adjustment plan was on its way. The Argentineans named it *el modelo*, a shortened name for the economic model. The *modelo* included a policy of "opening the borders" to cheap imports, and it produced the highest rate of unemployment Argentina had ever experienced by destroying its national capacity for production of material goods. The *modelo* turned a formerly rich country by South American standards into a poor, deeply dependent nation. The mass of people who fell below the poverty line (from 10 percent in 1975 to almost 60 percent in 2002) and the 26 percent unemployment were clear indicators that something was wrong. In December 2001, following looting and massive insurrections, the *modelo*—the IMF

Written especially for *Ruminations on Violence*.

poster child of the 1990s—collapsed as capital flew out of the country in search of more stable investment opportunities.

The unemployed workers developed strategies to call attention to their plight. Massive road blockades and other direct actions that included attacks to multinational corporations and government buildings spawned a nonhierarchical, horizontally led movement. Following Menem's presidency, on December 10, 1999, Fernando de la Rúa was elected on a platform that promised to change the economic situation. However, his administration followed exactly the same pattern as that of his predecessor. The December 2001 mass mobilizations, looting, and attacks to banks—partially triggered by the confiscation of the middle classes' savings and a declaration of a stage of siege by de la Rúa—brought his government down. After three short-lived congressionally appointed presidencies, Eduardo Duhalde was appointed president on January 1, 2002. Although he remained president until May 25, 2003, his government became powerless after the Massacre of the Pueyrredón Bridge on June 26, 2002, where hundreds of unemployed workers were injured and two were assassinated by the police—just outside of the once proud city of Buenos Aires.

Argentina's economy has partially recovered today by abandoning IMF economic recipes. However, poverty is still rampant although unemployment has decreased to 12 percent.

As part of my work as coordinator of the Argentina Autonomista Project, I hosted a delegation to southern Argentina for the purpose of visiting unemployed workers and factories under worker control. In the town of Cipolletti I interviewed Uberlinda, a 40-year-old organizer. What follows is a fictionalized narrative, partially derived from that interview and from information given to me about Urberlinda by other people who knew her well.

From Uberlinda herself, I learned that she had her children in high school, and that she survived by picking up cardboard from the dumpster since she was very young. From my other informants in the unemployed worker movement I found out that she had been institutionalized following the "accident" that killed her children inside the cardboard hut where they lived. Although the fire started by accident, it is no accident when a cardboard hut burns and children die. The event might be better described as a natural consequence of living under subhuman conditions.

My informants in the movement also told me that Uberlinda was a key person in the security of the road blockades, along with her 15-year-old boy. Uberlinda's narrative and presence deeply impacted me. I could not shake off my mind that we were of the same age, but she looked decades older, lice infested, and much stronger than I did at the time we met. I wrote the narrative that follows in an attempt to reconcile the complex realities which make up the struggle that is Uberlinda's life.

Uberlinda, the Cardboard and the Fire

At the end of the tunnel, there were the burning coals of a *brasero* (brazier). The iron bucket was the only source of heat for the hut with cement floor and cardboard walls. Uberlinda saw the world for the first time in this slum outside of Cipolletti, Río Negro, Argentina.

First her mom and her dad. Then her lover and her husband. Later, the nurses and the police. The hurt would come in cold red waves. It would stain the cardboard walls.

Fourteen years old and no shoes. Lice painting the paths of shame on her skull.

Below-zero temperatures at times. Uberlinda found the dumpster. Spectral landscape of half-burnt garbage. A search for cardboard to be sold for a few coins.

The psychiatrist reported that her mother died when she was four. Her father's multiple partners abused her. At fourteen she escaped with a man. Ensio, looking like a god in his factory overalls. Oil digger in Cultral-Co, nearby.

Turned around. Soft from inside. Melting brown skin. It was quick. Just a little pain. Not much of anything, but it did open a door out of her father's house for her.

Later, Uberlinda, following the rules of the hospital, had her legs tied to the stirrups. Fire burning through her. Again, the cold red waves that engulfed her from within. The closer she gets, the more it hurts. Then it's all over. Slapped by the doctor, the baby wails. Her breast is warm and the baby relaxes and sleeps.

An accident. Just an accident. Uberlinda, who got to the slum too late to help, watched her children burn. Flames and guilt and anger. Then and there, she stopped noticing her lice. Her lice followed her everywhere, since the beginning of time.

Once, Uberlinda's lice followed her into the asylum. They did not abandon her, not even when she hit her head against the wall in her delirium, confusing the padded walls of the confinement room with the cardboard walls of her burning home.

Ensio, from god in overalls to drunk in rags. The gringos took the oil and dumped the Ensios. The *piquetes* (picket lines) spread throughout the country. Fire on the national highways. Stones, rain, highway asphalt. Guards in riot gear. Masked men, women and children in rags. Stones and sticks against lead bullets. The judge, a woman, stood on a tank. A small body on a war machine. In a direct democracy assembly with the people, she heard their cry and commanded the Guard away.

Juan, Uberlinda's 15-year-old, threw stones with amazing aim. They banged against the acrylic shields that protected the soldiers' faces. All of them masked. The National Guard charged. From behind the burning tires, Uberlinda took aim. The molotov described an almost perfect arc on the dark sky. For a second, it lit up a war scene and then it was all fire and pain.

The prosecutor reported that Uberlinda was arrested in a piquete in the town of Cipolletti, charged with obstruction of a public highway, attack to National Guard officers, damage to property, and disorderly behavior.

The police station, dirty and small. Uberlinda and many women. Sweat, anger and, for the first time, *compañeras* to break bread with. Uberlinda learns a new word: solidarity. It's the feeling that helps her to stay strong when the sergeant—a woman—bangs Uberlinda's head against the wall. Outside, the people of Cipolletti riot until a judge releases the *piqueteras* and *piqueteros*.

Uberlinda, with two of her surviving children in high school, still picks up cardboard to survive and continues to organize with the autonomous piqueteros of Cipolletti. For the past few years, some families have been receiving $50 a month plus some food from the government. Uberlinda bakes, plants a garden, gossips, and sometimes fights with her compañeras. Despite President Néstor Kirchner's payoff to the IMF, the debt to foreign investors continues to be paid with Uberlinda's blood, cardboard, lice, and fire.

13

Negotiating Dangerous Spaces
Mundane Encounters with Prostitution and AIDS in Northern Thailand

Ida Fadzillah

INTRODUCTION

One can clearly see the effects of violence on youth and children in war-torn regions, in areas of famine and great poverty, and in places with organized crime run rampant. However, it takes more observant eyes to perceive how violence—whether physical, emotional, or symbolic—is experienced by the young in places of less overt distress. When attention is shifted, however, to focus on young people's experiences in such places, it becomes clear that violence, especially potential violence, is experienced in unique and unexpected ways. The effects of the physically and psychologically brutal sex industry, for example, can be perceived by some girls as beautiful, and as safe.

This essay examines the lives of teenage girls in rural Northern Thailand and explores how their perceptions and interpretations of their lives have been shaped by the presence of certain factors—specifically, an active transnational prostitution network[1] and a pandemic AIDS crisis engulfing the region.[2] Largely because of these factors, the girls of this study, who are between the ages of 12 and 17, experience their village and homes as places laced with invisible intrusions of what I term "mundane violence"[3]—that is,

---

Written especially for *Ruminations on Violence.*

[1] Phongpaichit et al. 1998.
[2] Bond et al. 1997.
[3] This term is similar to Scheper-Hughes' concept of "everyday violence," which she explores in her ethnography *Death Without Weeping* (1993). One way that "mundane violence" is different, though, is that I use it as a "generational" term emphasizing the perspective of children and youth that highlights the experience of violence as something one is born into.

spaces of potential social and physical dangers that at times might appear quite enticing and thus require constant, daily negotiation and monitoring by the girls as they work to transform into mature, responsible, and successful women. Their experience of violence within their landscape of home[4] is thus age-specific, linked to their perspective as young people who saw themselves as neither children nor adults. It is also culture-specific, shaped greatly by the factors previously mentioned and by the resulting and causative stories and stereotypes attached to the geographic region. This essay thus seeks to present Northern Thai spaces of mundane violence as ensconced within a series of concentric circles defining village girls' identities, beginning with the body of the Thai state—that is, the discourses circulating through the major Thai cities in the North, and the world discourses about Thailand in general—and ending with an interpretation of the villagers' actual physical bodies.

THE GOLDEN TRIANGLE

Thailand is a nation both blessed and plagued by its thriving sex industry, and for decades social scientists have scrutinized its sex workers and sex tourism industry.[5] This academic scrutiny has contributed to an image of Thailand as a nation of female exploitation and acceptable sexual commodification. It must be emphasized at the outset, though, that this image is by and large an inaccurate one: Thailand, as anyone who has visited can attest, is a place as moral and as virtuous as any other. However, Thailand has a sex industry that is disproportionately large, with an estimated 800,000 women out of a female population of approximately 27 million being involved in sex work.[6] A significant percentage of these prostitutes are from Northern Thailand.[7] They are predominantly young women from agrarian backgrounds, recruited by agents, brothel owners, or friends, and generally have a short span (of less than three years) of work in brothels.[8]

Northern Thailand is also part of the "Golden Triangle," a label originally referring to a geographic area intersecting parts of Thailand, Myanmar, and Laos that is a major site of opium and heroin production, with approximately 60 percent of the heroin sold in the United States originating from this area.[9] Undergraduates at Chiang Mai University (the largest university in Northern Thailand, located in Chiang Mai Province) informed me of the

---

[4] For more on the anthropology of space and place, I recommend Basso's ethnography *Wisdom Sits in Places* (1996) and Low and Lawrence-Zuaniga's reader, *The Anthology of Space and Place* (2003).

[5] For example, see Bishop and Robinson 1998; DaGrossa 1989; Hantrakul 1981; Jeffrey 2003; McCamish 1999; Montgomery 1998, 2001; Odzer 1997; Saengtienchai et al. 1999; Tannenbaum 1999; Truong 1990; Van Wijngaarden 1999; Watanabe 1998; and Wilson 2004.

[6] This is according to Phongpaichit (1988), though she and others have quoted other estimated totals that range from 20,000 to 2 million.

[7] Phongpaichit 1988; DaGrossa 1989; Odzer 1997.

[8] Phongpaichit 1988.

[9] Phongpaichit, et al. 1998:87.

other current meaning behind the term "Golden Triangle": it now also refers to the vagina of the Northern Thai woman, which is a "golden triangle" because of its surefire ability to produce great wealth.

Prostitution has made inroads into this region for several reasons, including the stereotype of the North as having the most beautiful and desirable women in the country, and the better organized regional networks feeding into the sex trade and embedded deep in the northern villages. *Tok khiew*, or "green harvest," originally meant "pledging green padi" for loans when farmers did not have enough to sustain themselves before harvest.[10] It now connotes an elaborate system of village-based loans, with farmers pledging their daughters' sexual labor to pimps and brothel owners.[11] One of the main reasons for the success of such ventures is the fact that Northern Thai women have a reputation among the general population as being more beautiful—more fair-skinned, taller, and more soft-spoken—and thus more desirable as sexual partners. They are also perceived by others throughout the country as "bolder" (*gla*), and more sexually aggressive, both seen as positive characteristics. Additionally, the North is one of the poorer regions of Thailand, though interestingly not the poorest. One woman from Chiang Mai, an administrative assistant at Chiang Mai University, spoke to me of how some Northern girls were forced into prostitution by their parents because of poverty: "If you visit some villages in Chiang Rai [Province] for example, you won't see any teenage girls there. They have all become prostitutes. These poor girls, they have no choice."

These were the images and stories that others associated with village girls in Chiang Rai Province, but how did the girls themselves experience the prostitution industry? Did they see themselves as having "no choice" about their future? I lived in the northern village of Baan Khmer[12] for 18 months, from 1996 to 1998, to explore this question more fully.[13]

SUCCESS AS TILE-ROOFED HOUSES

What I found most interesting in all my time in Baan Khmer was the almost constant and predictable action of the girls as we walked around the village, talking about their "homes." They often pointed out large, concrete houses surround by elaborate fences, with television antennas and sometimes satellite dishes, and expensive cars parked in the open garages. The roofs tended to be made of expensive tiles that glistened in the sunlight, and the houses looked clean and new. In Baan Khmer village there was such a house

---

[10] Hantrakul 1981.
[11] Bond et al. 1997:196.
[12] A pseudonym, as are the names of all the girls in this article.
[13] While I have not returned to Baan Khmer, I did conduct additional fieldwork for three months in Bangkok in the summer of 2001. What I found was that the business of sex work had flourished through the Asian economic crisis of the late 1990s, and that the image of Northern Thai girls as desirable prostitutes was as strong as ever.

or two on every street, always situated between two much smaller, usually wooden one-story dwellings with wooden or thatched roofs. My companions would make a point of singling out the new houses, saying something to the effect of "You see that house? The daughter of the woman who lives there now built that. The daughter works in Bangkok as a prostitute and gives her parents a lot of money. She bought that car for her brother. But she doesn't come to visit very often."

The same is said about the expensive cars that can be seen zooming around the village at certain times of the year. During national holidays or at harvest time, I would sit with my friend Odd (who was 28 years old and owned a video rental store along the highway) and watch cars go by, usually driven by young women wearing heavy makeup and jewelry. "Have you seen them before?" Odd asked me the first time we watched these cars together.

> They work in the city and have come back for the holidays to show off their new clothes and cars. Sometimes they have foreign boyfriends, too. These girls come back to make religious offerings at the temple. Even though everyone knows where the money is coming from they don't care, they still take the money. You know what these girls do, right? You see that nice cement house on the corner? The family's daughter built that for them. She bought her brother a new car too. Her mother says she works in a factory in Bangkok, but everyone knows she is a prostitute.

When they did come home—usually during the holidays or to help with the rice harvest or planting—the bodies of these girls too carried the symbols of success. "Look at her, have you seen her before?" Nim (16 years old) asked me:

> She came up from the city yesterday to visit her parents. I talked with her yesterday, and she was wearing a lot of makeup and gold jewelry. And her clothes were really expensive looking. She looked really "cool" (*thae*).[14] Then she had to get ready for the ceremony and changed into "normal" (*thammada*) clothes, just like mine.

From the perspective of my field research, it seemed that these aspects of the social landscape—the houses and the cars, the clothes and the jewelry—told the story of "cosmopolitan" life much more loudly than the actual words or stories of city girls themselves. Most of the teenage girls with whom I spoke were still in school for most of the year and had limited experience with actual day-to-day life in the big city, occasionally visiting Bangkok or Chiang Mai City only for vacations, school trips, family visits, or festivals. In addition, they rarely had the opportunity to visit the workplace of their older sisters and other female relatives and friends. Thus, the girls perceived the women's "success" and "freedom"—as represented through living and work-

---

[14] The term *thae* is used by young people to describe something "cool" or "in fashion." It is different from Mill's term of *thansamay*, which translated loosely refers to something that is seen as "cosmopolitan" or "modern." The former term is used constantly by the teenagers when referring to each other's clothing or accessories.

ing in the big city—only secondhand, through the goods bought, built, worn, and displayed. None of these symbolized the violence, trauma, and early death also associated with working in the prostitution industry.

The incentive for working in prostitution was thus reinforced because its rewards were equated with notions of female success: as a prostitute, not only was your beauty (as measured through your acquisition and use of Western clothes, goods, and perhaps foreign boyfriends) socially and economically legitimated, but you could also dot the landscape with symbols of your material success. The gleaming roof tiles, the iron gates, the satellite dish, are local reminders of the benefits and rewards of leaving the village for city life. Frequently the women whose money built the houses or bought the cars were not present, but their actual physical presence is almost unnecessary to complete the picture of "success" for village girls. These monuments—interspersed with the poor, unimpressive dwellings of those not fortunate enough to have daughters working in Bangkok—speak of filial piety, of filial obligations met, and of economic and social prosperity. And so, an intriguing question to be asked at this point is perhaps not "why do so many girls enter into prostitution," but "why don't more girls enter into prostitution"? One answer to that could be the highly visible AIDS infection rates affecting an alarming number of the Northern Thai population.

A Procession of Funeral Effigies

One of the most serious repercussions of the sex industry is the HIV epidemic spreading throughout the country. Thailand has a high incidence of HIV infection and death, and Northern Thailand is the area of highest HIV/AIDS concentration in the country. Between October 1984 and October 1994 there was an average of 201 AIDS cases per 100,000 people in the North, compared to 32.8 AIDS cases per 100,000 for the whole country. Chiang Rai Province had the highest rates within Northern Thailand, with 233.4 AIDS cases per 100,000 people.[15] Happily, the rates have dropped slightly in the North, to 92.91 cases per 100,000 people,[16] and in 2001 the numbers in Chiang Rai Province were reported to be 93.3 cases per 100,000.[17] However, these numbers still represent the highest rates of HIV/AIDS cases of all the provinces in the country.[18] These high rates can be explained partly through the increasing amount of migrant workers who leave the countryside to work in the cities. They get AIDS in the urban setting, but then when they return to their families or to get married, they transmit the disease to their mates and their children.[19]

According to Bond et al. (1997), the commercial sex industry in Thailand is the biggest reason behind such high rates of transmission. The rapid

---

[15] Singhanetra-Renard 1997: 80.
[16] Thailand Population and Housing Census 2000.
[17] Public Health Office, Chiang Rai, 2002.
[18] Phoolcharoen et al. 2003.
[19] Singhanetra-Renard 1997:80.

rise in HIV infection rates among prostitutes and the common use of prostitutes by Thai men suggest that commercial sex exposure is one way that a large percentage of men acquire HIV.[20]

How did the frequency of AIDS in the village affect girls' perceptions of themselves? On the most basic level, the presence of individuals with HIV-related symptoms and those who have died from AIDS-related complications exposed Baan Khmer girls to the threat of the disease. They had all seen the physical effects of AIDS. They were also well aware that AIDS can be transmitted to men and women of all ages, occupations, and classes. They saw people with AIDS at school, in the hospital, in public transportation, and in their homes. They were also participants in the funerals that took place for these victims, and the girls realized as well as anybody that AIDS was something that has affected the entire village, regardless of age, sex, or occupation.

For me, the most discomforting aspect of the girls' landscape was the frequent procession, down our dusty road, of elaborate funeral effigies surrounded by mourners. The effigies, made of paper mounted on thin wooden frames, took on shapes of religious significance such as Buddhist spires or temples and were transported to the temple grounds, where people threw wooden sticks or paper flowers inscribed with their prayers into them, and then all was set ablaze. In a nearby village there is an active business in making these effigies. There, competing businesses exist side by side along the main road, busily constructing the fantastic shapes in bright, glittering colors. In this neighboring village even the sundry-goods stores sold miniature effigies because of the reputation of the village as being the center for this craft. These funeral effigies, in which the body is placed and subsequently cremated, differ significantly, depending on the deceased persons for whom they are created. For example, if the deceased had been old and respected, the effigy would be white. If the deceased were not elderly, the effigy would usually be red. Unfortunately, I observed an inordinately large amount of red funeral effigies being carried towards the temple grounds.

While funerals were part of the entire village scene, they seemed to affect the girls in particular, for those who died were frequently relatively young and had close relationships within the teenage community (with their teachers, or as parents of their friends, for example). The girls of my study regularly attended funerals during the year I conducted field research. Nim and her friend Oy, who was sixteen years old at the time, went to a particularly sad funeral just one month after I arrived at the village, for a young female teacher who had died of AIDS. The woman's husband had died of AIDS the year before, and they had a three-year-old daughter who would now be taken care of by relatives. There were funerals for a policeman, another female teacher, the wife of a man who had contracted AIDS while working overseas, and for many more. The girls attending the funerals often described men who died of AIDS as playboys who had caught the disease from fooling around

---

[20] Bond et al. 1997:185.

and then had passed it along to their wives and later their children. Interestingly, I never heard of a funeral being held for a woman who was described as a prostitute, or of a woman who had passed the disease along to her husband because she was fooling around.

At these funerals, people would council me on the current superstitions. "Don't drink the water or eat the food," one person warned me, though traditionally it would be a great insult to the deceased's family if guests turned down their hospitality. Others have also told me that at funerals for those who have died of AIDS they go to pay their respects but do not usually eat or drink the refreshments, echoing the sentiment of one who said to me by way of an explanation, "I know they say you can't get AIDS from eating or drinking, but you never know."

Teenagers, both girls and boys, have attended the funerals of those in their community and family who have died of AIDS; they have also seen the physical deterioration that AIDS causes on the landscape of the human body as well. In the primary school, I asked a group of twelve year olds if they had ever seen a person with AIDS. They all said yes, each clamoring with the others to tell his or her story first. They had all visited the hospital at one time or another, where on any given day there would be at least one person dying of the disease. One girl said she saw a male acquaintance who was dying of AIDS at the hospital when she went to visit her sick aunt: "But he was very skinny. He used to be really fat, but it was like he was all dried up. And his skin was very black. He actually looked like a piece of dried fish, all black and skinny like that." Another girl in the group recounted,

> One time when I was taking the *song-thaew* [taxi] to the other side of the village a woman got on who was going to the hospital. She was in a lot of pain, but we didn't know what to do to help her. She had AIDS and was covered with sores. No one wanted to touch her. She had a hard time sitting down on the trip, and then she got out of the *song-thaew* at the hospital. I don't know what happened to her. It was very sad, but I was scared too.

In both the elementary and secondary schools, the children were well aware of the presence of AIDS. While most of the children in school did not have the disease, some in the kindergarten classes did. They stood out from their classmates because of the knit caps they wore to hide their bald heads. Some of them were orphans whose parents had died of the disease, and the teachers and other students frequently discussed these children as suffering from their parents' own follies. Teachers in the Baan Khmer primary school told me how hard it was to teach these children because "you don't know what to do with them." According to the teachers, many of the children in the Phratom 6 (sixth grade) have lost a parent to AIDS. Some have even lost brothers and sisters. They get their own food to eat during meals and don't share their eating utensils.

One of the most significant results of the almost "mundane" nature of the presence of AIDS in the village is the faulty perspective the teenage girls had developed regarding the means of getting HIV: while in Western and medical literature on the Thai situation there is a high correlation perceived between being a prostitute and getting AIDS, this correlation was not made by the girls themselves. They saw AIDS as something that was "given" by playboy men to their wives and children, not as something caught by being a prostitute. In the girls' imagination, a faithful wife has as much risk of dying of AIDS as a prostitute. Thus, while AIDS was highly visible and publicized, it did not deter girls from entering into prostitution. What it actually did was to strongly discourage girls from settling into committed relationships with men at an early age and remaining in the village. Their safest act, in their eyes, was to get out of the local arena. Though much of the reason for these local deaths was that most villagers who fell ill while working abroad or in the city came home to die, the village was still perceived by girls as a locus (and point of origination) of much danger, suffering, and death.

Conclusion

Violence exists for the young in many rural spaces as "potential" or "future" danger, and it exists largely due to conditions underscored by poverty. Northern Thailand, however, has in its favor a stereotype or mythology that seems at the outset to be charming. Their women are perceived to be the most beautiful, the most desirable, and the most ardent in the nation. Because of this image, the prostitution industry has a stronghold in this region that will continue far into the future. However, the girls who are being born and raised within this region constantly focus on both the "beautiful" side of prostitution—the nice houses, pretty clothes, and new cars—and the "ugly" side, that of HIV-AIDS. Only from talking to these girls on their own level, and trying to see their home through their eyes, does it become clear that AIDS is not perceived by them as a disease of prostitutes but rather one that is associated with mothers, teachers, and friends—even those who remain virgins until marriage and faithful to their husbands. Thus, the village girls believe that danger does not necessarily lie on the path of prostitution, but rather on the road to rural womanhood. For many, it seems logical that the safest thing for a girl to do is to get out of the village, which has become the space where the danger is perceived to reside. According to this logic, young women can perceive prostitution as the best "choice" in a space of multiple possible terrors.

References

Basso, Keith. 1996. *Wisdom Sits in Places: Landscape and Language among the Western Apache.* Albuquerque: University of New Mexico Press.

Bishop, R., and L. Robinson. 1998. *Night Market: Sexual Cultures and the Thai Economic Miracle.* New York: Routledge.

Bond, Katherine C., David D. Celentano, Sukanya Phonsophakul, and Chayan Vaddhanaphuti. 1997. "Mobility and Migration: Female Commercial Sex Work and the HIV Epidemic in Northern Thailand." In *Sexual Cultures and Migration in the*

Era of AIDS: Anthropological and Demographic Perspectives, ed. Gilbert Herdt, 185–215. Oxford: Clarendon Press.

DaGrossa, Pamela. 1989. "Kamphaeng Din: A Study of Prostitution in the All-Thai Brothels of Chiang Mai City." *Crossroads: An Interdisciplinary Journal of Southeast Asian Studies* 4(2): 1–7.

Hantrakul, Sukanya. 1981. "Prostitutes and Human Rights in Thailand." *Human Rights in Thailand* 5(3):5–17.

Jeffrey, Sheila. 2003. *Sex and Borders: Gender, National Identity, and Prostitution in Thailand.* Honolulu: University of Hawaii Press.

Low, Setha M. and Denise Lawrence-Zuaniga (eds.), 2003. *The Anthology of Space and Place: Locating Culture.* Malden, MA: Blackwell Press.

McCamish, Malcolm. 1999. "The Friends Thou Hast: Support Systems for Male Commercial Sex Workers in Pattaya, Thailand." In *Lady Boys, Tom Boys, Rent Boys: Male and Female Homosexualities in Contemporary Thailand*, ed. Peter A. Jackson and Gerard Sullivan, 161–192. Binghamton, NY: Harrington Press.

Mills, Mary Beth. 1999. *Thai Women in the Global Labor Force: Consuming Desires, Contested Selves.* New Brunswick: Rutgers University Press.

Montgomery, Heather. 2001. *Modern Babylon: Prostituting Children in Thailand.* New York: Berghahn Books.

———. 1998. "Children, Prostitution, and Identity: A Case Study from a Tourist Resort in Thailand." In *Global Sex Workers: Rights, Resistance, Redefinition*, eds. K. Kempadoo and J. Doezema, 139–150. London: Routledge.

National Statistical Office. 2000. *Key Indicators of the Population and Households, Population and Housing Census 1990 and 2000.* Bangkok, Thailand: Social Statistics Division, Population and Housing Statistics Branch, Population and Housing Census. Retrieved February 26, 2007, at http://web.nso.go.th/eng/en/stat/poph/poph.htm.

Odzer, Cleo. 1997. *Patpong Sisters.* New York: Arcade Publishers.

Phongpaichit, P. 1988. *From Peasant Girls to Bangkok Masseuses.* Geneva: International Labour Organization.

Phongpaichit, Pasuk, Sungsidh Piriyarangsan, and Nualnoi Treerat. 1998. *Guns, Girls, Gambling, Ganja: Thailand's Illegal Economy and Public Policy.* Chiang Mai: Silkworm Books.

Phoolcharoen, Wiput, Viroj Tangcharoensathien, Sombat Tanprasertsuk, and Chutima Suraratdecha. 2003. "Thailand's Health Care Systems: Responses to the HIV Epidemic." Panel presentation at the Sixth International Conference on Healthcare Resource Allocation for HIV/AIDS, Washington DC, October 13–14.

Public Health Office. 2002. "The AIDS Situation in Chiang Rai Province, Thailand." Chiang Rai City: Department for the Control of AIDS and Venereal Diseases.

Scheper-Hughes, Nancy. 1993. *Death Without Weeping: The Violence of Everyday Life in Brazil.* Berkeley: University of California Press.

Saengtienchai, Chanpen, John Knodel, Mark VanLandingham, and Anthony Pramualratana. 1999. "'Prostitutes are Better Than Lovers': Wives' Views on the Extramarital Sexual Behavior of Thai Men." In *Genders and Sexualities in Modern Thailand*, eds. Peter A. Jackson and Nerida M. Cook, 78–92. Chiang Mai, Thailand: Silkworm Books.

Singhanetra-Renard, Anjali. 1997. "Population Movement and the AIDS Epidemic in Thailand." In *Sexual Cultures and Migration in the Era of AIDS: Anthropological and Demographic Perspectives*, ed. Gilbert Herdt, 70–86. Oxford: Clarendon Press.

Tannenbaum, Nicola. 1999. "Buddhism, Prostitution, and Sex: Limits on the Academic Discourse on Gender in Thailand." In *Genders and Sexualities in Modern Thailand*, eds. Peter A. Jackson and Nerida M. Cook, 243–260. Chiang Mai, Thailand: Silkworm Books.

Truong, Thanh-Dam. 1990. *Sex, Money and Morality: Prostitution and Tourism in Southeast Asia.* London: Zed Books.

Van Wijngaarden, Jan W. De Lind. 1999. "Between Money, Morality, and Masculinity: Bar-Based Male Sex Work in Chiang Mai." In *Lady Boys, Tom Boys, Rent Boys: Male and Female Homosexualities in Contemporary Thailand*, ed. Peter A. Jackson and Gerard Sullivan, 193–218. Binghamton, NY: Harrington Press.

Watanabe, Satoko. 1998. "From Thailand to Japan: Migrant Sex Workers as Autonomous Subjects." In *Global Sex Workers: Rights, Resistance, Redefinition*, eds. Kamala Kempadoo with Jo Doezema, 114–123. London: Routledge Press.

Wilson, Ara. 2004. *The Intimate Economies of Bangkok: Tomboys, Tycoons, and Avon Ladies in the Global City.* Berkeley: University of California Press.

Convict Narratives from Postcolonial India
The Criminalized Woman in Phoolan Devi's Stories

Basuli Deb

INTRODUCTION

Through a study of postcolonial narratives from India, this essay explores how women who challenge caste atrocities are violently criminalized.[1] *India's Bandit Queen: The True Story of Phoolan Devi*[2] and *The Bandit Queen of India: An Indian Woman's Amazing Journey from Peasant to International Legend*[3] are the central texts considered here. These works are about Phoolan Devi, who was born into a lower-caste sharecropping family in India in the 1960s. She transformed herself from a violated girl into a tough outlaw, avenging caste outrage. In 1983 she negotiated her surrender to the government of India and was elected to the Parliament in 1996. She was finally assassinated in 2001.

Reading the life writings of "Phoolan Devi as convict" narratives that allow for a reconstructive reading of women's criminality, I analyze the caste politics of the criminalization of women through the organizing characters of the girl child and the concubine. Subsequently, exploring the roles of the warrior goddess, I examine the social militancy of these women against such caste oppression. Thus, in my reading the lower-caste female leader becomes both the target of oppression and the source of resistance.

Written especially for *Ruminations on Violence*.

---

[1] Please refer to the end of the article for a complete list of characters, in order of appearance, to better follow the narrative analysis.
[2] Sen 1993.
[3] Devi, Cuny & Rambali 2003.

CRIMINALIZATION OF WOMEN: PENALIZED FOR BEING SOCIALLY DEVALUED?

Gender, caste, and class oppression intersect to express social malady in distinct ways. Such social deprivation, manifested as criminality, is violently penalized by the state's legal mechanism of social control. The "material reality of women's lives within social structures" that leads to their militant challenges to the social order is disregarded (Danner 31).[4] Phoolan Devi's stories narrate how, in the context of India, women's resistance to caste-based social devaluation leads to their criminalization. My reading of *India's Bandit Queen* (*IBQ*) and *The Bandit Queen of India* (*BQI*) emphasizes the revisionary attempts of convict narratives to portray how and why the category of the woman criminal came to be. What role does lower-caste women's struggle against gender roles, regulated by both the state and its adversaries, play in their criminalization?

The Girl Child

The figure of the girl child in Phoolan Devi's life writings becomes especially poignant because it uncovers the alliances between the family and the state in criminalizing her poverty.[5] Devi's prison diary enabled Mala Sen to reconstruct her through the biography *India's Bandit Queen*. Quoting from the diary, Sen contextualizes Devi's criminalization against violent socioeconomic deprivation. Devi's literate uncle (Bihari) had cheated her illiterate father (Devidin) by bribing the village headman "who kept the land records, to transfer all [. . .] [of Devi's] grandfather's property into his name" (*IBQ* 31). It sets in motion the class connection between the empowered male relative and the civic structures that initiate the criminalization of Devi. In Devi's mediated autobiography, *The Bandit Queen of India*, when the family seeks justice from the law after Bihari's son (Mayadin) steals their tree, the policeman retorts: "'How dare you accuse Mayadin? He is already a rich man,' [. . .] 'what would he want with your tree?'" (*IBQ* 63). The tree, which was reserved as Devi's marriage dowry, was destroyed.[6] Her social death through the loss of the tree—her personal property—is a touching metaphor symbolic of the destruction of her prospects of a good husband: "He was in Mayadin's cart, dead, and cut into pieces! They had murdered him! That was the noise I

---

[4] I am indebted to Danner for this insightful perspective on the relationship between gender and criminalizaton. However, while she argues that "state apparatus assumes the task of controlling the behavior of women where superior male advantage is threatened" by women's access to material resources, mine is a postcolonial reading of how caste plays a significant role in the criminalization of women. See Danner 1996 (39).

[5] Rajeswari Sunder Rajans' understanding about the relationship among women, institution, family, and the state has been helpful in shaping my argument about the figure of the girl child in Phoolan Devi's convict narratives. See Rajan 2003 (97–106).

[6] Money, valuables, or property that the bride's family offers to the husband's family during marriage.

146   Part IV: Narrating Violence

had heard in the night, the noise of axes dismembering my handsome tree. I saw the pinkish-yellow heart of the tree bleeding its rich juice" (58). The tree is metonymic for a slain husband, hence Devi is described as widowed. As a violent tussle ensues over the tree between the little girl and her older cousin, the extended family becomes a significant site of physical brutality against the girl child. It also sets the stage for the criminalization of the girl child for her resistance to the violence committed upon her.

In the later episode of the girl child's marriage to the widower (Putti Lal), this pattern of physical violence is again manifested because of the vulnerability of the girl child created by poverty, gender, and age. The Child Marriage Restraint Act of 1929, enacted by British colonial governance, prohibited the formalization of child marriages. However, once the marriages were conducted they were not marked as illegal or null. India gained its liberation from British foreign rule in 1947. The postcolonial state in 1978 amended the act only to increase the age of consent to eighteen for women and twenty-one for men.[7] In *India's Bandit Queen* Sen situates the Indian penal code in the socioeconomic realities of the postcolonial nation: "Present laws in India prohibit both child marriages and the payment of dowries." However, "[t]hey are only used to extract bribes and intimidate those whom the authorities wish to prosecute. Otherwise, age-old traditions are not only allowed to continue but encouraged within village society" (36).[8] In the absence of sincere national efforts to eradicate poverty, the criminalization of these marriages is often tantamount to the penalization of poverty rather than crime, as with that of Devi's sister. This is because poor parents are frequently compelled to secure their uneducated daughter's future as soon as possible.

The Bandit Queen of India depicts how such parents are able to protect both their daughter's future and her present welfare through the local custom of *gauna*. In fact, it is really the violation of the customary law of *gauna* (an agreement guaranteeing a certain time only after which the child bride moves in with her husband) that leads to the domestic violence that Devi experiences in her conjugal family. The atrocity of the marital rape of eleven-year-old Phoolan by the thirty-year-old Putti Lal is communicated through graphic images of bestiality and monstrosity. Putti Lal becomes "a man who ate women," a strong demon with "hairy limbs," who "smelled disgusting, like a hyena," causing the child bride unbearable pain with his "nauseating

---

[7] "The Child Marriage Restraint Act of 1929 had raised the age of consent from 12 to 14 for females and 14 to 18 for males. The age limit had been further raised from 14 to 15 for females by an amendment in 1949." See Narrain 2005.

[8] *The Bandit Queen of India* recounts how Devi's uncle Bihari "managed to put a stop to three marriages" arranged for her sister Rukmini: "'The girl is a minor,' he told them [the groom's family]. 'She's only fourteen years old and her father wants to sell her! It's against the law.' He conspired with the Pradhan [village leader, probably Brahmin] and they brought the police with them." The traumatized Rukmini contemplated suicide after the incident. Powerful relatives can thus harness the resources of the state to conspire against the girl child and her poor family. See Devi, et al. 2003 (51).

serpent" as he threatened to knife open her hymen for his pleasure (99). Physical violence follows the child's flight from rape. She feels her "scalp on fire as he yanked out whole tufts" of her hair to discipline her into submission to his sexual desire (105). It is the girl child's rebellion against this horrific marital abuse that consolidates the criminalization of her marital status by both her extended family and her conjugal family. Putti Lal and Mayadin initiate a criminal proceeding in the *panchayat* (village council) against Devi's family for kidnapping her from her husband, though the case is lost.

The text traces how rebellion becomes the only means of attaining justice for the poverty-stricken, lower-caste girl child. At fourteen or fifteen, Devi realized that she "was a woman who belonged to a lowly caste" and "[f]aced with power and rupees [Indian currency]". . . "used any trick [. . .] [she could]." Deprived of the inherited land by Bihari, the family turns to sharecropping, which is rife with the exploitation of women's labor. The girl resists it: "I encouraged the other girls to sabotage the crops if the landowner wouldn't pay us" (*BQI* 155). In one such episode the daughter of the *Pradhan* (village leader) turns violent when Devi's family declines her demand for free labor from them. The Pradhan intervenes as Devi opposes his daughter's attack on them. This culminates in an episode in which Devi unleashes her wrath publicly against the upper-caste Pradhan by grabbing him by his genitals when he beats her in retaliation.

This episode ultimately defines the girl child's aberrant sexuality: "I had become a disreputable girl in the eyes of the villagers, someone the young men thought they could treat how they liked because she belonged to no one, she had no husband to protect her" (169). She attracts the attention of the son of the *sarpanch* (village headman) and she earns a reputation as an erotic object of men's desire. Her self-defense against his sexual advances leads to her gang rape at gunpoint before her parents. Sen recounts her ethnographic encounter with the myth of Devi's sensuality. The young girl's romance with her married cousin, Kailash, is circulated as folklore long after his death: "One old woman told me, 'Phoolan Devi used to dance naked in the moonlight for that man!'" (*IBQ* 48). As her deviant sexuality becomes a symbol of resistance to the traditional concept of femininity, it becomes necessary for the state to place her under surveillance and control. She is falsely implicated in a *dacoity* (robbery) at Mayadin's house in order to prevent her from addressing the land dispute between her family and Mayadin's in the high court where Mayadin did not have connections. The police custodial torture of the young girl starts with stripping her in front of her father and coercing her to admit to the crime she had not committed. In *The Bandit Queen of India* Devi recalls: "[T]he officers dragged me naked out of the cell and down the corridor into another room." Grisly torture follows: "They put my hands under the legs of the chair, and one of them sat down on it. Some of the others stepped on my calves with their heavy boots" (196).

This narrative of selective torture of lower-caste women in police custody in India is reflective of the custodial brutality inflicted on other tribal women in India. The custodial abuse of Dopdi Mehjen in the short story "Draupadi" by the Indian author, Mahasweta Devi, portrays the plight of one such woman. Arrested for murdering a landowner who refused "untouchable" sharecroppers like Dopdi water from his well during a severe drought,[9] Dopdi is gang raped in police custody and "her breasts are bitten raw, the nipples torn" (35). Representation of custodial violence like this in convict narratives are really commentaries on the criminalization of lower-caste and tribal women in India who are caught in the throes of social devaluation. This kind of social rejection is prompted by the lack of private property, exploitation of labor, patriarchal domination of women, and the role of the nation-state in upholding caste deprivation.

The Concubine

India's Bandit Queen and *The Bandit Queen of India* also chart the complex terrain of caste that operates within communities in resistance against the postcolonial nation-state. This section explores how lower-caste women who join such communities to protest against injustice are further quarantined within them. The figure of the concubine in Devi's convict narratives launches a robust critique of how statist criminalization of resistant women's sexuality is extended by the subversive community of bandits. This is played out over the body of the lower-caste woman through a violent caste politics.

Once again, the narrative constructs caste-gender violence as initiated by the alliance among patriarchal structures—this time of the family, state, and banditry—as Devi is "convinced that Mayadin had been the instigator" of her abduction by the bandits. This would assure Mayadin's future assistance to the gang: "He was, after all, a 'senior citizen' of the village and had influential friends in the panchayat" (*IBQ* 70). The character of caste-based female criminality is movingly captured through Sen's citation of an official press conference in 1983. In it Devi stands the logic of criminalization on its head as state authorities become social offenders for negligence of their duty to protect citizens under the threat of violence:

> Today I am a criminal who should be hanged. But what happened when I was abducted and raped? Where were the police then? I had gone to the police on the day of my abduction to ask for protection, yet today the policemen are officers and Phoolan Devi a murderer. (*IBQ* 124)

This caste war on the level of the bureaucratic structures of the nation-state is again enacted through the contest for leadership of the bandit gang. The brutal rivalry between Babu Gujar Singh and Vikram Mallah is played out on the body of the lower-caste woman. Gujar belonged to the warrior

---

[9] "Untouchability" was abolished in 1950 by the Constitution of independent India, and its practice in any form has been forbidden: "The enforcement of any disability arising out of 'untouchability' shall be an offence punishable in accordance with law." See Constitution of India, Art. 17.

caste of Khatriyas. On the other hand, Mallah was part of the lower-caste Sudras, as was Devi. Under the leadership of Gujar, "the hierarchy in the gang had more or less reflected the social order as it stands in villages." By killing Gujar and "taking over leadership of the gang, he [Mallah] had completely reversed the balance of power within it" (75).

The violence between Gujar and Mallah is provoked when Gujar "repeatedly raped her [Devi] during the first two days of captivity" (72). The rape is not merely the rape of Devi by Gujar, but the rape of the lower-caste community by the upper-caste. This upper-caste arrogance is depicted through the dehumanizing sequence on the second day when a drunk Gujar "dragged her [Devi] by the arm from one man to the next, asking if anyone wanted 'a taste of this Sudra [low-caste] whore.'" Reading Sen's biography against Devi's mediated autobiography, *The Bandit Queen of India*, enables us to understand how Mallah's intervention between Gujar and Devi renders Devi's body merely into a sign of caste honor: "'Why are you trying to protect her?' asked one-eye. 'Why her? We've had so many other girls before. What is it about this one?'" Mallah replies: "I told you not to touch her. She belongs to my community" (240). Returning to *India's Bandit Queen*, Gujar says that no "Mallah dog" would stop him and declares: "I'll teach you to remember that this is a gang made up of Thakur [warrior-caste] men . . . not fishermen" (74).[10] The fight ends in Mallah shooting Gujar dead.

However, for the only woman in the band, protection from violence can only be bartered: "That night, at another campsite, Vikram Mallah informed her that she was now his woman and therefore beyond the reach of other men." Mala Sen offers a clinching summary of the groundwork of the relationship between Mallah and Devi which later flourishes into love and marriage: "When asked by a journalist, soon after her surrender, why she had become Vikram's mistress so readily she replied: 'A piece of property has no choice.'" (76). In another touching reflection of her complicated feelings, Devi confesses in her testimonial: "But many years later, thinking about it, I would ask myself why didn't this man, if he loved me as he said, just let me go? Then I wouldn't have become a bandit like him" (*BQI* 270). For all intents and purposes, the woman bandit thus remains sexual property for both upper-caste and lower-caste male leadership. Hence, romantic love within banditry is secured by caste politics as well as by the contest of prowess between males.

As Mallah's upper-caste mentor, Shri Ram, is released from prison and joins the band, the caste war is restaged in the conflict between mentor and protégé over Devi. Mallah is killed, and in a culminating spectacle of public shaming for transgressing caste hierarchy by repelling Shri Ram's advances, Phoolan Devi is paraded naked through the villages of the Chambal Valley in northern India: "I saw crowds of faces and I was naked in front of them. Demons came without end from the fires of Naraka [hell] to rape me" (370).

---

[10] As Thakurs and Gujars are subcastes of Khatriyas, ranked just below the Brahmins, the Mallahs are subcastes of Sudras, who belong to the lowest rung of the caste system.

The theme of concubinage brings together the stories of Phoolan Devi and Dopdi Mehjen in Mahasweta Devi's "Draupadi." The name Dopdi is the colloquial form of Draupadi in the classical epic *Mahabharata*, in which Draupadi was married to five husbands and provides an exceptional instance of polyandry, "not a common system of marriage in India." Her honor is waged in a game of dice between her husbands and their rival cousins. Mahasweta Devi's short story rewrites the classical epic "by placing Dopdi first in a comradely, activist, monogamous marriage and then in a situation of multiple rape."[11] As in stories of non-Hindu tribal women like Dopdi Mehjen, the convict narratives of lower-caste Hindu women like Phoolan Devi revise conventional notions of the feminine in the founding epics of Hinduism by redefining the traditional relationship of the protector and the protected between men and women.

DEFYING THE DEFINITION: RECAST(E)ING THE WOMAN CRIMINAL

The framing of the lower-caste woman as the goddess becomes a point of entry to understand how the caste dynamics of criminalization is unsettled through a politics of faith.

The Warrior Goddess

It is an uneasy combination when the lives of lower-caste women, militant against the Hindu caste system, are mythologized as the exploits of Hindu warrior goddesses. However, can there be an alternative and a more empowered reading of such an allegorical representation? What kind of values do such goddess-identified lower-caste women take up in the context of caste-marked minority politics on the national and the global platform?

Durga and Kali become the reigning metaphors for the mythical subtexts of *India's Bandit Queen* and *The Bandit Queen of India*. The searing agony of Devi's marital rape by Putti Lal invokes the fierce iconography of Durga: "There was nothing I could do to stop him. But I swore to the goddess Durga who drank the blood of demons that he would pay for the pain he caused me" (*BQI* 127). She returns to castrate Putti Lal and leaves him bleeding and naked by the wayside. The text is again articulate with Devi's goddess-identified rhetoric of empowerment after she survives the police custodial torture: "I began to wonder if there was some force in me they were all trying to crush [. . .] I resolved to hang onto this force that was a gift of Durga" (200). Finally, in a mythic tableau in which Devi literally reincarnates Durga's slaying of the demon Mahisasur, Devi unleashes the rage of the goddess in a bedlam of castration and carnage. In a spectacle of sexual revenge, she strips the village men who had once protected the torturers who had raped and paraded her naked through the village. Likewise, she marches them naked

---

[11] Spivak 1998, 10.

through the village. The text records her bloody ecstasy: "I beat them between their legs with my rifle butt. I wanted to destroy the serpent that represented their power over me . . ." (396).

This personal vengeance is translated into cosmic retaliation, embodying peace for all that is feminine when the violent upper-caste male is sacrificed before the warrior goddess. He had outraged the village women, raped his daughter and daughter-in-law, and engaged in bestiality and pedophilic violations of young boys: "His serpent first, then his hands, then his feet . . . I cut them off. I did it before the image of the Durga, to give her peace" (*BQI* 398). This is the resilient rage of Mahasweta Devi's Dopdi Mehjen. Unlike the classical Draupadi who prays to Lord Krishna to prevent her public stripping by her husbands' cousins, Dopdi "remains publicly naked at her own insistence." Spivak summarizes: "the story insists that this is the place where male leadership stops" (11). Like Phoolan Devi who emasculates her torturers by refusing to continue in the realm of shame, Dopdi declares: "There isn't a man here that I should be ashamed. I will not let you put my cloth on me" (36).

However, it is only with the unprecedented massacre of twenty-two high-caste men by Devi that her fierce devotional justice marks the electoral politics of postcolonial India. In her introduction to *India's Bandit Queen* Sen recounts:

> The Thakurs (landowners) of UP organized demonstrations in neighbouring towns calling for justice, and the government in Delhi, led by Indira Gandhi, could not ignore their protest, for they delivered "block votes" from just such isolated hamlets scattered throughout the region. (xix)

With her entry into the realm of national politics, the press reconstructs Devi in the image of Kali rather than Durga. She "wielded the fearsome sword of Kali, the patron saint of thuggees" [bandits] (*IBQ* 408). Sarah Caldwell argues: "Whereas Kali embodies the pure power of destruction and is a manifestation of ultimate disorder, Durga is self-controlled and protective, a representative of the true cosmic order" (174).[12] This shift in iconicity from Durga to Kali is also played out on the eve of Devi's surrender to the Indian government as women pray to her, "whispering in confidence that she was the reincarnation of Kali, warrior goddess worshipped throughout the Chambal Valley" (*IBQ* 215).

Nonetheless, such a reading of female criminality can be criticized as problematic in the current Indian context of majoritarian Hindu politics against the Muslim minority. The Rashtra Sevika Samiti—the women's wing of the paramilitary Hindu nationalist organization Rashtriya Swayamsevak Sangh—mobilizes the fierce divinity of Bharatmata and Ashta Bhuja. They are symbolic of a violent feminine Hindu nationalism against a demonic Muslim male sexuality.[13] However, I argue that the figure of the goddess-

---

[12] Caldwell's argument (2004, 160–78) has been particularly helpful in locating the goddess discourse in *The Bandit Queen of India*.
[13] See Bacchetta 1994 (134–7).

identified woman bandit opposes such majority politics because Phoolan Devi's warrior goddess is not derived from mainstream Vedic Hinduism, but from the pre-Vedic Tantric and Shaktic practices of the Hindu minority who the Sangh was to exclude from citizenship.[14]

In India, Tantric and Shaktic practices of Kali have been traced to pre-Aryan times via archaeological evidence of the worship of fertility through the mother goddess.[15] The Brahminical religion of the Aryans who migrated to India around 1500 BC restricted the powerful sexuality of these female divinities by "providing orthodox male deities as husbands for the mother goddesses" (Liddle & Joshi 52–4). In a Tantric/Shaktic reading of Phoolan Devi as the militant goddess, the lower-caste woman resists being appropriated by Vedic Hindutva in which the woman remains "inconsequential without relationships with men." Through her Tantric/Shaktic practice she "maintains the world and fights without male directions and support against male demons" (Pathak & Sengupta 295). Such an understanding of militancy refuses Rajeswari Sunder Rajan's democratic feminist argument that salvaging the goddess to empower women will inevitably lead to a majority stand.[16] Rightfully so, because the Samajwadi Party with a largely lower-caste constituency, instrumental in Devi's release from prison and in shaping her political career, failed to contain her resistive feminist vision of a separate women's wing of the party. For many lower-caste women in India like Phoolan Devi, *bhakti* (devotion) to the warrior goddess remains a matter of personal faith—an everyday practice rather than an institutionalized religion.[17] *Bhakti* is "widely recognized as a historical challenge from within to the caste-fixed inflexibility of high Hinduism" (Spivak 2001,126). As a subcultural practice which gave "the lie to caste and scripture," *bhakti* "opened doors for women's agency" (127). By overwriting the faith of lower-caste women in the interest of national unity in the secular democratic nation-state, one fails to step out of the colonial frame which established the nation-state as the marker of political identity and indigenous faith as an impediment to modernization. In the transnational realm of feminist politics it is lower-caste women like Phoolan Devi who unsettle the dominant logic of Euro-American political correctness. In this secular agnostic world of left elitism she injects her own

---

[14] See Pathak & Sengupta 1995 (293); Bacchetta (135).
[15] See Liddle & Joshi 1986 (54).
[16] See Rajeswari Sunder Rajan 2001 (212–26).
[17] Debjani Ganguly emphasizes the importance of defining caste as everyday practice rather than through historical movements against injustice. However, I explore how convict narratives define caste through everyday practices like that of *bhakti* which nonetheless take up revolutionary dimensions, often influencing the international arena of anti-discrimination politics through collaborative storytelling. Ganguly's insistence on the need for a subversive theorization of *bhakti* has triggered my interest in the issue: "Even Ranajit Guha, who formulated a way of interpreting the domain of power and politics in South Asia that would resist both secular-historicist readings of India's past and the paradigm of modernization, is unable to theorize *bhakti*. He does not, however, talk of the democratic potential of *bhakti*." See Ganguly 2005 (xxii, 175).

brand of faith—*bhakti*—derived from practical rather than scriptural Hinduism—itself a minority culture in the global scenario.

Conclusion

Although Devi defined her choice of a personal faith in proto-Hindu religious icons, her convict narratives uphold her militancy against the oppressive social configuration of Hinduism. However, though Devi did not step into it, there is surely an ongoing postcolonial reclamation of the lower castes through the mobilization of goddesses in the interest of Hindu religious revivalism in India. Nevertheless, one cannot discount that the category of caste has returned to forge new opportunities for progressive politics through transnational political citizenship.[18] Caste has come to take on a new significance in the postcolonial nation-state. In the electoral politics of India votes are mobilized through caste alliances. As such, the lower castes are increasingly able to form an opposition to the higher castes by forming their own political constituencies via national elections. Such political access has enabled the lower castes and the casteless to place themselves on the national and the transnational map of historic injustice by relocating caste from the realm of religion to that of racial discrimination. The Scheduled Castes and Scheduled Tribes Prevention of Atrocities Act was passed by the Indian government in 1989.[19] Though caste politics affects other countries, its discussion in the international arena had been blocked for so long mainly by the government of India.[20] In the wake of the July 25, 2001, assassination of Phoolan Devi, caste was staged for the first time by the UN at the World Conference against Racism, Racial Discrimination, Xenophobia and Related Intolerance on August 27–September 1, 2001.

Characters

(In Order of Appearance in this Essay)
India's Bandit Queen and
Bandit Queen of India
    Phoolan Devi: Protagonist
    Bihari: Devi's uncle
    Devidin: Devi's father
    Mayadin: Bihari's son
    Putti Lal: Devi's husband
    Rukmini: Devi's sister
    Pradhan: Village leader

"Draupadi"
Dopdi Mehjen: Protagonist
Draupadi: Namesake (Classical Epic)
Lord Krishna: Draupadi's Friend
Surya Sahu: Landowner

---

[18] Nicholas Dirks' (2001) insightful understanding of the progressive role of caste in the postcolonial context has been especially informative for my comprehension of a postcolonial-transnational politics of caste.
[19] See Human Rights Watch 1999 (218–45).
[20] See Footnote #2.

154   Part IV: Narrating Violence

                Sarpanch: Village headman
                 Kailash: Devi's cousin
     Babu Gujar Singh: Bandit leader
       Vikram Mallah: Gujar's gang member, Devi's partner
                Shri Ram: Mallah's mentor

References

Bacchetta, Paola. "'All Our Goddesses are Armed': Religion, Resistance and Revenge in the Life of a Militant Hindu Nationalist Woman." *Against All Odds: Essays on Women, Religion and Development from India and Pakistan.* Ed. Kamla Bhasin, Ritu Mennon, Nighat Said Khan. New Delhi, India & Quezon City, Philippines: Isis International & Kali for Women, 1994. 133–56.

Caldwell, Sarah. "Subverting the Fierce Goddess: Phoolan Devi and the Politics of Vengeance." *Playing for Real: Hindu Role Models, Religion, and Gender.* Ed. Jacqueline Suthren Hirst & Lynn Thomas. Oxford & New York: Oxford University Press, 2004.

Constitution of India. Art. 17. <http://indiacode.nic.in/coiweb/welcome.html>.

Danner, Mona J. E. "Gender Inequality and Criminalization: A Socialist Feminist Perspective on Legal Social Control of Women." *Race, Gender, and Class in Criminology: The Intersection.* Ed. Martin D. Schwartz and Dragan Milovanovic. New York & London: Garland Publishing, 1996. 29–48.

Devi, Mahasweta. "Draupadi." *Breast Stories.* Trans. Gayatri Chakravorty Spivak. Calcutta: Seagull, 1998. 19–38.

Devi, Phoolan, Marie-Thérèse Cuny, & Paul Rambali. *The Bandit Queen of India: An Indian Woman's Amazing Journey from Peasant to International Legend.* Guilford, CT: Lyons Press, 2003.

Dirks, Nicholas B. *Castes of Mind: Colonialism and the Making of Modern India.* Princeton & Oxford: Princeton University Press, 2001.

Ganguly, Debjani. *Caste, Colonialism and Counter-Modernity: Notes on a Postcolonial Hermeneutics of Caste.* London and New York: Routledge, 2005.

Human Rights Watch. *Broken People: Caste Violence against India's Untouchables.* New York, Washington, London, & Brussels: Human Rights Watch, 1999.

Liddle, Joanna & Rama Joshi. *Daughters of Independence: Gender, Caste and Class in India.* London, UK and New Delhi, India: Zed and Kali for Women, 1986.

Narrain, Siddharth. "Ambivalence in the Law." *Frontline* 22, 14 (Jul 02–15, 2005). <http://www.hinduonnet.com/fline/fl2214/stories/20050715004802300.htm>.

Pathak, Zakia & Saswati Sengupta. "Resisting Women." *Women and the Hindu Right: A Collection of Essays.* Eds. Tanika Sarkar & Urvashi Butalia. New Delhi, India: Kali for Women, 1995. 270–98.

Prove, Peter. "Working Paper on Discrimination on the Basis of Work and Descent: Call for Submissions." Retrieved Nov. 6, 2000, from <http://www.ambedkar.org/UN/WorkingPaper.htm>.

Rajan, Rajeswari Sunder. *The Scandal of the State: Women, Law, and Citizenship in Postcolonial India.* Durham & London: Duke University Press, 2003.

———. "Feminism and the Politics of the Hindu Goddess." *Feminist Locations: Global and Local, Theory and Practice.* Ed. Marianne DeKoven. New Brunswick, NJ, & London: Rutgers University Press, 2001.

Sen, Mala. *India's Bandit Queen: The True Story of Phoolan Devi.* New Delhi: HarperCollins, 1993.

———. Introduction. *India's Bandit Queen: The True Story of Phoolan Devi*. By Mala Sen. New Delhi: HarperCollins, 1993. xix–xxiv.
Spivak, Gayatri Chakravorty. Draupadi: translator's foreword. *Breast Stories*. By Mahasweta Devi. Trans. Gayatri Chakravorty Spivak. Calcutta; Seagull, 1998. 1–18.
———. "Moving Devi." *Cultural Critique* 47 (2001): 120–63.

Part V

Violence as an Aesthetic

Sou Marginal Mesmo (I Am the Real Hoodlum) Using Violence as a Resource in Brazilian Hip Hop

Derek Pardue

> I'm not surprised that the audience applauded the violence, because I wanted them to be complicit in it. I wanted them to be involved in it, because you have to ask yourself after the movie is over how they feel about their complicity in these violent acts ... because if it's done in such a way that the audience is repulsed and held outside of the movie, then I've actually lost the opportunity to deliver to them the paradox of enjoying something that morally you find reprehensible.
>
> —David Cronenberg[1]

Not only do we as humans practice physical violence in many forms, but we also engage in various expressive forms of violence as a symbolic field of power and knowledge. In urban Brazil, hip hoppers are entrenched in the business of representing violence. Their differences of opinion regarding violence have led in great part to stylistic innovation over the past several years. While there exists significant variability among Brazilian hip hop styles and messages, locals use the categories of "positive" and "marginal" in their characterization of a particular group or the scene as a whole. For their part, "positive" hip hoppers employ universalist, spiritual, and/or African diasporic perspective to their performance. Contrary to its conventional connotation, "marginal" in this case refers to the dominant, most common style and attitude. Central to the "marginal" hip hopper (person) and hip hop style (aesthetics) is the representation of violence. In this essay I discuss the mean-

---

Written especially for *Ruminations on Violence*.

[1] Comments made by film director Cronenberg at a press conference during the 2005 Cannes Film Festival regarding his film, *A History of Violence*.

ings behind making violence an aesthetic (i.e., something appreciated as a commodity or as "being cool"). In addition, I demonstrate how violence has become part of a complex rhetoric of truth in Brazilian hip hop. For many hip hoppers in São Paulo, a "good" performer is one who is able to, extrapolating David Cronenberg's statements about film to hip hop, make the audience aware of their "complicity" in violence. Violence is not only an act of performative flair but also one of ideological elicitation.

Unlike the monetary situation of rappers and more general hip hoppers in the United States, especially at the "mainstream" level, there is relatively little money to be made in the business of hip hop in Brazil. This factor along with others, including variable systems of capitalism, masculinity, racial identity, and notion of humility, distinguish the meanings of U.S. and Brazilian hip hop cultural practices. One of the by-products of such differences is encapsulated in the following Brazilian hip hop slogan made famous by popular South Side São Paulo rapper Sabotage in 2002: "Hip hop is an obligation" (*Hip hop é compromiso*). The "obligation" is with respect to representation; and although there is significant variability in the methods and forms of hip hop representation, hip hoppers of all ages, styles ("marginal" or "positive"), and levels of public visibility understand that violence is part of hip hop. In fact, Sabotage, a figure from a "marginal" past who helped popularize "positive" hip hop, was murdered on January 24, 2003. In the following pages, I discuss why and how local hip hoppers in São Paulo, Brazil, the center of Brazilian hip hop, use and deploy violence as an aesthetic marker in the making of compact disc cover art and T-shirts as well as in the defining of hip hop in public debate. I have selected three ethnographic scenes to illustrate the "materiality" and "performativity" of violence, respectively.[2]

VIOLENCE AS A HIP HOP ESSENTIAL

Hip hop's *raison d'être* is the representation of "reality" in the (sub)urban periphery (*periferia*), and thus practitioners tend to be heavy-handed and overtly ideological in their approach to forms and practices of hip hop. In addition, most hip hoppers argue that in the performance of "reality" there is a chance for change or what is heralded in the community as *transformação* (transformation). The social fact that daily violence constitutes a significant part of hip hop "reality" in São Paulo requires that hip hoppers—those who are "real" and not "fake" or "wannabes"—must appreciate the impact of violence on the essential constitution of that "reality," with the foundational goal of narration and representation.

---

[2] I am referencing the small but important body of literature on the "materiality of violence" within contemporary cultural criticism of global expressive arts. For example, see Aldama and Lockhard (2002). In addition, I borrow "performativity" from feminist literature regarding the status of gender and sexuality as achieved and further "performed" categories rather than ascribed ones. For example, see Butler (1990) and, in the case of Brazil, see Kulick (1998).

Such an awareness of hip hop "obligation" and "reality" was not immediate in coming, although some emcees/rappers and B-boys (various practitioners of street dance, including poppin', lockin', and break dance) were explicit about the need to represent violence early on in Brazil's hip hop history. For example, Thaíde, a foundational figure of Brazilian hip hop as B-boy and emcee, wrote and rhymed lyrics directly related to police violence and social stratification in his 1988 hit song "Homens da Lei" (literally "Men of the Law," discussed later in this essay). It wouldn't be until the mid-1990s and the rise of Mano Brown and the Racionais MCs (Rational Emcees) rap group that violence embodied in the marginal style would emerge as a systematic narrative and representational paradigm.[3]

Most pertinent to this essay is the keyword "marginal." The term, which loosely translates into English as hoodlum, criminal, or delinquent is, in fact, a geographical term. It derives from the periods of industrialization and urbanization in post–WWII Brazil, in particular with regard to São Paulo and Rio de Janeiro. The decades of the 1950s, 1960s, and 1970s saw a major shift in domestic demographics as millions of Brazilians migrated from locales in the Northeast (Bahia, Pernambuco, northern Minas Gerais states) to the Southeast. As municipal governments were both unwilling and unable to keep up and provide basic infrastructure for the arriving masses, many newcomers built their own homes and created their own communities in what came to be known as the modern "periphery."[4] Tensions and conflict over basic services have resulted in both the cultivation of alternative networks of livelihood and infrastructure, some of which involve organized crime, and the general perception that the *periferia* naturally breeds a certain type of person—an uneducated, traditional, tragic figure with criminal tendencies. This is the *marginal*, a discursive and ideological imposition of "natural" hierarchy based on sociogeographical dynamics. For many in hip hop, it is precisely the long-standing, pejorative notion of what marginal means in Brazil that they try to subvert in an act of empowerment. In essence, many marginal hip hoppers, such as Shabazz (described below) are saying: "Yes, we are marginal but we demand the right to define ourselves. Through hip hop we are able to do just that."

In terms of violence, hip hoppers find themselves in a difficult and often precarious position, because they know that to report violence in a transparent manner without any other message or "consciousness" may alienate them from local hip hop and general community activists,[5] who preach citizenship through critique of both the State or the "system" (*o sistema*) and

---

[3] I discuss such histories and style developments at length elsewhere (Pardue 2004).
[4] Some examples of the literature pertaining to São Paulo's urbanization and social stratification include Sevcenko 1993; Caldeira 2000; Fabris 2000; Holston 1991; Magnini 1992; Maricato 1979; Ponciano 2001; Rolnik, Kowarick, and Somekh 1991; Sachs 1999.
[5] Since Brazilian hip hop was founded on tenets of "community" and "social change," many hip hoppers interpret straightforward reports of daily violence as reinforcing the "system" and the commonly held knowledge about the "periphery."

organized crime (*o lado do crime*). The ensuing loss of face is a significant concern for hip hoppers upon consideration of the fact that pure economic commerce still does not drive the majority of hip hop in Brazil. There are no Brazilian versions of the U.S. rapper "50-Cent"—artists who command hundreds of thousands of fans through repetitive verses of thug life and detailed conspicuous consumption (i.e., "bling").

Furthermore, hip hoppers are not gangsters. Although some hip hoppers (most famously the fallen rapper Sabotage) have had past experiences in lower-level drug trafficking—the most common and accessible position of power and violence—the overwhelming majority of hip hoppers have explicitly rejected this lifestyle and have intentionally turned to hip hop as a cultural and political solution (*solução*) to violence and crime. Solução is another keyword in hip hop mantras of reality, transformation, and agency.[6] Those who have engaged experiences with crime almost always claim hip hop as a salvation (*salvação*) from their past life of crime and explicit violence.

With that said, violence pervades the landscape, the psyche, and the discourse of *periferia* in contemporary São Paulo. It is unavoidable as it manifests itself in brutal police sweeps to periodically "clean up" the periphery, bloody territorial skirmishes by drug trafficking youth armies, precarious living conditions with entire neighborhoods located in mudslide or hazardous watershed areas, and daily discourse from the media (late afternoon television programs, cheap tabloid "popular" newspapers, etc.). These sources of information maintain the "common sense" notion that the *periferia* is a place of senseless violence and tragedy. Hip hoppers know and (as Marquinhos—an elder statesman whose pop music participation bridges the soul, disco, funk, and early hip hop periods in São Paulo—continually told me), hip hoppers *feel* (*a gente sente*) the periphery. They know most of the local criminal elements. During the long walk from the last bus stop (the end of the line) to his house in Jardim São Rafael on the extreme East Side of São Paulo, Marquinhos explained:

> We [present day criminals and I] grew up together. I give recognition to them. They know me; they know I've always been here and I understand the way things work. I chose hip hop. I do not agree with everything they do, but there is mutual respect between us. It's normal. At least they are not police officers. They [police officers] have no morality. With them there is only rage. That's it.

In sum, violence stands as a rich but conflicted resource of hip hop representation. Ultimately, hip hoppers, especially rappers, must choose whether they want to emphasize *reality* or *transformation* as their creative drive to per-

---

[6] While many hip hoppers, in practice, hedge their bets with regard to violence and crime due to various conflicting pressures, some have taken a public stand against the commercialization of guns, for example. In October of 2005, an initiative known as "SIM ou NÃO" [yes or no] was placed on the national ballot. Various hip hoppers created Aliança Hip Hop Pelo SIM (Hip Hop Alliance for Yes [to the banning of arms commerce]).

form. This brief epistemological background of Brazilian hip hoppers' construal of violence helps explain the three following ethnographic cases of representational methodology—compact disc cover art and T-shirt design (image) and public debate posturing (rhetoric).

BR: "No Funny Business"

In December of 2000 members of the Santo André group BR met to make a decision about the "look" of their brand of hip hop. While each member had different visions of the appropriate design and group members differed in the most effective way to actually get this job done, all members agreed that the "look" could go a long way in eliciting a special recognition among consumers—*algo diferente mas não fugindo a realidade cotidiana* (something different but getting away from the reality of daily life). Indeed, the trick is to create distinction, often encapsulated in the term *independente* (independent or underground), while simultaneously connected to the common genre of everyday life narratives. Alex, Urubu (literally "vulture"), DJ Reino, and leader Cérebro ("brain") met in the São Paulo downtown *galerias* (malls) with their *aliado* (ally) and contact, Jota (a fanzine writer from Jundiaí, a city on the outskirts of the metro area). The demo CD was completed, but the debate now centered on the cover.

I had arranged a meeting with Urubu and when I arrived at the designated *lanchonete* (grilled sandwich and juice stand), the members of BR had clearly only begun to discuss the visuals of their CD demo. Passing around group photos, magazine cutouts, and ketchup, Urubu and Cérebro, in particular, argued for a cover that featured a *chapada* (a sharply focused image): They felt that the profile (*perfil*) of BR was "in your face, straight up, no funny stuff" (*Tudo na cara, sem comédia*). "Let's use that picture from the show in Jundiaí with our *aliado* Jota. It's crazy." This desired effect could be most effectively achieved with a photo in 100% sharp focus, with defined boundaries of colors. In this case, *chapada* refers to an image with a relatively small radius of focus (i.e., f-stop on a conventional camera set very low) to emphasize the contrast of the focal point with the surroundings. The members of BR were following the aesthetic of Brazilian rappers Ndee Naldinho and Gog, as they linked the intense focus to their purpose of an "in-your-face" approach to rap and hip hop in general.

Jota made contact with members of BR back in 1999 during an "all elements" (all four hip hop practices: rap, DJ, graffiti, street dance, or B-boy/girl) show held in the public plaza in Santo André. I met Jota at the Jundiaí show, a cultural event sponsored by the local Department of Culture as part of the annual Grape Festival. Urubu had asked me to make the trek out to Jundiaí and take some photos. It was, in fact, one of these black-and-white pictures that Urubu and Cérebro had identified as *chapada*. It was perfectly sharp and also perfectly ripe for recontextualization. Urubu focused on the faces and cut away the tranquil surroundings of the immense public park where the event took place. Group members went back and forth: "*Joga a gente num alvo*—It's like Naldinho. We are a target (*alvo*). *O sistema* (the system) is like that. We are not artists. No, [let's] just use our eyes and we'll be looking down on the *periferia*. It's serious." It had to be "in your face." This is *chapada*—the "perfect" depiction. The members of BR saw themselves as unavoidably in focus and as a target of a number of forces, explicitly named as the "system" but implicitly associated with police violence, unemployment, and state abandonment.

Unfortunately, BR never advanced past the demo stage. For various reasons, they never were able to release a commercial product. In early 2001 DJ Reino joined the millions of unemployed in the São Paulo metro area.[7] For months he couldn't afford transportation fare to attend any group meetings or important hip hop events. In fact, he walked miles during the week simply to interview for potential jobs. Urubu became serious with a new girlfriend and Alex became a father of twins. They had intended to *somar*, to join other hip hoppers in what they had interpreted as a movement of reality representation. The story of BR is not a success story of artistic genius and entrepreneurial savvy; rather, it is a story that represents the dominant intention of São Paulo hip hoppers.

Participants connect hip hop ideologies and communicative graphics with the material and social conditions of *periferia* places. Hip hop participants preach art as "work" and beyond mere "representation" or "mimesis." Art, in this sense, is productive as the form and content engage in dialogue to affect a potentially resistant signifying practice. The following fieldwork vignette demonstrates such an articulation.

"Marginal" Gore and Empowering Narration

In March of 2002, I met DJ Giba in what appeared to me to be a festival of gore performed in local hip hop style. This seemed to be a typical "marginal" hip hop event. Some days prior, DJ Giba, the key hip hop figure at the community radio station Radio Alerte, had invited me to a hip hop event sponsored by the editor of *Rap Brasil*, one of the leading hip hop magazines in the country. Located in a nameless downtown nightclub, the show featured a series of local DJs and rappers. They competed for an interview spot in an upcoming issue of *Rap Brasil*. The master of ceremonies, magazine editor Rogério, tried to keep the audience interested and hyped by constantly promising the appearance of Gog, the legendary rapper from Brasília now living in nearby Campinas and recording in São Paulo. Gog had brought his "family," a group of young rappers and DJs he was promoting.

---

[7] According to the statistics collected by IBGE (Brazilian Institute of Geography and Statistics), the main agency of demography in Brazil, the national rate of unemployment in the second half of 2001 hovered between 5.3% and 5.5%. In the metropolitan area of São Paulo the percentage was nearly double this figure, and in areas classified as "periphery" or "suburbs" the rate was nearly 18%.

After an hour of walking in circles in the bizarre after-hours neighborhood wasteland called Bom Retiro, I finally found the club. This area of São Paulo's downtown is a haven for underground sweatshops, where Korean, Brazilian, and Bolivian entrepreneurs exploit recent Bolivian and Korean immigrants (legal and illegal). It is a space of *mutirões*, group housing projects organized by local human rights workers such as Regina of Gaspar Garcia.[8] By nightfall, it is an empty and dangerous place. Clubs such as this evening's hip hop locale remain nameless for reasons of security and market turnover. Property values are at rock bottom and risks of violence are high, and therefore there is little motivation to invest in a theme-oriented nightclub. It changes from hip hop to *forró* (a genre of Northeastern folk music) to heavy metal to whatever.

I found DJ Giba glowing. He admired Rogério and felt honored to be a judge for the contest. We watched the rappers together, and in between acts I asked Giba about his scores and his approach to being a judge. We screamed back and forth to be heard, and I finally convinced him to reveal his categories of evaluation: message, consciousness, reality, DJ performance, and rhyming skill.

After the third or fourth group, I couldn't help but notice that all the lyrics were about death and the gory details of *periferia* violence. One rapper, in particular, sported a homemade T-shirt and baseball cap featuring guns and blood as visual motifs. I asked Giba about the name of the group, *Solução* (Solution): What kind of "solution" was this? Giba explained that, in fact, he knew this *moleque* (kid). He lived near Radio Alerte in a typical East Side, working-class, "periphery" neighborhood and often called in to ask questions and participate in live interviews with rappers and DJs during the radio shows. Giba went on to say that through these conversations he knew that this rapper modeled himself after Facção Central (Central Faction), a group Giba himself admired. Giba impressed upon me the importance of telling stories of violence. "*É muito radical fazer isso aí*" (this very act [talking about daily violence] is radical), according to Giba.

As part of his radio shows, Giba and listeners share stories of daily violence. Giba claimed that through his radio shows, communities have formed. "We exchange information and we learn from each other." Although in his role of judge Giba felt that Solução needed to work on their stage performance and rhyme schemes, he gave them high scores on message, consciousness, and reality. As an aside, Giba commented to me that he appreciated the T-shirt and cap, because they signaled a basic, but important, "attitude" that "*não tem mais silêncio na periferia*" (we [those in the *periferia*] are no longer silent). For Giba, the members of Solução, and others, the gory details of violence and death are not merely spectacle and fanfare; they are part of (re)imaging and (re)imagining the *periferia*. For them this marks an end to the taboo of aestheticizing the elements of daily life.

---

[8] The namesake of the organization, Gaspar Garcia, was a Spanish *frei* (Catholic "brother") who was involved with various literacy programs in Nicaragua and was killed during the civil war in the 1980s.

POLICE VIOLENCE AND HIP HOP DENOUNCEMENTS

In the last ethnographic scene I move from image to rhetoric. Most frequently, hip hoppers articulate violence as a "reality rhetoric" to the tense relations between periphery neighborhood residents and members of the police.

One of hip hop's main continuities with past forms of African American and Latino/Latin American popular expression is the denouncement or indictment.[9] In Brazil this is known as the *denúncia* and since 1997 and the release of the rap recording *Sobrevivendo no Inferno* (Surviving in Hell) by the now legendary group Racionais MCs, the *denúncia* has become the leading narrative paradigm for Brazilian rappers. As a generic term in Brazilian Portuguese, *denúncia* conventionally refers to written or verbal reports about crime. Hip hoppers' appropriation and refashioning of the "indictment" as a source of narrative creativity and potential power as an agent of change fall squarely within the long-standing history of "flipping scripts" as evidenced in a variety of terms ranging from the fairly innocuous "bad" to the controversial "nigger/a." Whereas in the United States, the United Kingdom, and France, much of hip hop rescripting of terms revolves around race, Brazilian hip hoppers' use of "indictment" is one more riff in a series of keywords that focus on the conditions of violence and the individual character of the marginal.

Essentially, what Mano Brown, the front man of the Racionais MCs, MV Bill from Rio de Janeiro, and so many other lesser known and relatively anonymous youth have done is to transform the song lyric into a long, detailed report describing the daily acts of prejudice-based violence exercised by police and, to a lesser extent, by members of local organized crime syndicates. As a commodity, the *denúncia* succeeds to the extent to which the composer/rapper is able to impose his (seldom her) report through refined narrative skills. Such skills include intonation, rhyme scheme, vocal emphasis, and cohesion between word and sound in his collaboration with the DJ and sound engineer (often the same person).

The above layout serves as a background to the following ethnographic description of a public debate held in July of 2005. In early 2005, a group of twelve individuals from a variety of institutions including youth community centers, hip hop cultural centers, and "alternative" education committees organized the fifth annual "Hip Hop Culture Week" under the auspices of the NGO Ação Educativa (literally, Educational Action) located in downtown São Paulo. Each day of the week corresponded to a different main topic. For Wednesday, the topic of debate was "Violence: Hip Hop's Accomplice." The coordinators invited local B-boy and neighborhood activist Shabazz, elder

---

[9] The joining of African American and Latino (particularly Nuyorican and Chicano) in this phrase is a purposeful reference to what studious, knowledgeable (often older) hip hop aficionados know and what hip hop scholars Rivera, Flores, and others have demonstrated over the past decade—namely, that hip hop in the United States was founded as a "black" and Latino "thing" based on various common threads of existence, residential proximities, and artistic borrowings. For more detail, see Rivera 2003 and Flores 2000.

rapper Azul, and me. The debate was organized informally as a roundtable discussion with ample opportunity for audience members to ask questions, make interjections, and tell their own stories. My invitation to participate in the debate was the result of an attempt to include an educator, academic, journalist—someone who was a "professional" and a "sympathizer" with hip hop (or what is frequently glossed by hip hoppers as *o movimento*—the movement).

"Loss of Reflexivity" and "The Police are a Separate Race"

This general outline of Brazilian hip hoppers' relationship with violence helps one understand the underlying tension and ideological differences in the room that night in July of 2005. I began the debate by restating basic hip hop representational ethics and strategies—namely, that hip hop is built on knowledge of self expanded through a growing, dynamic "consciousness" of social economic, political, and cultural forces. Expression of the latter is glossed in the term *respect*. Hip hop is education because it forces the practitioner to engage the world, engage one's self, and ultimately formulate a sense of one's position within the world. In this popularized version of Paulo Freire's theories, education is the recognition of one's place in the world and the articulation of the various contexts and forces influencing such positions. Violence, both physical and symbolic, occupies the hip hop landscape and experience. Thus, by means of the four "elements" (rap or emcee, DJ, graffiti, and street dance) hip hoppers incorporate violence as both a demonstration of "real" knowledge and a provocation for others to engage their worlds in a similar manner. Due to the relative transparency of rap representation (descriptive language), I used rap lyrics to make my point explicitly. I cited the following two examples from the legendary rapper Thaíde and local rap crew Mira Direta (members of which have now become Os Alquimistas).

> Watch out people of São Paulo, from Osasco to the ABC
> The police are here to protect
> Corruption and extortion; this is the real law
> The big guys kill the masses and never go to jail . . .
> I didn't understand what they were grilling me about
> For them it's just for fun
> With their good image, more money is spent
> Is São Paulo [really] a safe state? . . .
>
> If they're [police] the ones that can escape death
> Then I also want to be like them
> Ignorant and disrespectful
> Hit any kid for no reason
> Walk freely without a care in the world . . .[10]

---

[10] Author's translation of an excerpt of the lyrics from Thaíde and DJ Hum's [Homens da Lei] ([Men of the Law]) on the compilation recording, *Hip hop Cultura de Rua* (El Dorado, 1988).

168   Part V: Violence as an Aesthetic

* * *

> Brazil, a divided country that others formed
> and because they were white,
> they think my people have to pay the bill.
> Clowns.
> We are the essence, black women and black men are the essence of Brazil . . .
> A question mark on top of the black man's head has been sighted . . .
> questions without answers . . .
> Stop, think, wake up, act. With a strong will,
> We can change all of this. [11]

In the case of "Men of the Law," I stressed Thaíde's call for reflection on police corruption and impunity. In his recent autobiography, Thaíde discusses the tense situations he and DJ Hum found themselves in during live shows, as the hired guards constantly threatened them not to sing "Homens da Lei." With "The Supposed Racial Democracy" I focused less on the content, a sharp critique of the ongoing ideology that race has nothing to do with social hierarchy in Brazil,[12] and rather highlighted the performance of reflective rhetoric.

Mira Direta's performance was effective and appreciated, because they demonstrated an important hip hop style of the period. As Brazilian hip hoppers considered themselves more "informed" about what hip hop knowledge and performance entailed, they began to explore hip hop aesthetics. By the mid-1990s many Brazilian rappers experimented with the high-speed rhetorical delivery akin to Das EFX, or even to U.S. rapper Busta Rhymes, balanced with an authoritative voice modeled on Chuck D from Public Enemy. The explosive and fast-paced sound production of The Bomb Squad (production team of Public Enemy) inspired mid-1990s hip hoppers in São Paulo to become more animated in performance and *assumir* (to "assume") a didactic posture of relating experience and showcasing knowledge. Mira Direta embodied this spirit as they screamed at the audience on that day in April of 1996 to "stop, think, wake up, and act . . . with a strong will, we can change all of this."

After discussing these two musical examples, I confessed to the audience that I worry about the status of violence in contemporary hip hop, because I

---

[11] Author's translation of an excerpt from Mira Direta's *A Suposta Democracia Racial* (The Supposed Racial Democracy), a field recording of a local performance in April 1996.

[12] The issue of "racial democracy" is one of the most documented ideologies and practices in all of the scholarship regarding Brazil. The foundational text that coined the term and historicized the notion comes from U.S.-trained sociologist Gilberto Freyre's *Casa Grande e Senzala* (1933). Despite the fact that dozens of scholars, community activists, politicians, and artists have critically deconstructed "racial democracy" as a functional framework to understand Brazil, current "common sense" and occasional publications, such as the recent Brazilian best-seller *We are not Racists* (*Não Somos Racistas*, Nova Fronteira, 2006), written in response to current initiative for racial quotas in Brazilian higher education, continue to appear and receive wide attention.

find fewer and fewer hip hoppers who employ scenes and language of violence as *reflexive*. I reserved the final few minutes to direct attention to a potential model—Afro Reggae. I cited a recent newspaper article outlining the efforts of the music-cultural group Afro Reggae[13] from Rio and their occasional workshops with police officers.[14] The article describes the intention of Afro Reggae members to create a middle ground and greater mutual understanding between locals and the police in Belo Horizonte, capital city of the state of Minas Gerais, through expressive culture (in this case graffiti). I ended my talk on a note of concern, wondering if we, too, as fans are following the urgent calls of Mira Direta to "stop, think, and reflect."

B-boy Shabazz stood up, took the microphone, returned to his seat across the public school desk being used as a coffee table in this context, and sat down. "Thank you doctor (*doutor*) for your interesting words." With that gesture, I felt slightly assured that I had succeeded in conveying a sensibility of informed appreciation and critical concern. That feeling of satisfaction, however, quickly disintegrated as Shabazz snickered and brushed me aside with a knowing laugh. Shabazz's use of "doctor" had been sarcastic. My last example of the workshops of Afro Reggae and local police in the metropolitan area of Belo Horizonte had obviously offended and enraged Shabazz. Judging from the audience reaction, Shabazz apparently was speaking on the behalf of many hip hoppers and by extension periphery dwellers. In an act of dramatic, highly performative deconstruction, Shabazz proceeded to take the keywords of "reflection" and "reality" from my talk and transform them into a vibrant platform of armed struggle against the police.

> Why am I laughing? I am trying to imagine a policeman, a person whose mission is to eliminate us in the periphery, to clean us out. ... I'm trying to imagine this person, if I can really call him a person, doing B-boy moves or doing spray-can art. Why am I laughing? That story about Belo Horizonte is propaganda. The police are another race. They're not like you or me. They massacre unarmed children. They supply drugs and arms to gangs (*bancas*) in our neighborhoods. As hip hoppers we have to tell these stories and motivate people to fight back. There is no conversation. That is the *reality*. It is one of war, or armed conflict. That is what I know. That is what everyone in Jardim Colombo and hundreds of other 'hoods (*quebradas*) know. Hip hop *reflection* should not be about limiting violence; no, it should be about more depictions of the daily violence that is killing us. That is what hip hop has always been—reports of *reality*.
>
> Do you all know what is happening in my neighborhood? I know some of you do. Let me tell you. Last Saturday, the police invaded a place where young people get together and hang out. This is not new. We've

---

[13] Greater attention worldwide has come to Afro Reggae through their involvement with Ford Foundation and in film with the recent release of *Favela Rising*, a documentary film about Afro Reggae told through the life experiences of its leader, Anderson Sá.

[14] The referenced article, "Police officers learn graffiti with youth," appeared in *Folha de São Paulo* on July 25, 2005, sec. C, p. 4.

been hanging out at this gas station on the Avenue for years now. The owner knows and he's fine with it. We listen to music, we dance, talk about whatever. There is no drug trafficking. Ok, you get it. Well, we're two fewer now. We lost two brothers. For what? These inhumane policemen invaded our space, because they thought one of us was involved with drugs. They couldn't find anything and decided to arrest all of us. We resisted. Two brothers ran and that was the wrong thing to do. They were shot. Brother Haroldo died immediately and brother Gerson lasted an hour. He couldn't fight any more. They're dead. That is the everyday in Jardim Colombo. This is what I know and what I think about. . . .

Shabazz continued for another 30 minutes, providing more details about the police reports, statistics of police violence, and police-related deaths in his neighborhood as well as within the district of Paraisópolis, the second largest favela cluster in São Paulo after Heliópolis. Paraisópolis is located immediately adjacent to Morumbi, one of the wealthiest neighborhoods in São Paulo. The sociogeographical significance of this was not lost on Shabazz, as he tended to connect rising police violence statistics with the fear and paranoia of neighboring bourgeois Morumbi residents.[15]

The audience exploded and various individuals demanded the right to speak. While a few engaged Shabazz with questions of clarification and philosophies of violence, the majority interpreted Shabazz's speech as a testimony and felt it appropriate to offer their own testimonies in the form of *denúncia*. In fact, except for a couple of curious teenagers and roaming, community journalists, I had been forgotten. Any potential conflict between Shabazz and me was soon ameliorated. We shook hands, clenched fists, and embraced. Through a brief period of e-mail exchange, it became clear that Shabazz's anger was structural and systematic, not personal. In retrospect, I realize the power of Shabazz's particular performance of violence, not for the content of what he stated or his perspective on violence and representation. Rather, what Shabazz achieved was the elicitation of narratives. As stated above, members of the audience, for the most part, were moved to tell their own stories. Through the informality of public debate, people created a real sense of collective memory related to police and everyday violence. For many, that can be as empowering as any "explanation" of violence.

AESTHETICS AND RHETORICS

In this essay I have interpreted three ethnographic scenes of hip hop violence. As is evident, the status of violence within Brazilian hip hop is an ongoing polemic. From its visualization to its narration, hip hoppers are divided as to the most effective strategy to take. As my fieldwork-based ruminations and analysis indicate, hip hoppers endure pressures of taste,

---

[15] See Caldeira (2000) for an extensive discussion of the history of fear and (in)security as part of urbanization in contemporary São Paulo.

ideology, and various armed forces on the ground. In the U.S. "mainstream"[16] rappers have simplified the aesthetics and rhetorics of violence and have led many critics to describe the late 1990s and early twenty-first-century hip hop as a process of "niggafication" full of "thugocentric" characters and iconography.[17]

Hip hop has always been about relating life experience, first and foremost, and under the rubric of "reality" or, in Brazil, *realidade,* hip hoppers have also always needed to make sense of violence. The stories told in this essay are trivial in the sense that they are told and circulated by virtually anonymous characters and scribes—no one destined for a high-profile career in the fledgling but viable Brazilian hip hop industry. It is precisely their ubiquitous quality that is significant, for at the mundane level, discourses and images of violence are still potent vehicles for elicitation. They influence thousands of poor, marginalized young men and women, the proposed target of Brazilian hip hop, to tell and retell their own stories of violence and daily life. Sometimes, such as in the case with DJ Giba and the member of the rap group *Solução,* these narrations lead to new energy in community building and social networking. In other cases, for example with the group BR, external forces of unemployment and family dynamics dissolve or divert any nascent formation of a productive hip hop/violence articulation.

As I learned on that night during the debate with Shabazz, one also needs to know his or her audience and understand the dynamics of reception. The politics of engagement, especially concerning issues with potentially dire consequences such as violence, are tricky. This is the theoretical and pragmatic challenge for scholars interested in representing violence. Following Marx's theories of class, Fanon's observations of race and colonialism, and Paulo Freire's manifesto of popular education, if one is to go beyond a situation of oppression, one must engage it directly. "Functionally, oppression is domesticating. To no longer be prey to its force, one must emerge from it and turn upon it. This can be done only by means of the praxis: reflection and action upon the world in order to transform it."[18]

References

Aldama, Arturo and Joe Lockhard. 2002. "Introduction: Aesthetics of Violence—Imagining Realities." In *Bad Subjects,* Vol. 61 (http://bad.eserver.org).

Boyd, Todd. 2002. *The New H.N.I.C.: The Death of Civil Rights and the Reign of Hip Hop.* New York: New York University Press.

Butler, Judith. 1990. *Gender Trouble: Feminism and the Subversion of Identity.* New York: Routledge.

Caldeira, Teresa P. R. 2000. *City of Walls: Crime, Segregation, and Citizenship in São Paulo.* Berkeley: University of California Press.

---

[16] "Mainstream" or "club" rappers are distinct from so-called "underground" rappers, who normally think of themselves as part of hip hop and thus as having a more complex sense of representation.

[17] See, for example, Rivera (2003), Perry (2005), and Boyd (2002).

[18] Freire 1970:36.

Fabris, Anna Teresa. 2000. *Fragmentos Urbanos: Representações Culturais*. São Paulo: Studio Nobel.
Flores, Juan. 2000. *From Bomba to Hip Hop*. New York: Columbia University Press.
Freire, Paulo. 1970. "Pedagogy of the Oppressed." Translated by Myra Bergmann Ramos. New York: Continuum.
Holston, James. 1991. Autoconstruction in Working-class Brazil. *Cultural Anthropology* 6(4): 447–465.
Kulick, Don. 1998. *Travesti*. Chicago: University of Chicago Press.
Magnini, Jose Guilherme Cantor. 1992. Quando o Campo e a Cidade: Fazendo Antropologia na Metropole. *Na Metropole. Sao Paulo*. ED. USP, pp. 15–53.
Maricato, Ermínia. 1979. Autoconstrução, a Arquitetura Possível. In *A produçãoCapitalista da Casa (e da Cidade) no Brasil Industrial*, Ermínia Maricato (ed.). São Paulo: Alfa Omega, pp. 71–93.
Pardue, Derek. November 2004. "Putting Mano to Music: The Mediation of Race in Brazilian Rap." *Ethnomusicology Forum* 13(2): 253–286.
Perry, Imani. 2005. *Prophets of the Hood: Politics and Poetics in Hip Hop*. 2nd Printing. Durham: Duke University Press.
Ponciano, Levino. 2001. *Bairros Paulistanos de A a Z*. São Paulo: SENAC.
Rivera, Raquel Z. 2003. *New York Ricans from the Hip Hop Zone*. New York: Palgrave Macmillan.
Rolnik, Raquel, Lúcio Kowarick, and Nádia Somekh. 1991. *São Paulo: Crise e Mudança*. São Paulo: Brasiliense.
Sachs, Céline. 1999[1990]. *São Paulo: Políticas Públicas e Habitação Popular*. Translated into Portuguese by Cristina Murachco. São Paulo: Editora USP.
Sevcenko, Nicolau. 1993. São Paulo: The Quintessential Uninhibited Megalopolis as seen by Blaise Cendrars in the 1920s. In *Megalopolis: The Giant City in History*, Theo Barker and Anthony Sutcliffe (eds.). New York: St. Martin's Press.

Omission, Silence, and Purity
A Statement on My Recent Work

Conor McGrady

For some time the core of my practice as an artist has been focused on issues relating to power, in particular that administered and wielded by states in the form of social control. The most recent work largely explores how architecture is used as an instrument of control in situations of conflict or civil unrest. Architecture, for the most part, is presented as a somewhat benign art form. From neo-classicism to modernist utopias and post-modern assimilation, architecture conjures up notions of civilization and progress on one hand and cultural heritage and statehood on the other. Less often is architecture referred to in terms of its duality, particularly when it comes to the issue of power. The architecture of prisons, military bases, and internment camps may be less "visible" culturally, but the existence of these and other such structures remind us that architecture continues to serve as a very visible and physical manifestation of power relations in contemporary society. From corporate headquarters to detention centers and lookout towers, to the use of checkpoints and modifications to the urban environment, it is the employment of architecture as a security device and repository of state power that currently interests me as an artist.

My practice, which consists of painting and drawing, has drawn extensively upon the conflict situation in Northern Ireland. The Northern Irish state was created in 1921 as a result of a protracted war of independence waged by Irish Republican Army guerilla against the British colonial presence. Ireland was Britain's first colony and remained so, despite constant resistance to British rule from the sixteenth century on. The war of independence resulted in the eventual creation of the Irish Republic, while Britain retained control of the six northern counties that became known as Northern Ireland. For the next fifty years the pro-British Unionist majority ruled this state with draconian powers, often employing military repression and intern-

Written especially for *Ruminations on Violence*.

ment against the minority community who desired an end to partition and the re-unification of the country. The minority community, known as Nationalists, was systematically discriminated against in housing, employment, and voting rights.

Inspired by the civil rights marches in the United States in the 1960s, this community took to the streets in demand of equality. The state's response was to attempt to crush the movement through police repression. The result was the re-emergence of the Irish Republican Army and a protracted armed struggle to end the British presence in the north.[1] Over twenty-five years of war followed, with cease-fires and a peace agreement signed in 1998. While the recent peace process has engendered significant changes, the Northern Irish state remains a deeply contested space, with much of the population polarized along ideological and class lines and with many of the core issues that led to the creation of the conflict still to be addressed.

As an artist, my response to growing up and living in a situation of civil unrest and state repression initially found its voice in paintings and drawings exploring violence, fear, claustrophobia, and the impact of living in a police state. These works, which were largely a gut-level response to the situation around me, contained the seeds of what was to become my later work. I grew up in the mainly Nationalist town of Castlewellan, near Belfast, and was raised in a community that was largely opposed to the British presence in the northern six counties. As an adolescent and teenager I was deeply affected by the violence around me yet retained the conviction that the British presence was historically illegitimate and was the source of both social and communal division and ultimately the cause of the conflict. While I did not agree with all of the actions of the groups opposing British rule, I fully supported the legitimacy of the struggle.

Politically I was initially drawn to anarchism and later socialism, and as a student I was able to apply social and historical analysis to the Irish situation in greater depth and to study the impact of imperialism globally. It became clear to me that the conflict in Ireland was not unique but was the product of very real divisions nurtured and sustained through British economic and geopolitical interests in Ireland, the same interests that colonial powers had historically exploited in Africa, Asia, and the Americas. While opposing the presence of British rule in Ireland, I also developed a greater understanding of class polarization in Britain itself. As a student in Newcastle Upon Tyne, in northeastern England, I witnessed the economic devastation that the policies of conservative government rule visited on working-class communities once dependent on mining and shipbuilding for a livelihood. I came to see that the violence of the state manifested itself not only in armed troops and the machinery of repression, but also in social and economic policies that resulted in the removal of the dignity and self-worth of

---

[1] For further reading see Kevin Kelley, *The Longest War* (Pluto Press, 1982), and Niall O'Dochartaigh, *From Civil Rights to Armalites* (Cork University Press, 1997).

ordinary people. It was as a student in Newcastle that I became convinced of the need for an art that called attention to and challenged the psychology of power and its all-too-prevalent manifestations.

Because painting and drawing cannot hope to compete with the media, it remains vital to understand the impact of the media in shaping perceptions of armed conflicts. In mainstream and popular media sources, discourse has tended to focus heavily on the violence of armed groups acting in opposition to the state or without its offical sanction. With the Northern Irish conflict in particular, there is a deficit in analysis and acceptance of the role of state violence up until the recent peace process. At the core of state violence lies the desire to preserve a particular ideology or social framework that wishes to remain impervious to change. Populations who actively desire change are often forced into violent confrontation with the state when democratic means of achieving change are shut down. In response to protest and armed confrontation the state then uses the various powers at its disposal to remove the threat. Power in the service of the state relies inherently on strategies involving both physical strength and secrecy. One of its ultimate goals is to enforce its acceptance through hegemony, which requires a compliant population who for the most part remain silent and accepting of the state's role and actions, which are deemed to be in their interest. Through censorship, carefully mediated news reportage and propaganda, states ensure that silence with regard to their abusive policies is enforced either through cover-up or by making their actions seem legitimate and therefore less subject to criticism.

Silence is one of the state's most important weapons in the propaganda war. In terms of Northern Ireland, successive British governments have consciously waged a propaganda war for the "hearts and minds" of the population. The views of those who disagreed with government policy, or who opposed it through protest and later through the use of arms, were silenced through outright media censorship and media strategies to demonize them and to render their voices invalid. As one of the desirable outcomes of media strategy, silence is also one of the goals of torture. In torture, physical and psychological violence are used to obtain information that in turn is used to remove and permanently silence activists and combatants who oppose the state. States also silence those opposed to them through imprisonment or through assassination with the use of covert death squads. The point is essentially to make a substantial sector of the population (those who oppose the state) disappear; to make them invisible; to remove their voices; and to remove them, either physically or though hegemony, from their stance of opposition to the state.

As an artist, I express this process of removal through the use of *incompleteness* or *absence* in my paintings and drawings. In the drawings, which are largely executed in gouache, ink, and compressed charcoal, violence becomes a form of omission, referring directly to the removal or containment of unwanted or subversive populations or individuals. The drawings are austere, usually with distilled or economical lines emphasizing the white void space of the paper. I deliberately use white paper as whiteness has connotations of purity, of sterility, of the "sanitized" space. In most of the drawings people are absent, alluding to state policies that attempt to contain and remove them. These policies, like torture, mirror surgical procedures in that something has to be extracted and removed (information and the insurgent population) in order for the state to heal what it perceives to be the cancer attacking the health and stability of its existence.

Some of the drawings refer to prisons, interrogation centers and military bases that were designed to keep people away from them as much as to keep people in (Fig 1). The secrecy that shrouds these institutions serves to keep the population silent and in passive acceptance of their existence. Occasionally what goes on within the walls of these places leaks out, and efforts are made to cover it up, as with both the recent revelations at Abu Ghraib prison in Iraq and the continued mistreatment of prisoners by U.S. military personnel at Guantanamo. The drawings employ silence and absence, as equated by the empty space within the picture plane, as strategies to draw the viewer into the work and experience a sense of liminal time, absence, or stasis. Through the inanimate nature of the objects produced, painting and drawing are perfectly adapted to carry a sense of stillness and the suspension of time. Both painting and drawing are a means of entrapment, trying to capture and pin down the component elements and affects of state power on people and places. As images and objects they are attempts to draw the viewer into a silent realm characterized by reflection and meditation, and to carry the weight of their subject matter by exuding a sense of disquiet or absence.

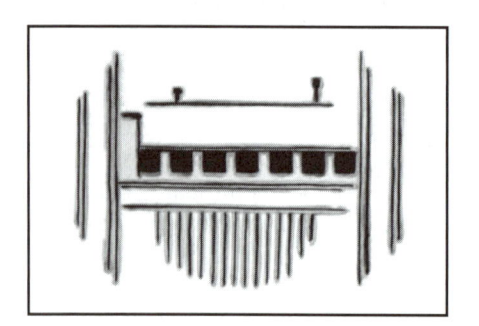

Figure 1. *Infirmary* (gouache on paper, 2005)

In many of the drawings that deal with urban spaces and housing developments, I work almost exclusively from memory. This is an attempt to strip out all extraneous details and depict the residue or imprint of public and domestic spaces subject to state control. The empty buildings and housing schemes in the drawings are not only subject to physical control by the military but in most cases were designed and planned with the help of military technicians to ensure containment of the population. In this situation the concept of private space does not exist; and these buildings and housing areas are subject to repeated military invasion, search procedures, and constant surveillance.

In some drawings I have expanded the scale in order to investigate their impact on physical space. While the small drawings are scaled down to create a sense of intimacy with the viewer, the large ones encompass or immerse the viewer in the urban arenas or natural vistas depicted within the picture plane.

In these cases I want the scale to reflect some of the issues that the drawings address. The perfectly controlled landscape, from a military point of view, allows for complete visual dominance in defense against unseen threats, somewhat along the lines of Bentham's Panopticon.[2] Yet despite the efforts of states to achieve this level of total visual control, urban and rural landscapes cannot be completely subdued through surveillance and still contain hidden threats (Fig 2). The landscape itself is both terrain to be conquered or controlled and the repository of the romantic ideal of the nation state. In a recent series of drawings the forest becomes both container of threat and desirable "arcadia" in terms of the state's conception of the land it occupies. The forest also contains symbolic imagery of stability and permanence. Trees are echoed in the rows and columns of military formations, symbolizing an impenetrable force that desires to remain impervious to defeat (Fig 3).

One series of four- by eight-foot drawings looks directly at housing schemes in Northern Ireland, exploring the use of urban planning designs such as the cul-de sac as a containment device. It also explores the idea that these areas evoke feelings of fear, contempt, and state-engendered vulnerability. Titles such as *Hole* and *Breeding Ground* (Figs. 4 and 5) refer to the routine dehumanization employed by state forces to the people living within them. The buildings become part of an almost perfect fascist landscape—neat, ordered and devoid of all forms of an overt human presence, all traces of insurgency "cleaned out." Another of these pieces, entitled *Cul-de-Sac*, is a nine- by forty-two-foot drawing on a gallery wall in New York (Fig. 6). The drawing occupies the viewer's full field of vision. The claustrophobic impact of the piece is enhanced by the narrowness of the gallery, where the viewer cannot step back far enough to take in the entire work. This work in particular draws attention to the inability of surveillance to be total and emphasizes the use of architecture and urban control to create a sense of domination and claustrophobia in the population. This piece also evokes feelings of physical and psychological restriction, bodily confinement, and stasis. Restriction of movement was a key tactic employed by the security forces during the conflict, and on a broader metaphorical level restriction of movement socially is at the root of the cause of the conflict. A sense of inferiority, second-class citizenship, and a liminal existence with little room for maneuver through political channels gave rise to a movement aimed at breaking social restrictions. The state's attempt to contain and remove this movement led to the protracted situation of conflict that characterized the past thirty-five years in Northern Ireland.

Another series of recent drawings are directly influenced by working for five months in lower Manhattan through the Lower Manhattan Cultural

---

[2] The Panopticon, designed by Jeremy Bentham in the nineteenth century, was a device employed in the design of prisons. It consisted of a circular structure with a central tower surrounded by cells. The person in the tower could see into each of the cells, while the occupants of each cell could view the tower from a small window in the door but could not view the occupants of the other cells.

178   Part V: Violence as an Aesthetic

Figure 2. *A New Horizon* (gouache on paper, 2005)

Figure 3. *Woods* (gouache on paper, 2005)

Figure 4. *Hole* (gouache on paper, 2003)

Figure 5. *Breeding Ground* (gouache on paper, 2005)

Center's residency program in the Woolworth building in 2003. Here, issues of domestic control and security in the United States fed into the work, in particular the impact of "security zones" on restriction of movement and access to "sensitive" buildings. In these drawings architectural modifications to buildings and the sealing off of streets in New York, dually aimed at protection and exclusion, take on the characteristics of similar structures in Northern Ireland and other police states where attack from within the body politic is expected at any moment (Fig. 7). Where these structures differ from their counterparts in Ireland is in their vulnerability. They tend to exist on a symbolic level, as "counterterrorism" measures aimed at making the public feel protected; yet they would not stand up to any real attempts to attack them or the buildings they aim to protect.

Towards the end of 2004 I created a small body of figurative drawings. The same sense of sparseness of line and visual austerity is still in place but is used to depict individuals with injuries sustained to their heads, limbs, and torsos (Fig. 8). Most of these drawings are taken from photos of people attacked and beaten either by the police or by right-wing groups in Northern Ireland. Here the body becomes the site on which the state (and its proxies) inscribes itself, where its ideology is physically imbedded into those who oppose it. Those who do not accept the ideology of the state or of opposing political groupings must literally and physically have that ideology beaten into them. The use of violence here is pedagogical, and the victims are treated as surrogate children who are "taught a lesson" in how they should conform to the status quo.

In the work I produced during 2005 and since I am further extending my research into the relationship between architecture and power though a study of fascist-era modernist architecture, neoclassicism, and the use of architecture as it is employed in the creation of the modern state's sense of identity. Public buildings such as libraries, museums, hospitals, and public spaces such as plazas and squares all serve as visible indicators of the benign or civilized face of the modern state. They represent order, stability and formality. Like the aforementioned drawings of trees, the columns of the neoclassical façade echo the military formation and even the romantic ideal of the forest itself (Fig. 9). There is an inherent duality at work in the creation of the public face of states that do not publicly acknowledge their hidden use of military control and the suppression of populations in opposition to them. This applies as much to Northern Ireland as it does globally. While the public face of the modern state is often the symbolic use of architecture, the neoclassical min-

Figure 6. *Cul–de-Sac* (Installation View) (ink drawing on wall, 2004)

Figure 7. *Box* (gouache on paper, 2003)

Figure 8. *Plastic Bullets IV* (gouache on paper, 2004)

Figure 9. *Façade* (gouache on paper, 2005)

gling with the postmodern, current architectural modifications geared towards protection and defense in the likelihood of potential attack are increasingly becoming the norm. In this sense, the state continues to project an air of stability and permanence while exposing its vulnerability through the modification of its sensitive or weak spots.

The aim of all these works is essentially to raise questions on the notion of political and, in particular, state power. It is my hope to engage the viewer in debate or dialogue on issues relating to the control of space and boundaries and to present ideas on how architecture and bodies are used as devices to enforce or symbolize social order. Ultimately the work is an attempt to create a space shaped by contemporary social experience, and to open that space for questions and criticism, both of the work itself and of the issues it addresses.

The Changing Qualities of Violence in American Popular Culture

Jack Levin and Eric Madfis

Media depictions of sex and violence are frequently blamed for amplifying America's social problems. Numerous media critics, both academic and otherwise, have attributed rising crime rates to the copious amounts of violence viewed by children on television screens and computer monitors across the nation.

The number of on-screen violent actions per episode, per day, per week, and so on has been quantified for decades. Overall, they have remained astonishingly constant and at a very high level. However, the subtexts and circumstances of these violent actions, which may be the truly significant precipitants of real-world violence, have not received nearly as much time or consideration. In terms of impact, it may not be a question of how much violence viewers watch that really matters, but what type and quality of violence they observe on-screen. We propose that the most dangerous media violence consists of (1) sadism and nastiness, including verbal humiliation and physical degradation; (2) realistic gore, including graphic depictions of blood and viscera; and (3) depictions of villains as celebrities whose violent actions are justified and go unpunished. Further, these particularly problematic forms of violence are exactly the types that have become increasingly prevalent on American television programs and in popular video games. Finally, technological advances such as the Internet and the increasing popularity of high-tech video games have created new venues for expressing the most dangerous types of violence.

Written especially for *Ruminations on Violence*.

VIOLENCE IN POPULAR CULTURE

Popular culture in the United States has become an important agent of socialization for most of America's youngsters. The typical child spends, on average, more than 38 hours weekly—almost five and a half hours on a daily basis—watching television, playing video games, listening to music, and surfing the Internet. For children aged eight and older, the contact with popular culture is even greater—almost seven hours a day (Kaiser Family Foundation, 2005).

Nearly three-quarters of the children in the United States live in a home that possesses at least three TV sets. It is no wonder then that children consume television more than any other form of mass entertainment. On a daily average, they watch TV some 2 hours and 46 minutes but spend only 20 minutes playing video games and 21 minutes using a computer for fun. Even listening to music, occupying 1 hour and 27 minutes of a typical child's time daily, is in second place to watching television. In sum, the average child spends more time in front of the TV than in school (Kaiser Family Foundation, 2005).

Parental controls on their children's television viewing behavior tend to be weak—almost 50 percent of all parents fail to impose any restrictions on their youngsters' viewing behavior. In fact, some 53 percent of all parents permit a set in their child's bedroom; fifty-eight percent leave a set on while the family eats dinner. And only 5 percent of all parents watch TV with their children aged 8 and older (Kaiser Family Foundation, 2005).

Yet parents often express their serious concern about what they consider to be the harmful effects of the mass media. Eighty-five percent of American parents report that today's popular culture contributes to children behaving in a violent or antisocial manner. In fact, more parents rank television rather than video games and music as having the most negative impact on their children. Almost half believe that TV contributes "a lot" to their youngster's potential for adopting violent behavior (Kaiser Family Foundation, 2003).

The concern of parents regarding the impact of TV and other forms of mass entertainment on their children's violent behavior is apparently not misplaced. By the age of 18, the average American has viewed 200,000 acts of violence on television alone, including 40,000 murders. Gerbner (1976; 1998) has long reported that incidents which hurt, kill, or threaten to injure human beings occur in more than two-thirds of all prime-time TV programs and in 9 out of 10 weekend morning programs. In TV dramatic series, 63 percent of all major characters engage in some type of violent conduct.

THE CULTIVATION HYPOTHESIS

The entertainment context of mass culture gives it tremendous potential for subtle influence and peripheral learning. By reducing awareness of manipulative intent on the part of the producers of mass culture, the mediated music, comedy, and dramatic series eliminate the defensive posture of audience members who might otherwise be put off by a message obviously intended to change their attitudes or behavior (Brehm and Brehm 1981). Renowned media critic and communications professor George Gerbner articulated his widely researched cultivation hypothesis, according to which heavy exposure to media images functions in a powerful socializing capacity. Therefore, the dramatized depictions on television and in the movies shape viewers' understanding of reality. Prolonged exposure to the mass media creates and cultivates attitudes which are less based in reality and more consistent with a false, media-conjured version of the world. Thus, some studies have suggested that heavy television viewers tend to have an exaggerated sense of fear and mistrust—what Gerbner (1998) refers to as a "mean world view." They are unrealistically concerned about their own personal safety, about violent crime, and about law enforcement.

Recent studies suggest that the cultivation effect may be exclusively an American media phenomenon. Wober (1990) and Pingree and Hawkins (1981) revealed that British and Australian audiences' respective viewing of non-American television did not result in the fearful, mean-world syndrome. Although Wober did find a relationship between watching American crime drama and fear among British viewers, a study of the cultivation effect in Iceland (Kolbeins 2004) revealed that viewing American crime drama had no impact on Icelanders' level of fear or mistrust of others. Accordingly, the cultivation hypothesis may only apply in a sociocultural context in which a strong obsession with crime, violence, and the fear of both exists (Kolbeins 2004).

Bandura (1977) theorized early on that aggressive behavior involves detailed skills that can be learned. He demonstrated experimentally that individuals learn these antisocial skills not only from being rewarded or punished but also from the imitation of violent role models who are sanctioned either positively or negatively. Bandura argued that the mass media, and television in particular (before the advent of the violent video game), make numerous models for aggressive behavior readily available to the members of society. In a classic study, he determined that nursery school children who watched a video of a woman beating up a doll and then being rewarded for her actions were more likely than their control-group peers to become aggressive.

QUALITATIVE ASPECTS OF MEDIA VIOLENCE

Though it is difficult not to accept Gerbner's general premise that mean and fearful mind-sets may be cultivated by violent media depictions of the world in which we live, not all media violence is of the same quality; nor does it have the same impact on the audience. When Gerbner and his colleagues determined the amount of physical violence on TV in his Cultural Indicators Project, they did so by measuring the frequency of violent actions, the amount of time devoted to these violent actions, how often the violence was serious versus humorous, and how centrally significant the violence was to the overall plot (Gerbner, Morgan and Signorielli 1994; Signorielli, Gerbner, and Morgan 1995). These researchers did not, however, ascertain how frequently media violence was depicted as inconsequential versus realistic in its gory consequences, deviant and destructive versus glorified and romanticized, and benign versus sadistic and humiliating to its victims. Therefore, utilizing Gerbner's schema, the depiction of a sadistic rape/murder scene with plentiful gore caused by the homicidal behavior of an attractive villain would be counted only as a single violent act, in the same way that any natural disaster such as a hurricane would be counted (Blank 1977).

We believe that it is vital for researchers to focus on the qualitative differences in violent media imagery, not merely on the number of times they occur. Observers who would like to attribute the escalating rate of juvenile violence in recent years to the increasing depiction of TV violence will have to look elsewhere. Research on television effects has consistently shown that media violence has not been increasing over time. In her analysis of prime-time network television from 1993 to 2001, for example, Nancy Signorielli (2003) found that the quantity of media violence remained stable. Signorielli discovered that throughout the time period under investigation roughly 60 percent of programs in her sample contained violent episodes. Similarly, in its analysis of television programs from the 1994–1995, 1995–1996, and 1996–1997 seasons, the National Television Violence Study (NTVS) found little change in the quantity of violence over the four-year period (Wilson et al. 1998).

The NTVS analyzed an unusually large sample containing thousands of hours of programming. As a result, this study is particularly significant for our discussion. Not only did the NTVS fail to demonstrate any increase in the quantity of violent actions depicted on television over time, but it also highlighted the particular portrayals of violence and plot elements which may cause greater risks for youthful viewers to learn aggressive attitudes and behaviors. According to the NTVS, high-risk portrayals included (1) a perpetrator who is attractive, (2) violence that seems justified, (3) violence that goes unpunished, (4) minimal consequences to the victim, and (5) violence that seems realistic to the viewer (Wilson et al. 1998).

In a subsequent article, Wilson et al. (2002) focused more on the way in which media violence is presented and placed into a context. Based on the original dataset from the National Television Violence Study, the more recent research examined the prevalence of particular forms of violence including attractive and heroic male perpetrators, justified and rewarded violent behavior, the presence of weapons, "blood and guts" portrayals, and depictions of the victims' pain and suffering. These contextual characteristics were then compared not over a period of time but by whether they appeared on programs designed for children and adults.

The Changing Characteristics of Media Violence

We suggest that the forms of media violence noted as particularly destructive by previous investigators have become even more prevalent since the turn of the century, possibly contributing to a recent rise in the level of violent behavior committed by America's young people. First, *sadism* and *nastiness* have assumed a prominent position in prime-time television and other media. In the face of intense competition for sales and ratings, and eager to capture the largest possible share of the market, TV producers have introduced more and more programs which appeal to their audience's desire to witness pain and suffering.

Sadistic media fare seems to appeal widely to the needs of many Americans who are desperate to feel good about themselves, even if it occurs at somebody else's expense. In the 1960s, parents and psychologists complained about an opposing tendency—to present violence without consequences, so that young people growing up on media fare learned that violent behavior caused little if any pain and suffering in its victims. Some forty years later, the excessive depiction of victims' suffering as a result of violence may be desensitizing American youth to the very real effects of destructive behavior. On popular prime-time programs, they learn that it is socially acceptable to enjoy the suffering of others (Potter 1999).

According to psychoanalyst Erich Fromm (1973), the sadistic impulse is learned. It becomes operative in societies where individual needs remain unmet, leaving many with a profound sense of powerlessness. In the face of corporate mergers, big government, and global connections, there are growing numbers of Americans who feel incompetent to influence their own destiny, let alone the course of events in the larger society. Through sadistic media images, however, they are temporarily (and, in some case, vicariously) made to feel superior to the individuals being abused, tortured, or embarrassed on the tube.

Thus, contemporary television programs are far more willing than ever before to depict the physical anguish of helpless victims in dramatic series as well as the emotional humiliation of ordinary people on so-called reality television shows. Representing the former category, prime-time series such as *Vanished, 24, Prison Break,* and *Criminal Minds* realistically depict extreme forms of torture being performed by either protagonists (e.g., Jack Bower in the series *24*) or villains (serial killers). As far as humiliation is concerned, a number of reality programs now depend for their high ratings on embarrassing ordinary people. In episodes of NBC's wildly popular prime-time program, *Fear Factor*, contestants engage in a series of humiliating tasks. They are given electric shocks; forced to swallow something they find disgusting (e.g., sheep testicles, worms, cockroaches, live beetles); or buried in a tank full of scorpions, rats, or spiders. If they fail to meet a challenge, they are eliminated. If they perform, they move on to face the next horrific task. The contestant who completes all required tasks also wins the game.

WB's now defunct *Superstar USA* where "only the bad survive" also thrived on sadism. In what looked like a parody of *American Idol*, the worst singers on *Superstar USA* were deceived into believing that they had won the contest because of their superior voices. At the end of the game, they were then informed that the "winners" were actually the biggest losers—those contestants who couldn't carry a tune. Apparently taking its cue from *Superstar*, Fox's *American Idol* now spends week after week showing the worst possible singers, most of whom are absolutely incredulous when they are rejected from the competition. In the process, the vast television audience is provided with a cheap laugh at the expense of the most insecure and delusional contestants. Moreover, Simon Cowell's unsparingly blunt criticism of contestants on *American Idol* has made him a superstar celebrity in his own right. The same can be said for Donald Trump on *The Apprentice* ("You're Fired!") and Anne Robinson on *The Weakest Link* ("*You* are the weakest link. Goodbye!").

In addition to sadism, the mass media have become increasingly more obsessed with the *depiction of blood and gore*. Graphically depicted autopsy scenes showing realistically created images of corpses in varying stages of decomposition, being dissected by sage medical examiners now fill the prime-time hours. Thanks to its high ratings, what began on *CSI* has spread without apparent limits to *CSI New York, CSI Miami, Crossing Jordan, NCIS,* and *Law & Order* (including its two spin-off series, *Criminal Intent* and *Special Victims Unit*).

It isn't only television that has come to portray the graphic details of violence. In R-rated motion pictures, our youngsters are now being entertained on a daily basis by scenes of eviscerations, disembowelments, decapitations, and people being skinned alive. Moreover, thanks to videotape and DVD rentals available to children of any age, a ten-year-old boy can come home from school, grab milk and cookies from the refrigerator, and watch on his own high-def TV set a gruesome 20-minute gang-rape scene, a group of sadistic men torturing a young woman with an axe, or an attractive woman being nailed to the wall with a nail gun while romantic music plays in the background (Linz, Donnerstein and Penrod 1984; 1988). Monk-Turner et al. (2004) showed that American war movies since 1990 have become far more gruesome and gory, depicting in a realistic fashion even the most nauseating details of warfare. Moreover, Lachlan et al. (2005) found that the violence in the most popular video games of 1999 frequently was astonishingly gory and graphic. Even when compared with the televised portrayal of gun violence, Smith et al. (2004:600) found that video-game gun violence "is far more repetitive or extensive in nature" and "more likely to feature blood/gore." According to experimental evidence collected by social psychologists, a steady diet of graphic violence as depicted in television series, motion pictures, and video games may desensitize viewers, making them callous to genuine pain, suffering, and violence in the real world (Linz, Donnerstein and Penrod 1984; 1988).

Aside from sadism and gore, there has also been a *blurring of the lines between fame and infamy* in American popular culture. Throughout much of the American history of celebrity, stardom was typically bestowed on those regarded as paragons of virtue, either because of their business acumen, ability to entertain, competitive achievements, great courage, or unusual talents. In certain cases, criminals also received inordinate public attention, but usually because they were regarded as "Robin Hood" types, whose victims—banks and large corporations—were widely viewed as exploitative and unethical (Kooistra, 1989). In some cases, of course, very influential villains also received attention, but only so long as they were newsworthy and only in media specializing in news of a political, economic, or legal character. For example, Adolph Hitler made seven covers of *Time*; Joseph Stalin's image appeared on twelve.

A recent content analysis of the individuals featured on the cover of *People* magazine suggested that, from 1974 to 1998, the focus of the cover themes shifted away from celebrity careers toward a preoccupation with the stars' personal problems—illnesses, crime, and family/sex issues (Levin, Fox and Mazaik, 2005). Over the decades, moreover, the basis for *People* celebrities appearing in a cover story became decidedly more negative. Beginning in the late 1980s, the magazine heaped attention—perhaps inordinate attention—on the "accomplishments" of rapists, child abusers, drug addicts, and murderers. Serial killer Jeffrey Dahmer appeared on three *People* covers. Also featured were Ted Kaczynski (aka The Unabomber); Laurie Dann, who shot students in an Illinois elementary school; boxer Mike Tyson; and Lorena Bobbitt, who excised her husband's penis.

During the closing decades of the twentieth century, the celebrity criminals featured in *People*—not unlike their counterparts who sing, dance, or perform in major motion pictures—simply entertained the masses with their spectacular and bizarre criminal behavior. Former *People* editor Richard Stolley may have recognized this shift in emphasis when he suggested in 1977, "We haven't changed the concept of the magazine; we're just expanding the concept of star" (Gamson 1994:46).

The changing focus in the cover of a major celebrity magazine is only one of many ways reflecting Americans' growing tendency to place killers in positions where we formerly placed those considered to be virtuous. Some "art lovers" have paid thousands of dollars for the artwork of serial killer John Wayne Gacy; others have competed to buy cannibal Jeffrey Dahmer's refrigerator and the bricks of his apartment building. There are now several companies which sell murderer trading cards, murderer comic books, and murderer dolls and action figures. Some serial killers have their own Web sites; others have written books containing their poetry, artwork, and music.

By granting celebrity status to murderers and other villains, we may be inadvertently providing our young people with a dangerous precedent for gaining national prominence. One serial killer made his intention known when he asked in a letter to the police, "How many times do I have to kill before I get a name in the paper or some national attention?" The answer to his query is as clear as it is chilling: The larger a killer's body count, the greater his potential for achieving celebrity status (Levin, Fox and Mazaik 2005).

As the National Television Violence Study indicated, it is particularly problematic to show villainous celebrities whose violent actions seem justified and are rewarded. These images amount to the worst messages we can send to children—especially to those who desperately want to feel important among their peers. Yet, this negative imagery is nowadays in constant supply. Tamborini et al. (2005) found that professional wrestling exhibits the worst kind of violence, where the actions of the villains are justified, unpunished, and unlikely to show real consequences. Furthermore, whereas the professional wrestling of the past featured virtuous good guys versus clearly evil villains in a dramatized morality play, the professional wrestling of today merely pits two equally despicable villains against each other. In the absence of many decent and respectable competitors, it seems inevitable that the wrestling villains—those who violate the rules and apply deceptive practices—will still be envied if not beloved. After all, they are winners.

Another concern presented by the NTVS is the problem of creating violent characters with whom viewers may empathize or identify. In addition to Nancy Signorielli's (2003) finding of the stable distribution of violence over time, she also emphasized that the one notable change in recent years was that the "same amount of violence is committed by fewer characters who are essential to the story line" (Signorielli 2003:54). This newfound increase in character development and centrality of the perpetrators of violence may lead to viewers more easily empathizing or identifying with them and thus justifying or negating their crimes. An apt example is provided by the Jack Bower character in the Fox Network series *24*. Bower is clearly a heroic figure. He is always taking extraordinary risks, compromising his own personal safety for the sake of the nation, the president, or his family. But he is also depicted as a dyed-in the-wool sociopath, someone who will use any and all tactics—no matter how illegal or immoral—in order to catch a terrorist. Similarly, in the video-gaming world, Lachlan et al. (2005) revealed how "video-game characters have attributes that are likely to increase the extent to which some players perceive them as attractive and similar" to themselves.

The Effect of Context

It is all too easy simply to blame the media for violence in society. Taken out of context and treating the relationship between media portrayal and youth in isolation, we might expect that a steady diet of sadism, gore, and killer celebrity fare would contribute substantially to the destructiveness of our children. And, it is true that many youngsters—perhaps especially those already at greatest risk for expressing violent behavior—are essentially on their own when they attend to the media. Their parents work or are divorced. After school, they come home to an empty house, where they are free to watch sadistic and gory motion pictures and TV programs or to play violent video games. In a sense, television becomes a babysitter for parents who lack primary control over their children's activities. Thus, it becomes important to locate methods for reducing the real-world consequences of the media's impact on our children's violent behavior. Everything depends on the context in which they watch.

Japanese society provides an alternative to the American television-viewing context. Though Japanese television programs and motion pictures are extraordinarily graphic and sadistic (Henslin 2006), the level of street crime in Tokyo and other Japanese cities remains minimal. Indeed, the murder rate in Japan is about one-fifth that of the United States. In Japan, children rarely watch television alone. Instead, they view alongside their parents, extended kin, or a family friend who is available to monitor, interpret, and explain the issues of fantasy and morality which arise from being exposed to media violence on a regular basis (Fox and Levin, 2006).

When the option of family members watching television with children is unrealistic, there is new evidence that the schools may execute this vital mediating function by explaining the context and significance of violence to youth with programs like the project REViEW—Reducing Early Violence: Education Works (Rosenkoetter et al., 2004). This classroom-based intervention has produced promising evidence that television literacy programs may alleviate the most harmful effects on young viewers of violent television by discussing the consequences of violence in a level-headed and realistic manner.

In addition, in communities where parents cannot afford to provide their youngsters with healthy alternatives after school or during the summer months, it might take a large-scale, grassroots community effort to reduce the potentially disastrous effects of media violence on children. This means providing adult supervision for the children in *other people's* families. It suggests that after-school programs, summer jobs for teenagers, and adequate community centers are actually violence-prevention programs which are necessary in our modern world for combating the potentially harmful impact of the mass media.

References

Bandura, Albert. 1977. *Social Learning Theory.* Englewood Cliffs, NJ: Prentice-Hall.
Bandura, Albert, Dorothea Ross, and Sheila Ross. 1963a. "Imitation of Film-Mediated Aggressive Models." *Journal of Abnormal and Social Psychology* 66:3–11.
Bandura, Albert, Dorothea Ross, and Sheila Ross. 1963b. "Vicarious Reinforcement and Imitative Learning." *Journal of Abnormal and Social Psychology* 67:601–607.
Bandura, Albert. 1986. *Social Foundations of Thought and Action: A Social Cognitive Theory.* Englewood Cliffs, NJ: Prentice-Hall.
Blank, David M. 1977. The Gerbner Violence Profile. *Journal of Broadcasting & Electronic Media* 21(3):273–279.
Donnerstein, Edward, Daniel Linz, and Steven Penrod. 1987. *The Question of Pornography: Research Findings and Policy Implications.* New York: The Free Press.
Federman, J. (Ed.). 1997. *National Television Violence Study: Vol. 2. Executive Summary.* Santa Barbara: University of California, Center for Communication & Social Policy.
Fox, James A., and Jack Levin. 2006. *The Will to Kill: Explaining Senseless Murder.* Boston, MA: Sourcebooks.
Fromm, Erich. 1973. *The Anatomy of Human Destructiveness.* New York: Holt, Rinehart, & Winston.
Gerbner, George. 1976. *Television and Its Viewers: What Social Science Sees.* Santa Monica, CA: Rand Corporation.

Gerbner, George, and Gross, Larry. (1980). The violent face of television and its lessons. In Edward L. Palmer and Aimee Dorr (Eds.), *Children and the Faces of Television: Teaching, Violence, Selling.* New York: Academic Press, pp. 149–162.

Gerbner, George. 1998. "Fairness and Diversity in Television." In *Casting the American Scene.* Screen Actors Guild Report. Retrieved February 28, 2007, at http://www.media-awareness.ca/english/resources/research_documents/reports/diversity/american_scene.cfm.

Henslin, James M. 2006. *Essentials of Sociology: A Down-to-Earth Approach* (6th ed.) Boston, MA: Allyn & Bacon.

Kolbeins, Gudbjorg Hildur. September 2004. The Non-finding of the Cultivation Effect in Iceland. *Nordicom Review* 25(1/2):309–314.

Lachlan, Kenneth A., Stacy L. Smith and Ron Tamborini. December 2005. Models for Aggressive Behavior: The Attributes of Violent Characters in Popular Video Games. *Communication Studies* 56(4):313–329.

Levin, Jack, James A. Fox, and Jason Mazaik. 2005. Blurring Fame and Infamy: A Content Analysis of Cover-Story Trends in People Magazine. *Internet Journal of Criminology.* Retrieved February 28, 2007, at www.internetjournalofcriminology.com.

Linz, Daniel, Edward Donnerstein, and Stephen Penrod. 1984. The Effects of Multiple Exposures to Filmed Violence against Women. *Journal of Communication* 34:130–147.

Linz, Daniel, Edward Donnerstein, and Stephen Penrod. 1988. Effects of Long-Term Exposure to Violent and Sexually Degrading Depictions of Women. *Journal of Personality and Social Psychology* 55:758–768.

Monk-Turner, Elizabeth, Peter Ciba, Matthew Cunningham, P. Gregory McIntire, Mark Pollard and Rebecca Turner. 2004. A Content Analysis of Violence in American War Movies. *Analyses of Social Issues and Public Policy* 4(1):1–11.

Pingree, S. and R. Hawkins. 1981. U.S. Programs on Australian Television: The Cultivation Effect. *Journal of Communication* 31(1):97–105.

Potter, W. James. 1999. *On Media Violence.* Thousand Oaks, CA: Sage.

Potter, W. James, and Stacy Smith. Spring 2000. The Context of Graphic Portrayals of Television Violence. *Journal of Broadcasting and Electronic Media* 44(2):301–323.

Rosenkoetter, Lawrence I., Sharon E. Rosenkoetter, Rachel A. Ozretich and Alan C. Acock. 2004. Mitigating the Harmful Effects of Violent Television. *Applied Developmental Psychology* 25:25–47.

Shanahan, James. September 2004. A Return to Cultural Indicators. *Communications* 29(3):277–294.

Signorielli, Nancy. March 2003. Prime-Time Violence 1993–2001: Has the Picture Really Changed? *Journal of Broadcasting & Electronic Media* 47(1):36–57.

Signorielli, Nancy, George Gerbner, and Michael Morgan. 1995. *Violence on Television: The Cultural Indicators Project. Journal of Broadcasting & Electronic Media* 39(2):278–283.

Smith, Stacy L. and Edward Donnerstein. 1998. "Harmful Effects of Exposure to Media Violence: Learning of Aggression, Emotional Desensitization, and Fear." In R. Geen and E. Donnerstein (Eds.), *Human Aggression: Theories, Research, and Implications for Social Policy.* New York: Academic Press, pp. 167–202.

Smith, Stacy L., Ken Lachlan, Katherine M. Pieper, Aaron R. Boyson, Barbara J. Wilson, Ron Tamborini and Rene Weber. 2004. Brandishing Guns in American Media: Two Studies Examining How Often and in What Context Firearms Appear on Television and in Popular Video Games. *Journal of Broadcasting & Electronic Media* 48(4):584–606.

Smith, Stacy L., Ken Lachlan, and Ron Tamborini. March 2003. Popular Video Games: Quantifying the Presentation of Violence and Its Context. *Journal of Broadcasting & Electronic Media* 47(1):58–76.

Tamborini, Ron, Paul Skalski, Kenneth Lachlan, David Westerman, Jeff Davis and Stacy Smith. June 2005. The Raw Nature of Televised Professional Wrestling: Is the Violence a Cause for Concern? *Journal of Broadcasting & Electronic Media* 49(2):202–220.

Wilson, Barbara J., Stacy L. Smith, James W. Potter, Dale Kunkel, Daniel Linz, Carolyn M. Colvin and Edward Donnerstein. March 2002. Violence in Children's Television Programming: Assessing the Risks. *Journal of Communication* 52 (1):5–35.

Wilson, Barbara J., Daniel Linz, James W. Potter, Edward Donnerstein, Stacy L. Smith, E. Blumenthal and M. Berry. 1998. Violence in Television Programming Overall: University of California, Santa Barbara Study. *National Television Violence Study, Vol. 2*. Thousand Oaks, CA: Sage.

Wober, J. M. 1990. Does Television Cultivate the British: Late 80's Evidence. In N. Signorielli and M. Morgan (Eds.), *Cultivation Analysis: New Directions in Media Effects Research*. Newbury Park, CA: Sage.

18

Trigger-Happy

Nadine Wasserman

"My fellow Americans, . . . we begin bombing in five minutes." On August 11, 1984, this remark by President Ronald Reagan was broadcast during what he believed was merely a radio mike check. While it was intended to be a joke at the Soviet Union's expense, it speaks volumes about the American "tough guy" culture. While the United States is by no means one of the most dangerous places on earth, it does dominate the world arms market while simultaneously dominating popular culture. Yet, while there is no question that a vast array of American pop culture is awash in violent imagery, violent images are not specific to American pop culture. They crop up throughout history in cultures all over the world and are expressed in many different forms of media, from literature to the visual and performing arts. Visual media are particularly conducive to depicting violence and have been utilized ever since prehistoric humans began painting hunting scenes on cave walls. Artists often reflect upon the environment in which they work, thereby offering the viewer a new outlook on a particular subject. This essay will contextualize the art of three American artists who each offer a different perspective on American violence.

The "tough guy" individualist who goes it alone, against the odds, is an American icon that can trace its beginnings to the landing of the *Mayflower*, but it remains as one of many cultural myths about what it means to be an American. In fact, this myth fails to capture the reality that being an American is a varied, particular, and complicated experience. First, the legend conveniently ignores much of what happened in the "New World" prior to 1620. Not only the many indigenous peoples who lived here for thousands of years are left out of the official myth of America. The Spanish, who landed in 1513; the French; the Portuguese; and even the Popham Colony and the Jamestown settlement, which were both founded in 1607, were omitted. Despite the fact that America's terrain is considerably diverse, its culture is continually modified by subsequent generations and new waves of immi-

Written especially for *Ruminations on Violence*.

grants, and many different peoples endured hardship and pain to make these United States, it is the Pilgrims and the Western pioneers who continue to dominate the image of the American national character.[1] Somehow these two groups have come to embody the enduring American spirit. Perhaps it is because the United States is still a relatively young nation—and as such it is devoid of long-held traditions and of a true sense of place—which leads its citizens to cling to a patriotism based on symbols such as the flag and the 4th of July, and on a hero worship that paradoxically defies the democratic ideals of freedom and equality. Either way, in the end the popular "all-American" hero is more John Wayne as cowboy, soldier, or boxer than Pocahontas as diplomat. When it comes right down to it, Americans prefer an adventure story with clearly defined heroes who conquer their evil foes and live happily ever after.

Despite its veneer of rosy optimism, American culture harbors an undercurrent of phobias and fears. Perhaps this is because American history has been punctuated with its fair share of violent episodes. In addition to wars, its history has been altered by racial conflicts, labor and political struggles, gangsters, civil unrest, terrorists, and invasions. In Michael Moore's film *Bowling for Columbine*, a humorous cartoon that portrays America as a land built by fear is offered as an extremely abbreviated and obviously satirical version of history. A narrator shaped like a bullet tells a story that goes something like this:

> The pilgrims were afraid of religious persecution so they sailed off to new lands. On arrival in their new land they met "savages," and since they were afraid of them they killed them. But then they became afraid of each other, so they burned each other as "witches." They went to war with the British because they were afraid for their freedom; and after winning they still didn't feel safe so they passed the Second Amendment, which stated that every white man could keep his gun. This was helpful in maintaining both independence and slavery, which made the United States a rich nation. But after slavery was abolished some white people were still afraid, so they created the KKK. In 1871, the same year the KKK became an illegal terrorist organization, the NRA was founded; and soon politicians passed one of the first gun laws making it illegal for any black person to own a firearm. Later on, because of civil rights unrest, white people were so afraid that they fled to the suburbs and bought a quarter of a billion guns to keep out the urban hordes.

While this condensed history lesson is certainly partial, it makes an interesting point about fear and the often violent conflicts that result from human trepidation and anxiety, particularly when it comes to racial or ethnic interaction. In addition, it focuses on the significant role that weapons have played in U.S. history. It is important to note that today the United States spends more on defense than the rest of the world put together, despite the fact that

---

[1] Tony Horwitz, "Immigration—and the Curse of the Black Legend," *The New York Times* (Sunday July 9, 2006), Section 4, p. 13.

194 Part V: Violence as an Aesthetic

there is not a single other nation who could rival the current U.S. stockpile of weapons, submarines, destroyers, and jets.[2]

To be sure, weapons do play an important and crucial role in human history. Early humans certainly developed them as a necessary response to their environment. Since survival itself was rife with insecurities, humans learned to exhibit aggressive behavior in certain circumstances, particularly when hunting or when defending the community against predators. Thus, fear is a great motivator because it is an emotion that triggers a physical response in the body. However, as an emotion fear can be easily manipulated for political, ideological, religious, and economic gain.

In her book *Blood Rites*, Barbara Ehrenreich theorizes that once early humans mastered the methods by which to defend themselves, they repressed the memory of vulnerability and instead let their aggression get the better of them. Once they learned to vanquish other predators they turned against one another. Postulating that the resultant anxiety infiltrates both ritual and collective behavior, Ehrenreich writes,

> [O]ur particular and ambivalent relationship to violence is rooted in a primordial experience that we have managed…to almost entirely repress. And that is the experience…of being preyed on by animals that were initially far more skillful hunters than ourselves.[3]

Ritual and spectacle reassure us that we are no longer "prey." According to Sissela Bok in her book *Mayhem: Violence as Public Entertainment*, it is through spectacle that humans can test their reactions to violence without risk and can confront their fears of pain and death.[4] In sacrifice, the spectator enjoys identification not only with the executioner but also with the helpless person being sacrificed, and the spectator does not have to attend to the "victim" afterwards but can benefit from the emotions of pity and relief.[5] Violent spectacles keep people distracted and entertained. Thus, considering that humans have only been "civilized" for a few thousand years, it is not surprising that we still exhibit violent behavior.[6] In Hannah Arendt's seminal work *On Violence*, she observes that no one engaged in thought about history and politics "can remain unaware of the enormous role violence has always played in human affairs."[7] Given this reality, it is not surprising that humans are fascinated with violent imagery, not only as a way to make sense of their own homicidal urges but also out of their attempt to quell their own fears and

---

[2] James Surowiecki, "Unsafe at Any Price," *The New Yorker* (August 7 & 14, 2006), p. 32.
[3] Barbara Ehrenreich, *Blood Rites: Origins and History of the Passions of War* (New York: Metropolitan Books, 1997), p. 22.
[4] Sissela Bok, *Mayhem: Violence as Public Entertainment* (Reading, MA: Addison-Wesley, 1998), p. 27.
[5] Ehrenreich, p. 35; Bok, p. 43.
[6] Harold Schechter, *Savage Pastimes: A Cultural History of Violent Entertainment* (New York: St. Martin's Press, 2005), p. 9.
[7] Schechter, p. 8.

anxieties. The paradox is that while it is cathartic to watch something horrifying, it simultaneously perpetuates one's fears and anxieties.

The compelling question is not necessarily why we are attracted to violence, but rather when and if we will ever stop practicing it. Jane Goodall, after many years of studying primates, contends that humans have the intellectual capacity to move beyond violent behavior. Indeed, much research indicates that most people will go to great lengths to avoid violence unless they are responding to authoritative command or are motivated by self-defense, heroism, honor, or revenge, or they lack empathy for their victims. But while scholarship is inconclusive in terms of whether violence is instinctual and/or learned, the fact of the matter is that average people are capable of committing countless atrocities, and exhibiting a wide range of violent actions. Violence takes many forms, ranging from individual acts of aggression to state-sponsored wars or executions.

Though violence seems to be more pervasive than ever, the fact remains that contemporary humans are in reality quite sheltered from violence and that compared to the past, these are relatively peaceful times. In his book *Savage Pastimes*, Harold Schechter argues that even a century ago life was more brutal than it is today. He explains that since it is necessary to repress certain urges in order to be "civilized," people today need virtual violence as a substitute for their forbidden thoughts and actions.[8] According to psychologist Jonathan Freedman, "people were more violent in the centuries *before* television and movies were invented."[9] Similar to folk tales, literature, and visual art, television and movies/film are modern forms of storytelling that allow people to whet their appetites for the taboo.[10] Indeed, while all of these media have been used to depict violent subject matter, film and video are particularly well suited to representations of violence.[11]

Perhaps it was not accidental that the motion picture camera was developed during a time of increased moral aversion to public executions in Western societies.[12] Since some of the earliest films were dramatizations of executions, they essentially replaced the actual viewing of executions with special effects and illusion.[13] Schechter explains that the camera's "unique ability to conjure realistic images of shocking, violent death accounted, in large measure, for its explosive success."[14] He gives the example of Thomas Edison's 1895 Kinetoscope short, *The Execution of Mary, Queen of Scots*, which "consists of nothing more than a thirty-second scene of the title character stepping onto the scaffold, kneeling at the block, and having her head whacked off ... accomplished with the earliest known use of stop-motion photography."[15]

---

[8] Schechter, p.10.
[9] Schechter, p. 150.
[10] Schechter, pp. 6, 11.
[11] Schechter, p. 115.
[12] Schechter, p. 106.
[13] Schechter, p. 107.
[14] Schechter, p. 107.
[15] Schechter, p. 113.

Though preceded by Edison's short, the ultra-violent spectacle that now dominates the film industry originated in the films of the director Sam Peckinpah, who demonstrated a visual sensibility of stylized violence. Peckinpah was interested in the cathartic capacity of screen violence, but paradoxically he aestheticized violence while attempting to critique it.[16] In *Straw Dogs*, for example, the protagonist tries to respond rationally to the increasing violence perpetrated on him and his girlfriend, but in the end he resorts to violence as the only defense. In some ways the film functions as nostalgia for the myth of the American individualist as resistance fighter, gangster, cowboy, outlaw, or vigilante.[17] Interestingly, this same tough-guy image is perpetuated in the political arena today by unilateral decision making, invasion, and governmental attitude. It's hard to imagine that a head of state from another country would challenge an insurgency with the phrase "Bring 'em on!" as President George W. Bush did. Despite the fact that most Americans are relatively sheltered from actual bloodshed today, it would appear that the frontier mentality is still embedded in the American character. Perhaps Americans crave the violent imagery provided by film, television, and video games precisely because violence is often remote.

In his book, Schechter discusses his own childhood love of violent comics, TV westerns, and toy guns in the 1950s, a decade "stereotypically perceived as a Golden Age of innocence."[18] He makes the argument that the violence in these and other sources was more or less considered to be "wholesome, red-blooded, (and) all-American."[19] The precursors to superhero and horror comics, television westerns, action movies, and video games were the dime novels of the 1860s and, prior to those, the Davy Crockett almanacs. In these books the youth of America would read tales of "manslaughter, mayhem, and bodily mutilation."[20] Schechter points out that "there is absolutely nothing new about the public's prurient interest in sensational crime" and violence. The difference today is that rather than public executions there are popular entertainments, the news media, and the arts to fill the gap.[21] Rather than condemning these methods, Schechter sees them as a positive "sign of how much progress we've made in devising clever ways to satisfy those dark primal urges."[22]

Violent images are often products of their time, and therefore they not only mirror but also comment on the environment in which they were created. While fine lines exist between provocation and condemnation, perpetuation and documentation, and celebration and critique, it may prove more

---

[16] Stephen Prince, *Savage Cinema: Sam Peckinpah and the Rise of Ultraviolent Movies* (Austin: University of Texas Press, 1998), p. 103.
[17] John Fraser, *Violence in the Arts* (London: Cambridge University Press, 1974), p. 16.
[18] Schechter, p. 16.
[19] Schechter, p. 33.
[20] Schechter, pp. 30, 31.
[21] Schechter, p. 72.
[22] Schechter, p. 88.

dangerous to censor violent images because, ultimately, the ability to understand and process them is more productive than either suppressing them or denying their existence. By learning to analyze violent imagery we can overcome the feelings of numbness and overload that can lead to apathy and indifference. Our best defense against frustration and impassivity is to learn to critically evaluate what we see and experience. Access to ideas and imagery can help us to thrive and to remain resilient when faced with our own vulnerabilities and insecurities. In that sense it is the role of art to provoke us to greater awareness, understanding, and knowledge.

The artists Gregory Green, Paul Shambroom, and Robert Beck each approach the topic of violence in different ways. What they share is that they focus on the suggestive rather than the graphic in order to engage the viewer in a serious analysis of the topic of violence. Rather than offering overly didactic commentary, they offer the viewer an ambiguity that forces a contemplation of the complexity of the topic at a time when the United States is engaged in a "war on terror" and when the number of privately owned guns is at an all-time high, despite the significant evidence that access to weapons is a major cause of fatalities and injuries.

Gregory Green has spent his career exploring the relationship between violence and power. He has built bombs, missiles, satellites, and pirate radio stations. Gallery director Jeffrey Deitch explains that Green's work reveals "a peculiarly American way of thinking," reflecting the "fierce individualism and the paranoia that consume the angry men" in the suburbs of America who stockpile weapons in their bunkers.[23] Green was interested in terrorism before 9/11, exploring in his work the spectacle and aesthetics of violence as well as alternative strategies to gain power. In a 1994 interview with Benjamin Weil he explained that

> American culture needs evil as a surface of projection for hatred.... Hatred is a part of a larger process of assimilation. This is the consequence of a terrible fear of difference. Violence is an instrument of forced assimilation. It pertains to the "cowboy" aspect of American culture; it is an inherent part of the "frontier." Violence is a mundane part of American culture.[24]

Green further explains that anyone can build an arsenal from material bought at the corner store with information found in the library or on the Internet. Though his sculptures of bombs and missiles are not functional as weapons, they are technically precise enough that they could be armed with biochemical and nuclear devices. His art objects represent terrorism, vigilantism, or the ability to sabotage or unsettle governments; but they are also a warning of power gone awry. Instead of glorifying terrorism Green is inter-

---

[23] Jeffrey Deitch, *Young Americans: New American Art in the Saatchi Collection* (London: Saatchi Gallery, 1996).
[24] Benjamin Weil, "Interview with Gregory Green," *Purple Prose* 7 (Fall 1994), p. 76.

198   Part V: Violence as an Aesthetic

ested in questioning authority, destabilizing it, and working towards nonviolent strategies so that in the future violence will be obsolete. He explains that "nonparticipation is the greatest form of revolution. If an ever-growing number of people deny the existing system by refusing all forms of participation, then the legitimacy of the system is gone, and it will eventually collapse." Like Jane

Gregory Green, *Worktable #6*.

Gregory Green, *Bible Bomb #1898*.

Goodall Green believes that ultimately humans will move beyond violence and develop a "growing awareness of being one large group made of various identities, with a consciousness of shared common interests and goals."[25] Ultimately his art objects suggest violence rather than portray it in order to subvert the spectacle, because he feels that violence as entertainment is dangerous.

Paul Shambroom, like Green, prefers to rely on suggestion rather than overt presentations of violence. While there is a long history of documentary photography that focuses on the atrocities of war, Shambroom's photographs instead record the banal, behind-the-scenes boardrooms and storage facilities that are the less dramatic parts of the theatre of war and that represent the inner sanctum of American power. It took many years and much paperwork for him to gain access to these often restricted locations. Because of this the photographs themselves become representative of the inner workings of power as much as they are visual records. In his Nuclear Weapons series Shambroom writes that his "goal is neither to directly criticize nor glorify" but to "reveal the tangible reality of the huge nuclear arsenal" in the United States. He explains that

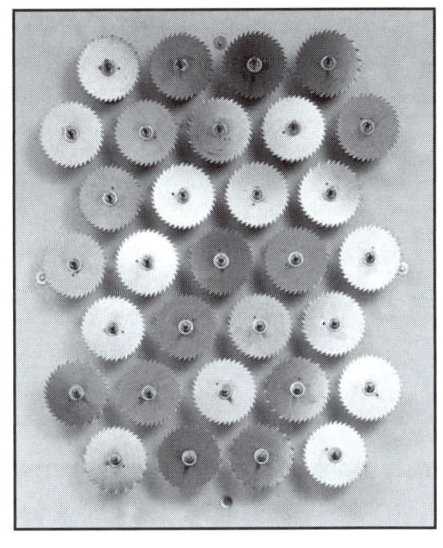

Gregory Green, *Thirty-One Blade Wall Installation* (blades rotate at 3200 rpm).

> [N]uclear weapons are still one of the dominant issues of our time, despite the ending of the Cold War. . . . [T]he burgeoning arms races among hostile nationalistic regimes compound the nuclear threat at the very moment when mankind could have been preparing to welcome a nuclear-free new millennium.[26]

In his more recent Security series, Shambroom captures the training facilities, equipment, and personnel involved in protecting America after 9/11. He explains that the series addresses "the tangible effects of international events on Americans' day-to-day lives, personal freedoms, and sense of security" and that it examines "fear, safety, and liberty" in the current climate. When looking at Shambroom's photographs it is easy to see why art critic Elizabeth Hoyt wrote that they imply a "masculine attraction to weaponry, suggesting that boyhood fantasies—war games first acted out with G.I.

---

[25] Weil, p. 79.
[26] www.paulshambroomart.com/art/nuclear%20weapons%20revA/index.html.

Paul Shambroom, *SWAT Team approaching House, "Terror Town,"* Playas, NM (from the Security Series).

Paul Shambroom, *1987 Honda Civic, 300 lbs. ANFO Explosive.* Energetic Materials Research and Testing Center (EMRTC), New Mexico Tech, Socorro, NM (from the Security Series).

Joes—are the fuel for all sorts of adult fears."[27] The images are often startling in their mundaneness as well as in the reality of what they represent. This stark contrast is what makes them all the more frightening. It is impossible to look at these images without making associations to what it is that they represent in terms of destructive capacity. The fact that the photographs are not filled with blood and gore makes them all the more compelling to look at. The viewer does not see the violence directly, but it is effectively implied.

---

[27] Elizabeth Hayt, "Paul Shambroom," *Art/Text* (May-July 1998), p. 86.

Robert Beck also uses the suggestion of violence rather than direct references. He is more interested in the trace of an event than in the direct representation of it. In his work Beck weaves oblique narratives that often combine staged or true-life crimes with his own personal history. His often banal subject matter projects an unnerving quality that suggests something dark and sinister has occurred. Several of his pieces emerge from an "all-American" childhood where hunting, gun culture, and the woods figure prominently. In *The Family Photo (Christmas 1968)*, three children pose with their rifles in front of a Christmas tree. The photo, in a deer-leg frame, is both festive and ominous, nostalgic and tragic, and the narrative within hints at both childhood innocence and malevolence. Beck, who is interested in the underlying evil beneath the ordinary, is influenced by the appeal of "true crime," in particular crimes perpetrated by and upon children. But rather than presenting a sensational version of events, Beck relies on suggestion and juxtaposition so that the viewer might develop his or her own interpretation. He of-

Paul Shambroom, *Untitled* (Ohio class Trident submarine, *USS Alaska* in dry dock for refit, Bangor Naval Submarine Base, Washington). NM (from the Security Series).

Robert Beck, *The Family Photo (Christmas 1968)*.

202   Part V: Violence as an Aesthetic

Robert Beck, *Anonymous*, oil crayon on paper (Slay Suspect).

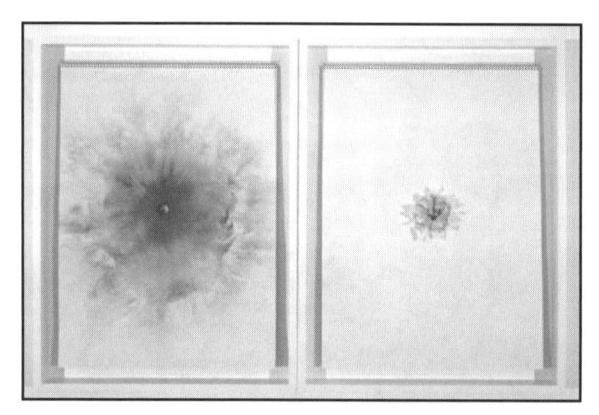

Robert Beck, *Untitled* (Daley .12 Over-Under/"Punkin" shells at close range). Gunpowder and drawing pads in two parts.

fers a type of forensic approach in which there is evidence but no determinate narrative. Due to the violent undercurrent of American life images that might otherwise appear innocent are influenced by sensational media and tabloid coverage of events. Beck explains that his work "begins with appropriation. . . . America is a violent culture, and I'm interested in contemporary American culture, and not to incorporate violence would be irresponsible."[28] Overall, it is the enigmatic nature of the work that causes the viewer to ultimately question his or her own tendency to seek out the gruesome and the sensational in an otherwise innocuous narrative.

All three artists broach the topic of violence as a condition of American culture, but through their subversion of a conventional sensational approach they ultimately force the viewer to consider the consequences of violence. While they each approach the topic differently, each chooses imagery that makes the viewer an active participant rather than a passive consumer of the merely sensational. This engagement forces the viewer to contemplate the topic, thus creating a dialogue that has the potential to enable social change. Ultimately, if violence is a part of human nature, it is in our best interest as a species to fully comprehend the consequences of that nature.

---

[28] www.crggallery.com/index.php?a=artist&b=1.

About the Authors

Kristin L. Anderson is an associate professor of sociology at Western Washington University. She is currently researching typologies of partner violence with the goal of helping us to better understand domestic violence as a gendered social process. She is also working on strategies that feminists can use to address the growing backlash against feminist perspectives on partner violence.

Jill Cermele is an associate professor of psychology and an affiliated faculty member of the women's studies program at Drew University. Her research focuses on women's resistance to violence and our perceptions of women's use of aggression in self-defense and other contexts. She is interested in the ways in which feminist research on women's use of aggression can further our understanding of the gendered nature of violence.

Basuli Deb has taught in various English departments in India, both at the undergraduate and at the graduate level before moving to the United States to join the doctoral program in English at Michigan State University. Her current work is on "Women and Militancy: Narratives from Guatemala, India, and South Africa." She has co-edited the journal *Directions: Discussions of Pedagogy, Gender, and Language*. Her publications include "The British Raj, Modernization, and India: Women, Transgression, and the Communism-Casteism Dyad in *The God of Small Things*" in *Atlantic Literary Review*. She is also co-editing a prospective anthology on "Writing Violence" which aims to publish the work of an international research group working in the field of representations of violence.

Peter Ellard is a historical theologian who teaches religious studies classes at Siena College in Albany, New York, where he is the director of the Reinhold Niebuhr Institute of Religion and Culture. He also serves as the chair of the Martin Luther King and Coretta Scott King Lecture Series on Race and Nonviolent Social Change. He teaches courses on world religions, religion and science, and the history of Christianity. His book, *The Sacred Cosmos: Theological, Philosophical and Scientific Conversations of the Twelfth Century School of Chartres*, is published by University of Scranton Press. He lives in the woods with his wife and family in New York State overlooking the Berkshires.

Ida Fadzillah is an assistant professor in anthropology at Middle Tennessee State University. Her work concentrates on gender and sexuality in Southeast Asia, with a focus on female youth cultures. Currently she is conducting field research on the burgeoning Laotian American community in Middle Tennessee to explore contemporary notions of local identity in an increasingly global South.

About the Authors

Richard B. Felson is a professor of crime, law, and justice and of sociology at Pennsylvania State University. His is currently doing research on domestic violence, race and regional differences in assault, alcohol use by offenders and victims, and the response of the criminal justice system to different types of assault. His books, including *Violence and Gender Reexamined* and *Violence, Aggression, and Coercive Actions* (the latter with J. Tedeschi) were published by the American Psychological Association.

Sculptor and photographer **Susan Graham** was born in Dayton, Ohio. In 1991, she moved to New York City to attend the School of Visual Arts. Susan has shown with various galleries and institutions including Holly Solomon Gallery, Photology Gallery in Milan, and the Bronx Museum of the Arts, Whitney Museum of Art at Phillip Morris. She was included in the show "Officina America," a survey of American artists curated by Renato Barilli in Bologna, Italy. In 2000, she was a resident artist in the Lower Manhattan Cultural Council's World Views program on the 91st floor of the World Trade Center. In 1999 and in 2002, she received fellowships from the New York Foundation for the Arts, and in 2001 she received a Pollock-Krasner foundation grant. Her work is currently included in Bang Bang, which travels from MIAM (Musee International des Artes Modestes) in Sete, France, to MAI (Musee des Arts ed de l'Industrie) in Saint Etienne, France. She is currently represented by Schroeder Romero Gallery in the Chelsea district of New York City.

Robert Hislope is an associate professor of political science, Union College. He received his PhD from Ohio State University. His research interests include comparative politics and ethnic and racial conflict. He has a particular interest in Macedonia and since 2000 has traveled extensively throughout the country, examining the interactions between ethnic politics, organized crime and government stability. Publications include: "Crime and Honor in a Weak State: Paramilitary Forces and Violence in Macedonia" in *Problems of Post-Communism*, 51(3) (May/June 2004); "Between a Bad Peace and a Good War: Insights and Lessons from the Almost-war in Macedonia" in *Ethnic and Racial Studies* (Jan. 2003) 26(1); and "Organized Crime in a Disorganized State" in *Problems of Post-Communism* (May/June 2002) 49(3).

Dustin Howes is an assistant professor of political science at St. Mary's College of Maryland. He has published in *International Studies Quarterly* and *Holocaust and Genocide Studies*. He is currently completing a manuscript that is tentatively titled *Toward a Credible Pacifism: Violence and the Possibilities of Politics*.

David Kaczynski is executive director of New Yorkers against the Death Penalty and the brother of Theodore Kaczynski—the so-called Unabomber—who was arrested in 1996 after David and his wife Linda approached the FBI with their suspicions that his brother might be responsible for a series of bombings that caused three deaths and numerous injuries over 17 years. Prior to joining NYADP, David was assistant director of the Equinox shelter for runaway and homeless youth in Albany, New York, where he counseled and advocated for troubled, neglected, and abused youth. David is currently writing a book on violence and healing with Gary Wright, who was seriously injured by one of Theodore Kaczynski's bombs in 1987.

William Leggett is an assistant professor of anthropology at Middle Tennessee State University. He writes about identity as negotiated through transnational encounters.

About the Authors

Jack Levin, PhD is the Brudnick Professor of Sociology and Criminology at Northeastern University in Boston, where he directs its Center on Violence and Conflict. He has authored or co-authored 27 books, most of which focus on aspects of violence and murder.

Leahanna Klement, native of Niskayuna, New York, is currently a senior at Union College in Schenectady, New York, majoring in political science and philosophy. She is passionate about educating and promoting awareness of sexual assault, domestic violence, women's rights issues, diversity affairs, and human rights violations. As a result, she is very active in her community as a resident advisor, a leader of various student-run organizations, and a co-founder of Tau Chapter of Latinas Promoviendo Comunidad/Lambda Pi Chi Sorority, Inc. She is also a member of Pi Sigma Alpha, the National Honor Society for Political Science, and hopes to attend law school in the near future.

Eric Madfis is a graduate student in the Department of Sociology at Northeastern University. His research interests are in multiple homicide, juvenile delinquency, and youth subculture and counterculture.

Conor McGrady was born in Downpatrick, Northern Ireland, in 1970. He studied at Cumbria College of Art and Design in Carlisle, UK, and at the University of Northumbria, Newcastle, UK, before receiving his MFA at The School of the Art Institute of Chicago in 1998. In 2000 and 2002 McGrady was awarded a Community Arts Assistance Program Grant from the City of Chicago. Most recently his work has been exhibited in the one-person exhibitions *Civil Abuse*, Ratio 3, San Francisco; *Social Security* at the Customs House, South Shields, UK; and *Purity* at Thomas Robertello Gallery in Chicago. In 2002 he was selected to participate in the Whitney Biennial at the Whitney Museum of American Art, New York. In 2003 he completed a five-month residency in the Woolworth Building, New York, through the Lower Manhattan Cultural Council's Studio Program. He currently lives and works in New York.

Carole Merill-Mazurek is the director of services to women and families, YWCA of Schenectady New York.

Graciela Monteagudo is an Argentine activist, community artist, and scholar. She holds an MFA from Goddard College and has worked internationally with diverse communities both on her own and with Bread and Puppet Theater. Some of her work has included coordinating puppet and street theater actions in Latin America and throughout the United States. Lately, Graciela has been touring internationally with academic multimedia presentations about Argentina. She is currently a PhD student at the University of Massachusetts in Amherst, Department of Anthropology, with a focus on gender dynamics and power structures in Latin American social movements and recovered factories in Argentina.

Daniel Mosquera is an associate professor of Spanish and Latin American Studies in the Dept. of Modern Languages and Literatures at Union College, Schenectady, New York. Professor Mosquera works, and has written articles, on New Spanish colonial historiography and Nahua devotional culture, Nahuatl theater, and Latin American cultural theory. He has also translated afro-Hispanic spirituals, work songs, and Pedro Calderón de la Barca's "Gran teatro del mundo" into English. More recently, he has written on the afro-descendant feast of St. Francis of Assisi (San Pacho) in Quibdo, Chocó, and has directed and co-produced two documentaries on the convergence of popular religious devotion and politics in the feast of San Pacho.

Derek Pardue is an assistant professor of anthropology and international and area studies at Washington University in St. Louis. His work has concentrated on the power of popular culture to shape contemporary understandings of race, class, gender, and nation. This point of inquiry has led to the publication of various articles on Brazilian hip hop and soccer as well as casual restaurants in the United States. His ethnography, *Hip Hop as Cultural Design: A Retelling of Marginality in São Paulo, Brazil*, is currently under review by Palgrave Macmillan Press.

Linda E. Patrik is a professor of philosophy at Union College. Trained in both European philosophy and Tibetan Buddhism, she works on creating opportunities for cross-cultural dialogue between Western and Asian philosophies. Her research in comparative philosophy has explored similarities between ancient Greek and ancient Buddhist theories on the best human life, feminist ethics of care and Buddhist ethics of compassion, Western and Tibetan pedagogical methods for teaching philosophy, and the phenomenological method and meditation. She met David Kaczynski in the seventh grade. After fortifying their trust in one another as lab partners in high school chemistry class, they became lifelong friends. The real chemistry experiment occurred later when they married at the ripe old age of 40.

Victoria Sanford is an associate professor of anthropology at Lehman College, City University of New York. She is the author of *Buried Secrets: Truth and Human Rights in Guatemala*; *Violencia y Genocidio en Guatemala;* and *La Masacre de Panzos* as well as co-editor (with Asale Angel-Ajani) of *Engaged Observer: Anthropology, Advocacy and Activism*.

Nadine Wasserman is an independent curator living in Albany, New York. She has organized a number of exhibitions dealing with the theme of violence including "Armed" at the Mandeville Gallery, Union College, Schenectady, New York, "Nothing to Fear" at the Art Center of the Capital Region, Troy, New York, and "In Cold Blood" at the Samuel Dorsky Museum of Art, State University of New York at New Paltz. She has previously held positions as Curator of Exhibitions at the Samuel Dorsky Museum of Art, Curator of the Wriston Art Center Galleries at Lawrence University, Appleton, Wisconsin, and Curatorial Assistant at the Museum of Contemporary Art, Chicago.